An Integrity in My Being

The inner experiences of these past years have changed the perception and meaning of the daily events of my life: achievement, sexual desire, anger, boredom, pleasure, money, relationships, work, and play. I no longer feel that one part of me is fighting another. I experience any integrity in my being that includes the deepest as well as the most superficial. More of the time, the moment—no matter what I am doing—is permeated with space, peace, equanimity, joy, and lightness

In this book, as in my others, I have attempted to share what I have found.

Bantam Books of Related Interest

Ask your bookseller for the books you have missed.

JOURNEY
of
AWAKENING

A Meditator's Guidebook

revised edition

by

Ram Dass

Edited by Daniel Goleman
with
Dwarkanath Bonner
and Ram Dev (Dale Borglum)
Illustrated by Vincent Piazza

BANTAM BOOKS
NEW YORK • TORONTO • LONDON • SYDNEY • AUCKLAND

JOURNEY OF AWAKENING: A MEDITATOR'S GUIDEBOOK
(REVISED EDITION)

A Bantam Book / August 1990

PUBLISHING HISTORY
Originally published June 1978

ACKNOWLEDGMENTS

We gratefully acknowledge the following people for quotations published here: Marie Idol, pp. 55, 56; Ram Tirth, p. 61; Surya Singer, pp. 62, 63; Soma Krishna, pp. 63, 64; K. K. Sah, pp. 68, 69; Maharaji, p. 69; K. K. Sah, p. 73; Soma Krishna, pp. 74–76; Father Ed Lavin pp. 76, 77; Saraswati Ransom, pp. 83, 84; Tara Bennett, pp. 85, 86; Saraswati, p. 181; and, Anjani, p. 217.

Grateful acknowledgment is made to the following publishers for permission to reprint copyrighted material: HARPER & ROW, PUBLISHERS, INC., for "Roshi Taft" in The Wheel of Death, *edited by Philip Kapleau: copyright © 1971 by Philip Kapleau. MACMILLAN PUBLISHING CO., INC., as well as the Trustees of the Tagore Estate and Macmillan London and Basingstoke, for poems XXIV, XXII, and XLI as they appear in* One Hundred Poems of Kabir *(originally published as* Songs of Kabir*), translated by Rabindranath Tagore; copright 1915 by Macmillan Publishing Co., Inc., renewed 1943 by Rabindranath Tagore. NEW DIRECTIONS PUBLISHING CORPORATION for portions of "The True Man," "The Man of Tao," "Symphony for a Sea Bird," and "When the Shore Fits" as they appear in* The Way of Chuang Tzu *by Thomas Marton; copyright © 1965 by The Abbey of Gethsemani. PRINCETON UNIVERSITY PRESS and ROUTLEDGE & KEAGAN PAUL LTD. for a poem by Ryokwan as it appears in Zen and Japanese Culture by Daisetz T. Suzuki, Bollingen Series LXIV: copyright © 1959 by Princeton University Press. RAMAKRISHNA-VIVEKANANDA CENTER for quotations from* The Gospel of Sri Ramakrishna, *Complete Edition, by Swami Nikhilananda, published by Ramakrishna-Vivekananda Center of New York, Inc., 1942. SHAMBHALA PUBLICATIONS, INC., for quotations from* The Jewel Ornament of Liberation *by sGam.po.pa translated by Herbert V. Guenther: copyright © 1971 by Shambhala Publications, Inc.:* The Myth of Freedom *by Chogyam Trungpa; copyright © 1976 by Chogyam Trungpa: and Visual Dharma by Chogyam Trungpa, Rinpoche: copyright © 1975 by Chogyam Trungpa, Rinpoche. UNITY PRESS, INC., for quotations from* The Experience of Insight, A Natural Unfolding *by Joseph Goldstein; copyright © 1976 by Joseph Goldstein. UNIVERSITY BOOKS, INC., for a portion of "The Song of Mahamudra" by Tilop as it appears in* Teachings of Tibetan Yoga *by Garma C.C. Chang, and for quotations from* The Hundred Thousand Songs of Milarepa *by Garma C.C. Chang; both copyright © 1962 by Oriental Studies Foundation. Every reasonable effort has been made to obtain appropriate permission to reproduce those copyrighted materials included in this volume. If notified of omissions, the editor and publisher will make the necessary corrections in future editions.*

ISBN 0-553-28572-6

Published simultaneously in the United States and Canada

Bantam Books are published by Bantam Books, a division of Random House, Inc. Its trademark, consisting of the words "Bantam Books" and the portrayal of a rooster, is Registered in U.S. Patent and Trademark Office and in other countries. Marca Registrada. Bantam Books, 1540 Broadway, New York, New York 10036.

PRINTED IN THE UNITED STATES OF AMERICA

COVER PRINTED IN U.S.A.

WCD   12 13 14 15 16 17 18 19 20 21

ACKNOWLEDGMENTS

In 1974 the Hanuman Foundation was formed to further the spiritual awakening in our society. One of its original projects was to promote the development of a broad base for meditation in the West. We began with a list of meditation facilities. As time went on we felt it would be more useful if we added explanations and advice by Ram Dass, and helpful quotations from a wide variety of teachers. The material mushroomed, and we found we had a book.

We approached Bantam for help in producing and distributing a full-sized book at the cheapest possible price. In the spirit of service and right livelihood the royalties from the sale of this book are being divided equally between the Hanuman Foundation and the author-editors. Thus in part the returns from this project will help to support further work of the foundation.

Four of us collaborated on this book, Ram Dass providing inspiration and text, Daniel Goleman organizing and editing, Ram Dev (Dale Borglum) nursing the project from the start and collating the directory, and Dwarkanath Bonner administering, designing, and helping edit.

The many other people who helped include:

The artists—Vincent Piazza, who with his ingenious pen gave birth to our concept of the little meditator; and Jay Bonner, who designed and drew the mandala dividers.

Laura Huxley, Soma Krishna, K.K. Sah, Father Ed Lavin, Tara Bennett, Saraswati Ransom, Surya Singer, Marie Idol, and Ram Tirth whose articles or portions thereof we are very pleased to be able to include.

Bill Alpert, Mirabai Bush, Richard Clark, Polly Constantine, David Graves, Willow Norris, Acharya Anagarika Munindra, Betsey Serafin, Swaha Smith, Brother David Steindl-Rast, and Robert Thomson, whose energy and assistance have been invaluable.

Lakshmi (Gael Malloy), who did several stages of typing with great patience and good cheer.

And Cecilia (Ceci) Hunt, our editor at Bantam, who helped us focus the book and gave us plenty of space in which to play.

And the many people who have permitted quotations to be used throughout the book, including Richard Clark and Whitall N. Perry. (A few of the quotations have come from secondary sources. The original sources were unknown to us so we left them out. We hope that you will pardon any lack of scriptural scholarship and appreciate, nevertheless, the transmission or transmutation.)

For us the preparation of this book has itself been a meditation. It has been permeated from the outset with the love and spiritual purpose that we have come to know and treasure through our guru, Neem Karoli Baba.

We offer it to you as an invitation to join in the feast.

Ram Dass
Daniel Goleman
Ram Dev
Dwarkanath Bonner

Contents

INTRODUCTION

When we make it in our society and then don't feel good inside—happy, at peace with ourselves—we are confused. As we strive for external security and success we anticipate that the pot of gold at the end of the rainbow will not only look good, but make us feel good. If it doesn't, we conclude that there is something wrong with us, that we need to "adjust." The assumption is that an adjusted being would be happy with success. But success usually turns out not to be enough to make us happy, and the therapeutic couch isn't necessarily appropriate for what ails us.

Disillusioned by the hollowness of success, some of us have sought fulfillment in revolution, others in "dropping out," and others in trying to milk more and more gratification from our environment—and some of us have sought a solution to our problems in other cultures, philosophies, or religions.

For me this search took me from being a psychology professor at Harvard University, through experimentation with LSD and other psychedelics, and finally to the Himalayas in India. There I came to understand that I would have to approach my inner being directly to find a lasting answer. Meditation has been the best way to do this.

There are innumerable meditative techniques deriving from many philosophies and religions. Over the past years I have sought training in and practiced a variety of these—and have profited greatly from each. The inner experiences of these past years have changed the perception and meaning of the daily events of my life: achievement, sexual desire, anger, boredom, pleasure, money, relationships, work, and play. I no longer feel that one part of me is fighting another. I experience an integrity in my being that includes the deepest as well as the most superficial. More of the time, the moment—no matter what I am doing—is permeated with space, peace, equanimity, joy, and lightness.

In this book, as in my others, I have attempted to share what I have found. In the final analysis what has been found is simple. The challenge is to say it simply. I hope you will find this book to be of use.

Ram Dass

JOURNEY
of
AWAKENING

1

GETTING
YOUR
BEARINGS

The Flow

There have been moments in your life when you were
pure awareness. No concepts, no thoughts like "I am
aware" or "That is a tree" or "Now I am meditating."
Just pure awareness. Openness. A spacious quality in
your existence. Perhaps it happened as you sat on a
river bank and the sound of the river flowed through
you. Or as you walked on the beach when the sound
of the ocean washed away your thinking mind until all
that remained was the walking, the feeling of your feet
on the sand, the sound of the surf, the warmth of the
sun on your head and shoulders, the breeze on your
cheek, the sound of the seagull in the distance.

For that moment your image of yourself was lost in the gestalt, in the totality of the moment. You were not clinging to anything. You were not holding on to the experience. It was flowing—through you, around you, by you, in you. At that moment you were the experience. You were the flow. There was no demarcation between you-sun-ocean-sand. You had transcended the separation that thought creates. You were the moment in all its fullness.

Everyone has had such experiences. These moments are ones in which we have "lost ourselves," or been "taken out of ourselves," or "forgotten ourselves." They are moments in flow.

It is in these moments of your life that there is no longer separation. There is peace, harmony, tranquillity, the joy of being part of the process. In these moments the universe appears fresh; it is seen through innocent eyes. It all begins anew.

> *The past has flown away.*
> *The coming month and year do not exist;*
> *Ours only is the present's tiny point.*

> —Shabistari

> The Secret Rose Garden of
> Sa'd Ud Din
> Mahmud Shabistari

We try so hard to overcome the separateness. More intimacy. More rubbing of bodies. More exchanging of ideas. But always it's as if you are yelling out of your room and I am yelling out of mine. Even trying to get out of the room invests the room with a reality. Who am I? The room that the mind built.

We spend so much effort to get out of something that didn't exist until we created it. Something that is gone in a moment. We've all had moments when there was no room. But we freaked. Or explained it away, ignored it, or let it pass by.

A moment. The moment of orgasm. The moment by the ocean when there is just the wave. The moment of being in love. The moment of crisis when we forget ourselves and do just what is needed.

We each come out again and again. We turn and look and realize we're out—and panic. We run back in the room, close the door, panting heavily. Now I know where I am. I'm back home. Safe. No matter how squalid the room is, no matter how unmade the bed, no matter how many bugs are crawling around the kitchen. Safe.

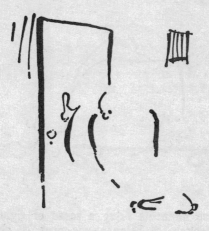

These moments appear again and again in our lives. For many people it first comes as a glimpse into other states of consciousness brought about by emotional trauma, drugs, sex, nature, or a love affair. This glimpse reveals to the person that there is something more. That he or she isn't exactly who he or she thought.

You may link these moments with the conditions out of which they arose. Perhaps it's the moment of sexual orgasm when you transcend self-consciousness. Perhaps it's a moment of trauma, of extreme danger when you "forget yourself." Perhaps it's when you are out in the woods away from people and you let down your defenses, loosen the boundaries of your self-consciousness. Perhaps when you are lazing by a stream. Perhaps when you are sitting quietly with friends you trust and love.

For surfers it is the moment when they come into equilibrium with the incredible force of the wave. For skiers it is when the balance is perfect. When our skills fit the demand perfectly, then there is no anxiety. Then we have proved ourselves. There is nothing left to do. In that moment our awareness expands.

These moments bring a sense of rightness, of total perfection, of being at-one-ment, of clarity, of feeling intimately involved with everything around you, of being free of the tension self-conscious thought brings. But you mistakenly identify the moment with the vehicle. You cling to these situations; you keep going back to them to recreate those moments. But you needn't cling to the situations that have triggered them in the past. These moments of flow can happen anywhere, anytime. Throughout life, each of us has had many of these moments. They are ephemeral. But such moments are the essence of meditation.

What concerns us in this book are the practices, that increase these meditative moments in your life, until ultimately your entire life is meditation-in-action. Then all of your acts are part of the flow of the universe. Why meditate? To live in the moment. To dwell in the harmony of things. To awaken.

IF I HAD MY LIFE TO LIVE OVER

I'd like to make more mistakes next time. I'd relax. I would limber up. I would be sillier than I have been this trip. I would take fewer things seriously. I would take more chances. I would climb more mountains and swim more rivers. I would eat more ice cream and less beans. I would perhaps have more actual troubles, but I'd have fewer imaginary ones.

You see, I'm one of those people who live sensibly and sanely hour after hour, day after day. Oh, I've had my moments, and if I had it to do over again, I'd have more of them. In fact, I'd try to have nothing else. Just moments, one after another, instead of living so many years ahead of each day. I've been one of those persons who never goes anywhere without a thermometer, a hot water bottle, a raincoat, and a parachute. If I had to do it again, I would travel lighter than I have.

If I had my life to live over, I would start barefoot earlier in the spring and stay that way later in the fall. I would go to more dances. I would ride more merry-go-rounds. I would pick more daisies.

—*Nadine Stair,*
85 years old,
Louisville, Kentucky

Relax

Thought Prison

Your ego is a set of thoughts that define your universe. It's like a familiar room built of thoughts; you see the universe through its windows. You are secure in it, but to the extent that you are afraid to venture outside, it has become a prison. Your ego has you conned. You believe you need its specific thoughts to survive. The ego controls you through your fear of loss of identity. To give up these thoughts, it seems, would annihilate you, and so you cling to them.

There is an alternative. You needn't destroy the ego to escape its tyranny. You can keep this familiar room to use as you wish, and you can be free to come and go. First you need to know that you are infinitely more than the ego room by which you define yourself. Once you know this, you have the power to change the ego from prison to home base.

All that we are is a result of what we have thought.

—The Dhammapada

The epitome of the human realm is to be stuck in a huge traffic jam of discursive thought.

—Chogyam Trungpa

The Myth of Freedom

Consider awakening on a usual morning. The alarm clock rings, you come out of sleep, focus enough to think "Alarm clock," and reach over to turn it off. Your thoughts might go something like this:

"It's time to get up. I have to go to the toilet. It's warm in here. Do I smell coffee perking? I could still sleep for ten more minutes. Oh, I forgot to do the dishes last night. I need to go to the toilet. Gee, my mouth tastes awful. I could still sleep for ten more minutes. What was I dreaming about? Who was that person in my dream? Wonder if it's warm outside. Boy, I'm hungry. What's that sound in the other room? I really need to go to the toilet. God, I wish I could stay in bed all day."

Thought after thought with the rapidity of a triphammer. Thoughts about what you hear, what you taste, what you smell, what you see, what you feel, what you remember, what you plan. On and on they go. A raging roaring river of thoughts pouring through you: "Think of me, think of me, think of me, me, me, me, me first, think of me." And so it goes all day, until you go to sleep.

You are totally in the control of your senses and thoughts. The alarm sounds and captures your attention, draws your awareness to it. But "you" are not your ears hearing the clock. You are awareness attending to your ears hearing. It's like when you're reading something so absorbing that you fail to hear someone enter the room. The sound of their steps triggers the processes of hearing, yet you do not "hear." For you are busy reading and thinking. Just as you are not your ears hearing, you are not your other senses either. You are not the eyes seeing, nose smelling, tongue tasting, or skin feeling. Only your thoughts are left. Here is where most people cannot escape. For they identify totally with their thoughts. They are unable to separate pure awareness from the thoughts that are its objects. Meditation allows you to break this identification between awareness and the objects of awareness. Your awareness is different from both your thoughts and your senses. You can be free to put your awareness where you will, instead of it being grabbed, pushed, and pulled by each sense impression and thought. Meditation frees your awareness.

A being whose awareness is totally free, who does not cling to anything, is liberated.

> *Wherever there is attachment*
> *Association with it*
> *Brings endless misery.*
>
> —*Gampopa*
>
> The Jewel Ornament
> of Liberation

We need the matrix of thoughts, feelings, and sensations we call the ego for our physical and psychological survival. The ego tells us what leads to what, what to avoid, how to satisfy our desires, and what to do in each situation. It does this by labeling everything we sense or think. These labels put order in our world and give us a sense of security and well-being. With these labels, we know our world and our place in it.

Archie Bunker was for many years a TV archetype of a bigot. He had definite labels for who everybody else was. As long as they stayed within the labels, he seemed content. When the world refused to fit his labels—when the black turned out to be a corporation vice-president or his doctor a woman—Archie's world collapsed.

Our ego renders safe an unruly world. Uncountable sense impressions and thoughts crowd in on us, so that without the ego to filter out irrelevant information, we would be inundated, overwhelmed, and ultimately destroyed by the overload. Or so it seems.

The ego has convinced us that we need it—not only that we need it, but that we are it. I am my body. I am my personality. I am my neuroses. I am angry. I am depressed. I'm a good person. I'm sincere. I seek truth. I'm a lazy slob. Definition after definition. Room after room. Some are in high-rise apartments—I'm very important. Some are on the fringe of the city— just hanging out.

Meditation raises the question: Who are we really? If we are the same as our ego, then if we open up the ego's filters and overwhelm it, we shall be drowned. If, on the other hand, we are not exclusively what the ego defines us to be, then the removal of the ego's filters may not be such a great threat. It may actually mean our liberation. But as long as the ego calls the shots, we can never become other than what it says. Like a dictator, it offers us paternalistic security at the expense of our freedom.

We may ask how we could survive without our ego. Don't worry—it doesn't disappear. We can learn to venture beyond it, though. The ego is there, as our servant. Our room is there. We can always go in and use it like an office when we need to be efficient. But the door can be left open so that we can always walk out.

Outside there is flow, no definition. We don't have to be thinking all the time about who we are. The tree is not saying, "I'm a tree, I'm a tree; I'm an elm, I'm not an oak, I'm an elm." It's just being an elm. Why couldn't we have the same harmonious relationship to the universe that the elm does? The elm is harmonious whether it's a seed, or a little sapling, or a huge elm, or a rotting dead tree. Not us. We fight the flow. We think. "I gotta stay young." Or, "It's horrible." Or, "I don't dare." That stops the flow.

> *The intelligent man who is proud of his intelligence is like the condemned man who is proud of his large cell.*
>
> —*Simone Weil*
>
> Simone Weil: A Life

If your mind is empty, it is always ready for anything; it is open to everything. In the beginner's mind there are many possibilities; in the expert's mind there are few.

—*Shunryu Suzuki*

Zen Mind, Beginner's Mind

Initially most people choose to meditate out of curiosity or to relieve psychological pain, increase pleasure, or enhance power. The goal of all these motives is to strengthen the ego. For as the ego gets more comfortable, happy, and powerful, its prison walls thicken. The ego's motives do not allow examination of the ego itself, nor allow insight that the ego is your prison. These motives paradoxically contain the seeds of freedom, because they lead you to meditate more. Meditation makes you more calm and quiet, and in this new stillness other motives, deeper motives, arise for going further into meditation. As your meditation develops beyond the level of ego payoffs, the prison walls begin to crack.

You might think of these deeper motives in many ways:

to answer the question, "Who am I?"
to awaken cosmic consciousness
to see things just as they are
to rend the veils of illusion
to know God
to tune to the harmony of the universe
to gain more compassion
to reach a higher consciousness
to become liberated
to be born again
to know the truth which lies beyond dualism
to transcend the wheel of birth and death
to abandon desire
to be free

These motives all describe the same peak from different points at its base. They all express a single desire: to escape the prison of ego.

> *From the moment you came into the world of*
> *   being,*
> *A ladder was placed before you that you might*
> *   escape.*
>
> —*Divani Shamsi Tabriz*
>
> Selected Poems from the
> Divani Shamsi Tabriz

In the process of pursuing my own deeper motives, the ego neuroses that once preoccupied me, my obsessions with sexuality, achievement, love, and dependency, haven't all gone away. What has gone is my preoccupation and my identification with them. Now they are merely quaint and fascinating, an interesting room or passing show rather than the huge mountains and crevasses and devastating potential disasters which once seemed to surround me on every side. Though I may get angry, I let go of the anger more quickly. And more important, I let go of the guilt connected with the anger. These feelings now simply arise and pass away, without my resisting or clinging to them. More and more I am just awareness.

The explanation is involvement without clinging. Not grabbing at anything. You may be attached to your lover: you say "my woman" or "my man." There's the clinging. It can be part of the flow of the moment to be with a man or woman, but if he or she disappears tomorrow, that's a new moment. No clinging. Your life just lives itself.

You're not sitting around saying, "How am I doing? Am I a failure in life? Am I a success?" You're not judging. Your life is just a process unfolding.

I'm a Ram Dass. I do whatever it is I do. I see people, teach, and write my books. I eat, sleep, and travel, get tired and irritable, go to the bathroom, touch, and taste, and think. A continuous stream of events. A flow. I am involved with it all, yet I cling to none of it. It is what it is. No big deal.

The man in whom Tao
Acts without impediment
Does not bother with his own interests
And does not despise
Others who do.
He does not struggle to make money
And does not make a virtue of poverty.

He goes his way
Without relying on others
And does not pride himself
On walking alone.
While he does not follow the crowd
He won't complain of those who do.
Rank and reward
Make no appeal to him;
Disgrace and shame
Do not deter him.
He is not always looking
For right and wrong
Always deciding "Yes" or "No."

—Thomas Merton

The Way of Chuang Tzu

The mind of a yogi is under his control; he is not
under the control of his mind.

—Sri Ramakrishna

The Gospel of
Sri Ramakrishna

Your duty is to be; and not to be this or that.

—Sri Ramana Maharshi

Talks with Sri
Ramana Maharshi

The Game of Awakening

We have built up a set of ego habits for gaining satisfaction. For some it involves pleasure; for others, more neurotic, it involves pain. As you look at many people's lives you see that their suffering is in a way gratifying, for they are comfortable in it. They make their lives a living hell, but a familiar one.

This network of thoughts has been your home since you can remember. Your home is safe and familiar. It may be sad and painful sometimes, but it's home. And besides, you've never known any other. Because this structure has always been your home, you assume that it is what reality is—that your thoughts are Reality with a capital R.

If you start to use a method that makes gaps in this web of thoughts of who you are and what reality is, and if it lets the sunlight in and you peek out for a moment, might you not get frightened as the comforting walls of ego start to crumble? Might you not prefer the security of this familiar prison, grim though it sometimes may be, to the uncertainty of the unknown? You might at that point pull back toward the familiarity of your pain.

That is the criticial point. For here is your choice: whether you truly wish to escape from the prison or are just fooling yourself. For your ego includes both the suffering and the desire to be free of the suffering. Sometimes we use cures halfheartedly, with the secret hope that the cures will not work. Then we can hold on to our suffering while protesting we want to get free. But meditation does work. It gives you moments of sunlight—of clarity and detachment. Sooner or later you must either stop meditation, do it in a dishonest way, or confront your resistance to change.

When you begin meditation you may approach it as you would a new course in school, a new method to learn, a new goal to achieve. In the past when you took a new course you studied the rules of the game so you'd do well. You wanted to receive a high grade from the teacher, to get approval, or to be more powerful. As you advance in meditation, these external motives fall away. You begin to feel a spiritual pull from within. It is profound and it is scary.

Most people start to meditate for psychological reasons. It's not that they feel a great yearning for God. They're just kind of miserable. Or they feel they'd be a lot more efficient if they had a quieter mind. Or that life would be more beautiful if their hearts were more open. Or that they would be more powerful if their minds were focused. Because this is all true, the mass movements in the spiritual community market their product to play on these ego motives. If there were nobody buying, they wouldn't be selling.

For example, I recently got a magazine on meditation. On the back page it shows a couple, both very gentle-looking people. He is putting his hand on her breast, and she's looking down sort of pleased-shy. The blurb says, "Very often the meditator is attracting more potential partners than ever before." And it's true. It's not a hustle, it's true. When everybody's light is veiled, as though they had dark clouds over them, even a little flicker of light makes the meditator seem special or attractive.

The game of awakening is very subtle. At first you may buy the package of meditation because you're nervous, anxious, uptight. You want to get rid of all your pain and and have a little pleasure out of life. But you really don't know what you're buying. They say, meditate and you can have a Cadillac, but they don't tell you that when you get the Cadillac it's liable to feel a little empty. By the time you get to the Cadillac, who it was that wanted it isn't around any more. See the predicament? Meditation changes your desires in the course of fulfilling them.

You may meditate in order to get rid of your pain and increase your pleasure. When you have moments where you see your suffering as just a set of thoughts that come and go, you begin to develop a new perspective. But as you see that pain and suffering come and go, you also see that pleasure passes. If you use meditation to avoid pain and to have more pleasure, in the bargain you also come to see the transitory nature of pleasure.

While at first you were motivated only to maximize your pleasure, you are now faced with what lies beyond pleasure and pain. Enlightened beings have always said that clinging to any experience or possession that is in time causes suffering, for everything changes. Both pleasure and pain are in time. To fully escape suffering, you must seek what lies beyond the polarities of pleasure and pain, beyond time.

Time is the grim reaper of it all, of all forms. Form is always changing. Time, change, flow. Going to hold on? Where? Remember Shelley's poem about Ozymandias? He had been king of a long-forgotten desert empire. All that remained to tell his story was a broken statue half-buried in sand. And on its pedestal it bore the inscription:

My name is Ozymandias, King of kings:
Look on my works, ye Mighty, and despair!

The great sages have warned again and again about things in time. Buddha said, "Cling not to that which changes," and Christ said, "Lay not up your treasures where moth and rust doth corrupt." Both are saying the same thing, though they use different images to talk to different people. The truth is one and the same.

There are many ways the message is transmitted. If you're ready, one Zen story can change your whole life. I've met people whose lives were transformed by some simple little story. *The Way of the Pilgrim. The Little Flowers of St. Francis.*

Everyone needn't go through the big public routes at all. The spiritual journey is individual, highly personal. It can't be organized or regulated. It isn't true that everybody should follow any one path.

Listen to your own truth.

It's characteristic of the ego that it takes all that is unimportant as important and all that is important as unimportant.

—*Meher Baba*

Discourses

All worldly pursuits have but the one unavoidable and inevitable end, which is sorrow: acquisitions end in dispersion; buildings, in destruction; meetings, in separation; births, in death.

—*Milarepa*

Tibet's Great Yogi Milarepa

There once was a king who was going to put to death many people, but before doing so he offered a challenge. If any of them could come up with something which would make him happy when he was sad, and sad when he was happy, he would spare their lives.

All night the wise men meditated on the matter.

In the morning they brought the king a ring. The king said that he did not see how the ring would serve to make him happy when he was sad and sad when he was happy.

The wise men pointed to the inscription. When the king read it, he was so delighted that he spared them all.

And the inscription? "This too shall pass."

> *The world is so constructed, that if you wish to enjoy its pleasures, you must also endure its pains. Whether you like it or not, you cannot have one without the other.*

> —*Swami Brahmananda*
>
> Discipline Monastique

Relative Realities

You have at this moment many constellations of thought, each composing an identity: sexual, social, cultural, educational, economic, intellectual, historical, philosophical, spiritual, among others. One or another of these identities takes over as the situation demands. Usually you are lost into that identity when it dominates your thoughts. At the moment of being a mother, a father, a student, or a lover, the rest are lost.

If you go to a good movie, you are drawn into the story line. When the house lights go up at the end of the film, you are slightly disoriented. It takes a while to find your way back to being the person sitting in the theater. But if the film is not very good and it does not capture you, then you notice the popcorn, the technical quality of the movie, and the people in the theater. Your mind pulls back from involvement with the movie.

The quietness meditation brings your life is like pulling back from the movie. Your own life is the movie, its plot melodramatic: Will I learn to meditate? Will I become enlightened? Will I marry, will I have children, will I get a better job? Will I get a new car? These are the story lines.

The autobiographical part of the book *Be Here Now* was initially called His-Story. Each of us has his story. History. To see your life as His-Story or Her-Story is to break the attachment to the melodrama of your story line. But be careful. This doesn't mean to push it away, to reject or deny it or consider it trivial. It merely means to surround the events of your life with quiet spacious awareness.

It is not that you erase all of your individuality, for even an enlightened being has a personality marked by all sorts of idiosyncrasies. An enlightened being doesn't necessarily have beautiful hair, sparkling teeth, a young body, or a nice disposition. His or her body has its blemishes; it ages and dies. The difference is that such a being no longer identifies with that body and personality.

Another way to understand the space you approach through meditation is to consider dreams. Perhaps you have never experienced awakening from a dream within a dream. But when you awaken every morning, you awaken from a dream into what? Reality? Or perhaps another dream? The word "dream" suggests unreality. A more sophisticated way of saying it is that you awaken from one relative reality into another.

We grow up with one plane of existence we call real. We identify totally with that reality as absolute, and we discount experiences that are inconsistent with it as being dreams, hallucinations, insanity, or fantasy. What Einstein demonstrated in physics is equally true of all other aspects of the cosmos: all reality is relative. Each reality is true only within given limits. It is only one possible version of the way things are. There are always multiple versions of reality. To awaken from any single reality is to recognize its relative nature. Meditation is a device to do just that.

Normal waking consciousness, dream states, emotional states, and other states of consciousness are different realities, somewhat like channels of the TV receiver. As you walk down the street you can tune your "receiver" into the world on any number of channels. Each way of tuning creates a very different street. But the street doesn't change. You do.

You see what you look for. If you are primarily preoccupied or tuned to the physical body, as you look at people you see them as man or woman, fat or thin, tall or short, attractive or unattractive. If, on the other hand, you are busy looking at personalities you might see them as introverted or extroverted, hysterical or paranoid, happy or sad. If you were tuned to astral identities you'd see a Leo or a Taurus, an angel or a demon. It's all in the eyes of the beholder.

Christ could walk up to you and you might see him as a pleasant carpenter, dressed plainly. You might think: interesting teacher, he has a nice vibe. If you were looking beyond that, you might see Him as Living Spirit.

Meditative awareness is a vantage poini from which you can focus on any event from various levels of reality. Take, for example, your relationship with your parents, spouse, or children. Most relationships are very reactive. Your parent comes along and says something to which you immediately react and the parent in turn reacts to you. These are habitual reactions, in which nobody really listens; there is merely a mechanical run-off between people.

If you are rooted quietly in your awareness, there is space. In the moment, after your mother or father speaks to you, you see the reaction you would usually make. But you also see the situation in a variety of other ways. You might see that your parent is in fact your parent only in this incarnation; from another level, like you, your parent is just another soul running off karma, living out the results of his or her past actions. You are part of each other's karma. To appreciate this allows you to understand your dialogue in terms of cause and effect. Or you might understand it from other vantage points: in Freudian terms or as a power struggle, or as a symptom of the generation gap, or perhaps your parent simply has a stomach ache. Or you might see this dialogue as God talking to God.

Every event in your life is incredibly significant on level upon level upon level. Were you to attempt to think of each of these levels at the moment someone says something, you would be swamped by an overwhelming number of thoughts. The meditative awareness is not one of intellectual analysis nor one of labeling different "takes" of reality. It allows all ways of seeing to exist in the space surrounding an event. Meditative awareness has a clarity that lays bare both the workings of your mind and the other forces at work in a situation. This clarity allows you to see the factors that determine your choices from moment to moment. Yet you don't have to think about it to grasp all this. You find that you know, you understand. In this inner stillness and clarity you are fully aware of the entire gestalt, the whole picture. With no effort your response is optimal on all levels, not just mechanically reactive on one. The response is in tune, harmonious, in the flow.

> *The manifestations of mind outnumber the*
>   *myriads of dust-motes*
> *In the infinite rays of sunlight.*

> —*Milarepa*

> The Hundred Thousand
> Songs of Milarepa

> *You carry heaven and hell with you.*

> —*Sri Ramana Maharshi*

> Talks with Sri
> Ramana Maharshi

What am I doing at a level of consciousness where this is real?

—*Thaddeus Golas*

The Lazy Man's Guide
to Enlightenment

2

SETTING OUT

What to Expect

When you begin to meditate you may notice changes right away. You may feel less anxious or more alert. You may be better able to concentrate, have more energy, be more at ease socially, or be more powerful intellectually. Or nothing much may seem to change. Don't count on anything dramatic. Most changes happen slowly.

There is a wide variety of experiences you will have during meditation itself, such as feelings of a pleasant calmness, a slight exhilaration, or, if you're fatigued, strong drowsiness. A common report is the feeling of the mind speeding up. Actually, this is not what is happening, but rather your awareness is standing back a bit so that for the first time you notice the normal speediness of your thoughts. Other kinds of experiences can include seeing images with your eyes closed, hearing inner sounds, or having inner smells, tastes, or new sensations in the body; these are less common. Outside meditation, you may find a sense of spaciousness in your life, a new peace.

All of these experiences, because of their novelty, have a great fascination. But they are best seen as markers along the way, signposts to be noticed, read, perhaps enjoyed, and then left behind as you go on.

There is no "best" or "right" kind of experience in meditation; each session is as different and unique as each day of your life. If you have ideas of what should happen, you can become needlessly disappointed if your meditation doesn't conform to these expectations. At first meditation is likely to be novel, and it's easy to feel you are changing. After a while, there may be fewer dramatically novel experiences, and you may feel you're not making any progress. In fact, you may be making the most "progress" when you don't feel anything particularly significant is going on—the changes you undergo in meditation are often too subtle to detect accurately. Suspend judgment and let whatever comes come and go.

Some people find meditation boring. They feel as if nothing is happening. This is another way in which the old you holds on tight; and it is important to be able to persist even through the experiences of boredom. Set yourself a period of time to seriously try meditation, perhaps a period of two weeks or a month in which you say to yourself, "No matter what I experience in meditation I will continue to do it regularly." This will give you a chance to get through discouraging experiences in meditation such as boredom.

On the other hand, the initial reaction to meditation may be just the opposite of boredom—ecstasy.

Many people find things happening after their first few meditative experiences that give them incredible enthusiasm and truly ecstatic states. This may lead them to proselytize, to want to tell others. I suggest that in the early stages you move gently and slowly. Don't overreact.

Positive experiences may well be followed shortly after by indifference. If you don't keep your experiences to yourself you may find yourself caught in a social situation in which you have created a monster of enthusiasm which you must pump up in a false way in order to be consistent. It is wise in all stages of meditation to be calm and not to make too much of any of your experiences, positive or negative. Merely notice them and keep on with your meditation.

Some people overreact to their experiences and go around saying that they're enlightened—they're the Buddha, they're the Christ. This is a self-deception. Others go to the other extreme and say they are nothing, they are unworthy. Both these positive and negative attitudes have to go.

Be open to whatever experiences come in your meditation. Don't get fixed on a model of what meditation is supposed to feel like. Set aside judging, being critical, having opinions. Meditation is giving up models and labels.

The less you expect, the less you judge, the less you cling to this or that experience as significant, the further you will progress. For what you're seeking is a transformation of your being far beyond that which any specific experience can give you. It is important to expect nothing, to take every experience, including the negative ones, as merely steps on the path, and to proceed.

When you practice zazen, just practice zazen. If enlightenment comes, it just comes.

—Shunryu Suzuki

Zen Mind, Beginner's Mind

Your Body

Body, posture, and health determine, in part, the quality of meditation. Until your meditation becomes deep it will be difficult, for example, to override physical pain. In a sitting meditation your neck may hurt, your spine feel tense, you may be restless and unable to find a comfortable position. If so, you should work on your body. Hatha yoga is designed to prepare your body to sit still. The series of stretching positions and movements (called asanas) help your body become straight, clear, and at rest for sitting. (There is a sample of hatha yoga in the section on movement in the next chapter.)

When you first start to do a sitting meditation, find any comfortable position with your back straight. If you sit on the floor, raise your bottom with a pillow. A straight back keeps you alert. Sit so you can stay still for a long time without moving or having to think about your body. If you're not used to sitting on the ground with crossed legs, don't try it right away.

A straight-backed chair is fine for beginners. Later, as your meditation gets stronger, you can gradually try sitting crosslegged, in a half lotus or full lotus. It doesn't really matter whether you sit on a straight-backed chair or crosslegged or lie flat on your back. It is important that your back and head be straight. If this is difficult, just be as alert as you can.

When I sit in meditation, first I find a comfortable position. If my body bothers me because of discomfort or pain, meditation is more difficult. I sit either in the half lotus on a firm pillow or in a chair. To sit half lotus (crosslegged with one foot resting on the opposite thigh), you may need to do hatha yoga postures daily to loosen up your ankle, calf, knee, and thigh. The advantage in sitting half lotus is that it is a very stable position. This physical stability makes it easier for you to enter meditative states. Then your body becomes a meditation temple.

> *I have visited in my wanderings shrines and other places of pilgrimage. But I have not seen another shrine blissful like my own body.*
>
> —Saraha
>
> Buddhist Texts

Food for Thought

Diet is important to your practice. Within certain limits the food you eat affects the quietness of your mind. Let your diet change gently and naturally; be honest with yourself. Don't force changes: to try to give up a food too soon merely makes you focus on it all the more. If you think of nothing else but juicy steaks while eating your soya burger, you're going too fast. The point is to let go of the thoughts as well as the food—your attachments are more important than whether you eat or abstain from certain foods.

Some foods make you more agitated and stimulated, so it's hard for you to sit quietly. Your sensitivity to such foods will change. As you come to feel lighter, for example, red meats may seem too heavy for you. Slowly your diet may shift away from meat, toward chicken, fish, eggs, and finally perhaps just fruits, grains, and vegetables. In the same way, you may drift away from sugar, alcohol, and cigarettes. Remember: there are no specific rules to this game. Beings have become enlightened eating anything and everything.

Be sure to honor your dietary needs of the moment. Be careful as you shift your diet not to upset your protein balance. If you are moving toward a vegetarian diet, use protein supplements if necessary. Keep up your vitamin intake as well, particularly B and C, minerals, and perhaps E. Flagging energy and anemia are obstacles to deep meditation.

Fasting is also useful to purify and cleanse your body. But be moderate. You should do extensive fasting only with the guidance of a teacher.

Along with growing awareness about your food, it is well to become more sensitive to what you feed your mind. Some spiritual systems, like macrobiotics, are built around diet. Very often, however, people focus on food with little attention to what they put in their minds. To eat sprouts, grains, and fruit and then watch sadistic violence and greed-ridden games on television is hardly feeding your spirit in a balanced way. Be conscious of both kinds of food.

As you progress you become less excited about collecting the melodrama of the daily news; for as you delve within yourself, you want less and less to feed your mind unnecessary images and thoughts that agitate it. You simplify what you talk about, what you watch, and what you read. You find yourself drawn to new kinds of books, perhaps books written by those who speak from the quiet of meditation. They are invaluable in creating a space in which your mind can become quiet also.

We stuff our minds with trivia just to fill the emptiness we feel. When I sit in a New York subway train and watch people read the *Daily News*, I see how much unnecessary information they are collecting. I once spent six months in a temple in India. I had no communication with the rest of the world. It was during an election period, and I did not know who was the new president of the United States. This was ironic, for as a psychologist one of the questions on tests I had given to mental patients was, Who is the president of the United States? When I returned from India, I found that in about one day of reading back issues of magazines, I caught up with the significant events of the last half-year. At the same time I escaped being preoccupied with the personalities, events, and drama of the news. One can be a responsible citizen without allowing one's mind to be captured by the media and their need to create news. There is a saying: "When you sweep out the temple courtyard, don't stop to read the old newspapers."

We act as if the human intellect were a runaway monster which must be fed continuously at all costs. I myself am becoming less of an information addict. Now I sit on the subway doing mantra or following my breath and end the trip tranquil and ready for the next mo-

ment. Meanwhile others, immersed in collecting information to feed their minds, end the trip more tense, fragmented, and speedy than when they started.

> *Do not therefore ascribe blame or praise to the eating (or not eating) of foods, or to the drinking (or not drinking) of wine, but ascribe praise, or woe, unto those who make use properly or improperly of meat and drink.*
>
> —*Palladius*
>
> Stories of the Holy Fathers

> *What need of so much news from abroad, when all that concerns either life or death is at work within us?*
>
> —*William Law*
>
> The Perennial Philosophy

The teaching which is written on paper is not the true teaching. Written teaching is a kind of food for your brain. Of course it is necessary to take some food for your brain, but it is more important to be yourself by practicing the right way of life.

—*Shunryu Suzuki*

Zen Mind, Beginner's Mind

Where to Meditate

Meditation is work. It helps to have a physical space to work in—a room or corner set aside for meditation. All you do there is meditate, study holy books, or chant. Do nothing there that's not part of your spiritual practice. If you have the choice, you may want to keep this corner of the room simple, just bare white walls. Or you may decorate it in keeping with its unique part in your daily routine. A candle or stick of incense may do. Or maybe add a few pictures of beings who inspire you—Christ, Buddha, or Ramakrishna. You might also keep a few helpful books there such as the Bible or the Bhagavad Gita.

When you sit down in that corner or go into that room, make sure that all you do there is meditate or study. Don't use it for any other purpose. Dedicate it to the awakening of your spiritual self. Such a space becomes invested with the effects of your every attempt at meditation. You consecrate it. If you keep its use

pure, the space fills with a vibration that smooths your way for meditation.

Find a quiet place, free of distractions. A beginning meditator is easily distracted. In deeper meditation it won't matter what your surroundings are, but in the beginning the outer quiet helps you find an inner silence. Familiar places, where there are few things that catch your attention, are best.

While it is desirable to have a specific space or a private corner for your meditation, it is not necessary. Once you have a meditative practice that suits you, you can do it most anywhere. You will find many ordinary moments in your life are perfect for meditation: when you are waiting in the dentist's office, or for the bus, or sitting on a subway. Moments which usually were times for boredom or wandering thoughts become a gift—a chance to meditate.

Often I have had my deepest meditations when I least expected them: not when I was sitting on my meditation cushion surrounded by other meditators, but while driving my car, or sitting in an airplane, or waiting in the Internal Revenue Service office, or standing in line in the New Delhi railway station. Even standing in a crowded subway you can go within. The stronger your meditation, the less your surroundings distract you. Eventually, you will be able to meditate anywhere, anytime.

> *When a monk goes into a tavern, the tavern becomes his cell, and when a haunter of taverns goes into a cell, that cell becomes his tavern.*
>
> —*Hujwiri*
>
> Kashf al-Mahjub

> *The happiness of solitude is not found in retreats. It may be had even in busy centres. Happiness is not to be sought in solitude or in busy centres. It is in the Self.*
>
> —*Sri Ramana Maharshi*
>
> Talks with Sri Ramana Maharshi

When to Meditate

When should you meditate? Timing, like place, is important in the early stages. Just as you should find a comfortable place to sit, you should find a convenient time of day for your meditation. If you've just eaten a large meal, you may become drowsy. If you're hungry, that too may interfere with your meditation. Most serious meditators practice at least twice a day, in the morning after awakening, and some time during the evening. The first sitting puts your mind in a relaxed state before your day begins. The second sitting refreshes you for the evening.

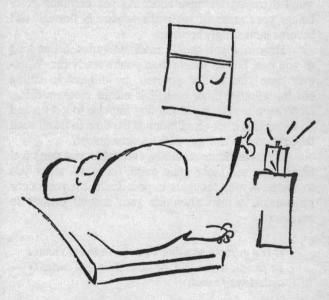

It's best to meditate each day at the same time in your daily rhythm—for example, before leaving the house each morning and before dinner each evening. Find or make times when you can be free of concerns and responsibilities for a while. Let someone else answer the phone or mind the children. The habit of meditating daily provides an outer framework for the inner process of meditation. So be regular.

In the beginning, twenty or thirty minutes is a good length for each meditation session. You can gradually extend the length of your sitting by increments of five minutes or so up to forty-five minutes to an hour, as your schedule and inclinations allow.

You can keep track of the time with a kitchen timer or with a watch, opening your eyes briefly to see if the time is up. These quick glimpses to check on time won't disrupt your meditation. As you continue practicing, your sense of when the session is through will become increasingly accurate.

How long you should meditate varies. Sit as long as you can, but no longer than you're ready for. Whatever time you set for yourself, be diligent in sitting out the allotted time, even if it means clockwatching. Don't stop meditating at the first impulse to get up and do something else—meditation is the time to let all such thoughts come and go, without attachment.

If you meditate regularly, even when you don't feel like it, you will make great gains, for it will allow you to see how your thoughts impose limits on you. Your resistances to meditation are your mental prisons in miniature.

It is a mistake to think that the sadhana cannot be practiced for lack of time. The real cause is agitation of mind.

—*Swami Brahmananda*

Discipline Monastique

With Whom to Meditate

Find other people with whom you can share your interest in meditation. They can become your support system. The nineteenth-century Indian saint Rama-krishna remarked that a beginner in spiritual life is like a young tree that needs to be circled with a fence for protection. This is the seeker's need for satsang, a group of fellow aspirants who strengthen one another's sometimes shaky faith on the journey. In sharing your experiences with other meditators you benefit from their feedback. You get a broader view of what's possible in meditation than you would have if you meditated alone.

To meditate with a group will certainly strengthen your practice. Your mind will create ruses to disrupt your practice. At those moments when you feel bored or agitated, if you were alone you might be inclined to stop and get up. An agreement to meditate with another person for a set time keeps you in place. When you sit with others, the pretexts that arise in your mind for quitting meditation are more often simply observed, rather than acted upon.

At a more profound level, meditating with satsang creates a group vibration that often intensifies your meditation. It's as if there is a summation of quieting thoughts that pass from one person to another. I have often come into meditation halls in Japan and in the United States where the hall itself would seem thick with these vibrations. Many churches and temples provide this peaceful space.

Your group could meet in someone's living room, light a candle and perhaps some incense, and sit quietly for an agreed period of time. Gradually you might add other activities done in a meditative spirit. For example, eat together afterward, or take turns reading aloud from books about meditation, or chant together.

Finding such a group may be as simple as checking bulletin boards or putting up a note in the laundromat, health-food store, or bookstore, asking if anyone would like to meditate with you one or two evenings a week. Maybe a friend would like to meditate with you. Or you might sit in at a Quaker meeting, for their form is itself meditative in nature. There may already be a neighborhood group that meets informally in someone's home, or in an adult-education evening course, or perhaps regular sittings of some meditation group.

The directory at the back of this book may help you find people with whom you can sit. There are listings for nationwide meditation organizations and for smaller meditation groups—perhaps there is one in your community. Each group has its own style and view, and in the long run, any one of them may or may not be attractive to you. Initially it makes little difference so long as you feel comfortable with the group. Later, with more experience, you may find you prefer to drop out of one group or join another. But don't waste too much time in the beginning by trying to judge this group or that, this individual or that. The important thing is to start meditating.

For where two or three are gathered together in My Name, there am I in the midst of them.

—*Matthew 18:20*

The New Testament

3

PICKING
A
PATH

Which Method is for Me?

Most people don't realize what a wide variety of possibilities there are among meditative practices. Perhaps because of mass advertising, they've come to identify meditation with a specific practice, like sitting with your eyes closed to repeat mantra, as in the TM technique, or facing a blank wall to empty your mind, as in zazen. The choice of methods available to help you gain inner freedom is actually quite diverse. There are many, many methods and groups to choose from, besides the few well-known names.

People sometimes are turned off by meditation when they begin with a method that is too hard for them. It helps to use a method which uses your natural tendencies, and so reinforces a positive attitude. At the outset choose a method that harmonizes with what you are already good at, a method that interests you. Follow it until you feel a strengthened connection to a quietness of mind, to a meditative awareness, to God.

Look at your life and see what has really turned you on. Perhaps you are very athletic. To sit motionless for an hour would be to fight your body. Instead you might begin with karate or kung fu and then go on to t'ai chi or some other moving meditation. If you are more sedentary or scholarly you might start by reading Krishnamurti or Buddhist doctrine and practicing vipassana meditation. An emotional person might find these practices too dry and be drawn instead to Sufi dancing or to singing or chanting. These are also forms of meditation.

As your meditation develops, you may find yourself drawn back to the methods you avoided when you began. You may get frustrated because the fire is not hot enough and you want to move faster than easier methods permit. So you work with one method after the next until all aspects—heart, mind, and body—are balanced. If you begin with one of them, sooner or later you will probably want to integrate the others as well. It makes no difference which technique you start with. Try to sense what you're ready for and what you need. Above all, be honest with yourself.

A useful tactic is to pick a method that feels right and do it for two weeks. During this trial run, agree with yourself, "I will treat all my negative reactions to this form of meditation as merely thought forms prompted by my ego to keep me from taking it seriously.

I will suspend judgment, criticism, and doubt." At the end of two weeks, you're free to evaluate the method. Or, give yourself three months or six months.

Plunge in. Eventually you have to stop trying to figure out where you are if you want to get somewhere else. Imagine Lindbergh flying from New York to Paris with only his little periscope sticking out of the *Spirit of St. Louis* to guide him. He can calculate his position from the stars, but all he sees is that there's a lot of ocean below. He doesn't really know whether he's miscalculated or not until he arrives. He's going on the faith that he's getting there and that it will all work out. That's what the spiritual journey is like. You need discipline to persist when the going gets rough or uncertain, faith to stick it out—to the end.

> *Does one really have to fret*
> *About enlightenment?*
> *No matter what road I travel,*
> *I'm going home.*
>
> *—Shinsho*

A Trial Run

If you've never done any meditation before, you can try one right now. First of all, quiet down a bit and find a comfortable seat. Your favorite armchair will do, or, if you want to sit crosslegged, try that.

Sit up as straight as you can without making yourself uncomfortable. Sooner or later you'll have to learn to sit with your back straight and your head, neck, and chest in a line. For the moment just get really comfortable. Stop reading for a few moments and get comfortable.

Now as you sit comfortably, your mind wanders. It turns to fantasies, memories. You think, what is this about, this meditation? What am I doing? If you don't hold on to any of these thoughts, but just let them keep flowing by, you are already in the act of meditation. This is it. You're doing it. But one of these thoughts may grab at you and lead you off into plans, fantasies, memories, or problem solving. Then you're just thinking, not meditating.

Here's a way you can keep from getting too lost in your thoughts. See your thoughts go by as if they were autumn leaves floating down a stream. But focus on the stream. The leaves drift by, being moved this way and that by the eddying water. On some there are drops of water that glisten in the sunlight. Let the leaves, the thoughts, float by, but keep your attention on the water itself. Your mind may dwell on a sound, a memory, a plan, or any of a thousand things. When you notice your mind clinging to any of these, these leaves, very gently bring it back to the stream, back to the water flowing. Let the leaves float by. Don't get angry because your attention got caught, for that anger is just another leaf. Don't get frustrated, because your attention will get caught thousands of times. Each time, very gently but firmly bring it back to the flowing water. Now try this meditation for a few minutes.

This is the beginning of the quiet mind.

Many Paths

Sitting quietly with eyes closed is only one of many ways to meditate. People can meditate while dancing and chanting the names of God, while making a cup of tea, or during practically any activity. And for those who meditate with eyes closed, there is a wide variety of inner practices. It is not what you do with your body but what you do with your mind that counts in meditation.

Sampling the variety of meditative practices in the sections that follow, you will come to appreciate that there is a wide range of possibilities. While all of the practices described here lead ultimately to the same result, each emphasizes different qualities of the meditative state. Thus, for example, one type of meditation will emphasize quietness of mind, another tuning to the forces of the universe, another compassion. I think of this difference as merely a matter of timing, for although each of these practices starts with one quality or another, ultimately all the qualities come into play in the course of the seeker's path.

To pursue any method brings you to more subtle considerations and more advanced levels of practice. What initially may have been irrelevant takes on significance later. For example, take mantra. When you begin to work with mantra, any one will do. Later, however, you become aware of nuances, such as the subtle differences between mantras and the states to which they bring you.

Each method reveals subtleties as you advance in it. Experiment until you find one that seems right for you. Then focus on it wholeheartedly, either on your own or with a teacher.

Concentration

Concentration is the root skill in all meditation practices. The meditator must be able to keep the mind fixed on a specific task or object, and let distractions go by, no matter which technique is used. This skill is simple in definition, but takes great patience to develop in practice. To begin developing concentration you need simply pick some object, thought, or part of the body and fix your mind on it for a fixed length of time. When your mind wanders, return your focus gently but firmly to the object of your meditation. Once you develop even a little concentration—which happens after a relatively short period of meditation—you will find it enhances all other methods of spiritual practice.

One simple exercise for bringing your awareness to a single object is concentrating on a candle flame. Place a candle in front of you a foot or so away and focus on the flame. As you look at the flame, countless thoughts will float by about the candle, the flame, meditation, sounds you hear, feelings in your body, and so forth. In each case you notice the thought, let it go, and merely come back to an awareness of the candle flame. By gently but firmly trying to keep your attention focused on the candle flame, you begin to see your thoughts and senses grabbing at your awareness. You become aware of the process of attachment.

This training in one-pointedness of mind is the first step in learning not to cling. The goal of meditation is to free your awareness from its identification with your senses and thoughts. So freed, your awareness permeates everything but clings to nothing.

> *The attainment of the one-pointedness of the mind and the senses is the best of austerities.*
>
> —*Sri Sankaracharya*
>
> **A Thousand Teachings**

> *The very essence of meditation is one-pointedness and the exclusion of all other considerations, even when these considerations happen to be enticing.*
>
> —*Meher Baba*
>
> Discourses

Try these directions for mindfulness of breathing, a basic concentration practice: When you're ready to meditate, close your eyes and bring your attention to the motion of your breath as it enters and leaves your nostrils. Keep your focus at the nostrils, noting the full passage of each in-breath and out-breath, from beginning to end. Don't follow the breath into your lungs or out into the air; just watch its flow in and out of the nostrils. If you can, notice the subtle sensations of the breath as it comes and goes. Be aware of each in-breath and out-breath as it passes by the nostrils, just as a doorman watches each person who comes and goes through a door.

Attend to the feeling of the breath. Don't try to imagine it or visualize it. Note the sensation of the breath just as it is, exactly as you feel it. You may feel the breath at the rim of the nostrils, or just inside the nose, or on the upper lip beneath the nose. The sensations you feel will change—you may sometimes feel the breath like the light touch of a feather, like a dull throb, or as an intense point of pressure on your lip, or in countless other ways. There is no "right" way for the breath to feel; just be aware of what is. Each time you notice your mind has wandered to other thoughts, or is caught by background noises, bring your attention back to the easy, natural rhythm of your breathing.

Don't try to control your breath. Simply watch it. Fast or slow, shallow or deep, the nature of the breath does not matter. Your full attention to it is what counts. If you have trouble keeping your mind on the breath, count each one up to ten, then start over again at one. Or, to anchor your mind on your breath, you can occasionally make a strong, deliberate inhalation and exhalation. Then let your breath return to its normal rate.

Whenever you realize you're thinking about something else, return your awareness to your breath. Don't try to fight off thoughts. Just let them go.

If sounds distract you, do the same: Let them be and simply start watching your breath again. If aches or itches bother you, slowly move or shift to ease them if you must. But keep your mind on breathing while you do it.

Your mind will wander, and when you first start to meditate you may be acutely aware of how active it is. Don't worry about it. Just keep returning your attention to your breath, letting go of whatever the mind wanders to. This is the essence of meditation: letting go of your thoughts.

Mantra

A word, a name of God, or a spiritual phrase that is repeated over and over again is known as a mantra. The practice of mantra is an effective way to concentrate your mind. But as important as concentrating your mind is what you concentrate on. Although the mind can focus on anything, only certain words can qualify as mantra. A mantra must connect you with the sacred. Most of them focus you on God through repetition of a divine name. A mantra provides a boat with which you can float through your thoughts unattached, entering subtler and subtler realms. It is a boat that steers itself—to the threshold of God.

The use of mantra sets up one thought, one wave, that repeats over and over again, dislodging your attachment to all other thoughts, until they are like birds gliding by. For example, you can quietly or silently repeat the Sanskrit mantra "Ram," a name of God. Just repeat "Ram, Ram, Ram, Ram." A billboard goes by and disappears into "Ram, Ram, Ram." If a passenger in your car asked what you were doing, you might tell him, "I'm saying 'Ram, Ram, Ram' " instead of, "I'm taking my foot off the accelerator." All you're thinking of consciously is the mantra, while the driving is taken care of automatically. In the same way you begin to see your life from the detached vantage point of the mantra.

Although groups like TM recommend that beginners not meditate more than twenty minutes twice daily, I have found it useful to sit quietly and do nothing else but practice mantra for longer periods. You can work concentratedly with mantra for an extended time, three or four hours, or even longer. In this way you will become intimate with the sound of the mantra and you will begin to surrender into it, to merge.

Offer all your thoughts as a sacrifice to the mantra. If you think, "This isn't going to work," take that thought and imagine yourself offering it to the mantra on a golden tray with a silk handkerchief, incense, and a candle. Offer it as you continue to repeat the mantra undisturbed. Keep offering your thoughts, your doubts, discomforts, boredom, even your sore throat.

Later, when you have gotten up to go about the business of the day, keep remembering the mantra; invite it to stay with you. You can coordinate the mantra with your steps as you walk or with any rhythmic activity. No matter what else you do, keep doing the mantra. If you are typing, each time you hit the shift key, "Ram"; if you are talking, each time there is a pause, "Ram."

One very effective and widely used method of remembering a mantra is the "counting" of beads with a rosary or mala. Any easily handled beads will do. You pass the beads across your fingers, bead by bead, with

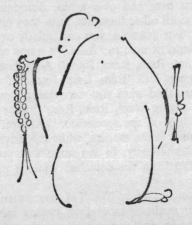

each repetition of the mantra. If your mind wanders, the activity of the hand or the touch of a bead will remind you of the mantra. The rhythm becomes more compelling, the experience more total as your body works in harmony with the mind. Also, you can use the beads to keep track of how many times you have repeated the mantra as part of your daily meditation routine.

As you practice you will notice that when your mind is calm the mantra will be delicate and subtle. When your mind is agitated the mantra will be as strong and gross as is needed. Just keep bringing your mind back to the mantra and let it make you more and more still.

Some examples of mantra besides "Ram" are "Aum," the one basic sound or totality of all sound; "Aum Mani Padme Hum" (pronounced AH-OWM MAH-NAY PAHD-MAY HOOM), the Tibetan mantra meaning "The All is a precious jewel in the lotus flower which blooms in my heart"; and the Buddhist mantra "Gate Gate Paragate, Parasamgate, Bodhi Svaha" (pronounced GAH-TAY GAH-TAY PAH-RAH GAH-TAY PAH-RAH-SAHM GAH-TAY BOW-DEE SWAH-HAH), which means "Beyond, Beyond, the Great Beyond, Beyond that Beyond, to Thee Homage." As far as you can think, as far in as you can go, these mantras keep going beyond, drawing you on until finally you go beyond any need of the mantra into the source of all thought.

There are various stages as your practice of a mantra deepens. An exquisite description of this process is found in *The Way of a Pilgrim*, written by an unknown Russian whose practice was to repeat the Jesus Prayer.

> *After no great lapse of time I had the feeling that the prayer had, so to speak, by its own action passed from my lips to my heart. Further there came into my heart a precious warmth. None of these things made me feel at all cast down.*

*It was as though they were happening to someone
else and I merely watched them. The prayer
brought sweetness into my heart and made me
unaware of everything else.*

How fast this takes place depends on how wide
open and ready you are. But before too long, if practiced continually, a mantra becomes somewhat auton-
omous, like a top spinning inside which every now
and then needs just a flick to keep it going. Eventually,
it will go on with no need of encouragement, as in the
case of the saint Kabir who said, "Ram practices my
japa [repetition of God's name] while I sit relaxed." It's
a blissful moment when you notice that happening:
Instead of doing mantra, the mantra is doing you.

If your spirit is ripe for it, you might only have to
hear a mantra or see it in a book to sense that it is the
right vehicle for you. Or you might try a particular
mantra and find, when you begin to use it, that nothing
happens. It may feel foreign and irrelevant as you
repeat it. Don't worry about your pronunciation. In the
course of time it will take care of itself. Give a mantra
a chance. Then, if it still feels strange and uncomfortable, perhaps it is not the right mantra for you. No
harm done. Just try another.

Mantras can range from a simple word or phrase
which you might want to work with, to the Sanskrit and
Tibetan mantras designed so that each syllable activates
a particular chakra or a particular type of consciousness. A powerful English mantra comes from Herman
Rednick: "I am a point of sacrificial fire held within
the fiery Will of God." Do this mantra while keeping your attention focused on the point between the
eyebrows. As you bring your energy to this point with
mantra, day after day after day, you gradually become
a channel of God's will.

The Hindu mantra "Aditya Hridayam Punyam,
Sarva Shatru Bina Shanam" (pronounced AH-DIT-
EYA HRI-DAEE-AHM POON-YAHM SAHRVA

SHAH-TROO BEE-NA SHA-NAM) means "When the sun is kept in the heart all evil vanishes from life." If you wish to practice this mantra, as you repeat it visualize the sun. Consider how the sun sends light and warmth on everything, good and evil alike. It doesn't say, "I won't shine on you because you aren't playing the game." It just keeps sending out light and warmth. Do this in the morning. Contemplate the sun, Aditya, and bring it slowly down into your heart. Feel its warmth and radiance in your heart. To send this warmth and love out you don't have to do anything; the sun is the emission of light. Let it shine. As you repeat this mantra and follow the visualization, you are tuning to the Self residing in your spiritual heart, or Hridayam. When the sun is kept in your heart, all evil vanishes from your life.

In the Bible is a natural mantra as simple as its name—the "Jesus Prayer" or "Prayer of the Heart." In Luke 18:13, it says: " . . . but the publican standing afar off, would not so much as lift up his eyes to heaven, but kept striking his breast, saying: 'O God, be merciful to me the sinner.'" This mantra has come to read: "Lord

Jesus Christ, son of God, have mercy on me a sinner." It may be reduced to as few as three words depending on the one who prays:

"Lord Jesus Christ, son of God, have mercy on me, a sinner."

"Lord Jesus Christ, have mercy on me, a sinner."

"Jesus Christ, have mercy on me, a sinner."

"Jesus Christ, have mercy on me."

"Christ have mercy."

If you discipline yourself to learn this mantra and repeat it constantly, it will sink down into your heart and after awhile it will go on by itself.

—Marie Idol

In the beginning was the Word, and the Word was with God, and the Word was God.

—John 1:1

The New Testament

It is in pronouncing Thy Name that I must die and live.

—Muhammad

Introduction aux Doctrines esotériques de l'Islam

*Thus abide constantly with the name of our Lord
Jesus Christ, so that the heart swallows the Lord
and the Lord the heart, and the two become one.*

—*St. John Chrysostom*

Writings from the Philokalia
on Prayer of the Heart

*Blessed is the person who utterly surrenders his
soul for the name of YHWH to dwell therein
and to establish therein its throne of glory.*

—*Zohar*

Major Trends in
Jewish Mysticism

*I am a happy man, indeed!
I visit the Pure Land as often as I like:
I'm there and I'm back,
I'm there and I'm back,
I'm there and I'm back,
"Namu-amida-butsu! Namu-amida-butsu!"*

—*Saichi*

Mysticism Christian and
Buddhist

Contemplation

Reading scripture, praying, and communing with nature are all forms of contemplation.

You should read enough of the thought underlying your spiritual practices to understand fully what you are doing. Use this study as seeds for contemplation. Collect a series of books written or spoken by beings who are liberated or attuned to higher states of consciousness. Quotations from some of these books are sprinkled throughout this one. Each day in the morning or evening open a book at random or read until you find a paragraph or a sentence with which to work. Reflect on it throughout the day. See your own life through the lens of the passage. Through this practice, in time, comes a transformation of your perception, your ways of understanding the nature of reality.

Contemplation can also be free-form. Thoreau wrote:

> *Sometimes, I sat in my sunny doorway from sunrise till noon, rapt in a revery, amidst the pines and hickories and sumacs, in undisturbed solitude and stillness, while the birds sang around*

or flitted noiseless through the house, until by
the sun falling in at my west window, or the
noise of some traveller's wagon on the distant
highway, I was reminded of the pass of time. I
grew in those seasons like corn in the night,
and they were far better than any work of the
hands would have been. They were not time sub-
tracted from my life, but so much over and above
my usual allowance. I realized what the
Orientals mean by contemplation and the
forsaking of work.

To some extent, and at rare intervals, even
I am a yogi.

The revery of which Thoreau speaks just happens
to us. To let your mind float around an idea or image
in a relaxed but focused way is the most familiar kind
of contemplation. It is not so different from the almost
formless prayer described by St. John of the Cross.
Prayer can range from a simple silent openness to a
very personal dialogue with God.

When you go apart to be alone for prayer, put
from your mind everything you have been doing
or plan to do. Reject all thoughts, be they good or
be they evil. Do not pray with words unless you
are really drawn to this; or if you do pray with
words, pay no attention to whether they are many
or few. Do not weigh them or their meaning. Do
not be concerned about what kind of prayers you
use, or whether you formulate them interiorly,
by thoughts, or express them aloud, in words.
See that nothing remains in your conscious mind
save a naked intent stretching out toward God.
Leave it stripped of every particular idea about
God (what he is like in himself or in his works)
and keep only the simple awareness that he is as
he is. Let him be thus, I pray you, and force

him not to be otherwise. Search into him no
further, but rest in this faith as on solid ground.
This awareness, stripped of ideas and deliberately
bound and anchored in faith, shall leave your
thought and affection in emptiness except for a
naked thought and blind feeling of your own
being. It will feel as if your whole desire cried out
to God and said:

> That which I am I offer to you, O Lord,
> without looking to any quality of your
> being but only to the fact that you are
> as you are; this, and nothing more.

Let that quiet darkness be your whole mind
and like a mirror to you. For I want your
thought of self to be as naked and as simple as
your thought of God, so that you may be
spiritually united to him without any fragmentation
and scattering of your mind. He is your being
and in him, you are what you are, not only
because he is the cause and being of all that exists,
but because he is your cause and the deep center
of your being. Therefore, in this contemplative
work think of your self and of him in the same
way: this is, with the simple awareness that he is
as he is, and that you are as you are. In this way
your thought will not be fragmented or scattered,
but unified in him who is all.

Leave your thought quite naked, your
affection uninvolved and your self simply as you
are, so that grace may touch and nourish you
with the experimental knowledge of God as he
really is. Look up joyfully, and say to your Lord,
in words or desire:

> That which I am, I offer to you,
> O Lord, for you are it entirely.

Go no further, but rest in this naked, stark,
elemental awareness that you are as you are.

—*St. John of the Cross*

The Ascent of Mount Carmel

*Hear, O Israel: The Lord our God, the Lord is
One! And thou shalt love the Lord thy God
with all thy heart, and with all thy soul, and with
all thy might. And these words, which I command
thee this day, shall be upon thy heart, and thou
shalt teach them diligently unto thy children,
and thou shalt talk of them when thou sittest in
thy house, and when thou walkest by the way,
and when thou liest down, and when thou risest
up. And thou shalt bind them for a sign upon
thy hand, and they shall be for frontlets between
thine eyes. And thou shalt write them upon the
door-posts of thy house and upon thy gates.*

—Deuteronomy 6:4–7

The Old Testament

*Everywhere, wherever you may find yourself,
you can set up an altar to God in your mind by
means of prayer.*

—The Way of a Pilgrim

Prayers are answered in the way they're asked.

—Ram Tirth

I felt it better to speak to God than about him.

—St. Therese of Lisieux

You pray to what you love; for true, whole prayer is nothing but love!

—St. Augustine

Nature is the easiest object of contemplation for our surroundings can inspire and lead us into the quiet unity of all creation. Surya Singer and Soma Krishna suggest these ways to open to nature:

As children, the play of the sun on rippling water brought us before God's throne. Did you ever see an infant gaze at a lightbulb or the moon? Spiritual techniques are discovered naturally by infants and little children: holding their breath, staring unblinking, standing on their heads, imitating animals, turning in circles, sitting unmoving, and repeating phrases over and over until all else ceases to exist. Stop thinking that meditation is anything special. Stop thinking all together. Look at the world around you as if you had just arrived on Planet Earth. Observe the rocks in their natural formations, the trees rooted

*in the ground, their branches reaching to the sky,
the plants, animals and the interrelationships
of each to the other. See yourself through the eyes
of a dog in a park. See a flower through its
essence. See a mountain through its massiveness.
When the mind allows its objects to remain
unmolested, there may be no mind and no object
—just breathless unity.*

— Surya Singer.

*To see the world in a grain of sand
And Heaven in a wild flower
Hold infinity in the palm of your hand
And eternity in an hour.*

—William Blake

Auguries of Innocence

*Devise meditations in which you draw nature into
your own being through your senses. You can
experiment with some of these:
Sit with your back pressed against the
trunk of the mightiest tree you can find and pull*

its strength into your spine with each breath. Lose awareness of where the tree trunk and your back become one. Thank the tree.

Rest an evergreen branch on the top of your head and let its power pour into you as though to fill an empty vessel. The overflow bathes you in green mist and you are renewed.

Hold a rock in your hand. Feel its texture, weight, and reconstruct its geological history. How old is it? Did it travel from deep within the earth or from space as a meteorite before it reached your hand? Become that rock.

Feed on the smell of fresh-cut grass, even the lawn, drawing the odor into your nose and mouth. Let it nourish body and spirit.

Taste the wind. What does it carry? Salt from the sea, perhaps? Or clean pine essence from the mountains, or parched desert air? Lick snow and rain from the wind's fingers.

Lie on the sun-warmed ground and share its gratitude as the generous rays kindle the soil's own latent life. Imagine that you are a seed. Watch yourself sprout and grow.

Listen to the ocean pound on the beach. Close your eyes and let the intensity of the sound fill your head, then your whole body, until you vibrate with it. Try to hear beyond the ocean to the roar of the raw primal energy in the universe.

Watch the flow of a river. Throw your burden of worry and negative emotions to the passing water to carry off. Breathe deeply to dislodge old crystallized tensions from around your heart, as the current sweeps away layer after layer of ancient woes on its way to the ocean. Visualize the ocean waiting, neutralizing all, and converting it back into pure energy once more.

—Soma Krishna

*There is a sadhu in Hrishikesh who gets up early
in the morning and stands near a great waterfall.
He looks at it the whole day and says to God:
"Ah, You have done well! Well done! How
amazing!" He doesn't practice any other form of
japa or austerity. At night he returns to his hut.*

—Sri Ramakrishna

The Gospel of
Sri Ramakrishna

*At Kugami
In front of the Otono,
There stands a solitary pine tree,
Surely of many a generation;
How divinely dignified
It stands there!
In the morning
I pass by it;
In the evening
I stand underneath it,
And standing I gaze,
Never tired
Of this solitary pine!*

—Ryokwan

Zen and Japanese Culture

*The voice of the mountain torrent is from one
great tongue;
The lines of the hills, are they not the pure body
of the Buddha?*

—*Zenrin*

The Gospel According to Zen

Devotion

Prayer, sitting with a picture of a holy being, singing to the Beloved—all of these are devotional meditative practices, the way of the heart. Devotion balances the more impersonal wisdom that comes from most kinds of meditation. It allows us to cultivate our humanity while we transform our consciousness. This outflowing of the heart toward the object of our devotion facilitates most other methods as well, through the flow of loving energy.

As an example, imagine a being standing before you, someone to whom you feel particularly tuned, such as Abraham, Christ, Mary, or Hanuman. This being is radiant, luminous, a being whose eyes are filled with compassion, a being in whom you feel the wisdom that comes from an intimate harmony with the universe.

Despite all of the impurities to which you cling, despite all your feelings of unworthiness, such a being loves you unconditionally. To sit before such a being, or to imagine such a being sitting in your heart, to be with that being and return the love, to see yourself reflected in such compassionate, unjudging eyes, to open more and more, as if to a beloved, to carry on imaginary conversations with such a being, opens you to compassion, tranquility, warmth, patience, to all the qualities of a free being.

This interpersonal quality of devotional meditation allows you to start from your psychological needs, to love, to be loved, to be in the presence of wisdom, compassion, and peace. When you are with a being who embodies these qualities, they rub off, and you feel more evolved, even to the point of recognizing the radiant light within yourself. This acknowledgment of your own beauty allows you to open even more to the beloved, until finally the lover and the beloved merge and you find out that what you had seen outwardly as perfection is a mirror of your own true being.

There are lower and higher stages of devotion. In the lower you romanticize the journey. You merely shift the focus of your melodrama from marketplace to temple. The images in the temple, the temple itself, your participation in worship, the love, say, of Christ, of Krishna, of Buddha, become preoccupations. You want to think about, talk to, play with, and open your heart to them. This level is romantic; you have fallen in love with your vehicle for going to God. But your love grows and your beloved becomes the whole object of your life, you tune to a deeper place within yourself. Then the emotional, romantic qualities of devotion give way to a new kind of love where finally you see all people as the beloved.

O Sadhu! the simple union is the best.
Since the day when I met with my Lord,
    there has been no end to the sport of our love.
I shut not my eyes, I close not my ears,
    I do not mortify my body;
I see with eyes open and smile, and
    behold His beauty everywhere;

I utter His Name, and whatever I see,
   it reminds me of Him; whatever I do, it
   becomes His worship.
The rising and the setting are one to
   me; all contradictions are solved.
Wherever I go, I move around Him,
All I achieve is His service:
When I lie down, I lie prostrate at His feet.
. . . I am immersed in that one great bliss which
   transcends all pleasure and pain.

   —Kabir

   One Hundred Poems of
   Kabir

Devotion is easy and natural and has no hard and
fast rules regarding how one should meditate.
By devotion one can realize the secret of love
itself. On this path the aspirant sees the universe
as the very expression of his Beloved.

   The only thing it requires is faith—implicit
faith. There is nothing to argue, it is beyond
logic. It is like learning to swim: a person cannot
enter the water unless he can swim, and swimming
is impossible without entering the water.

   There are various attitudes or feelings with
which one may approach the Beloved. You
might feel as though God were your child, like
the feeling of Yashoda (Krishna's mother) toward
her baby Krishna, or the feeling of Mary for the
infant Jesus. Or you could see God as a friend.
Again there is the attitude of the servant toward

his Master, where you serve the Lord as Hanuman serves Lord Rama in the Ramayana. Then there is the attitude of lover, where you see your Beloved with the love of husband or wife. . . . becoming the bride of God, like the gopis sporting with Lord Krishna, or St. Therese the Little Flower married to her beloved Jesus. Finally there is the attitude of peaceful contemplation of the great saints and sages, the ancient yogis of India.

There are many ways to open yourself, to make oneself more receptive to this love for God. One way is through satsang, the company of saints, contact with the living spirit of Truth and Love in other beings. Delighting in the stories and incidents of God in His many forms and incarnations—like the life of Christ, or Rama or Krishna—can also bring this love. Or by humbly serving at the feet of the Guru, the devotee can efface the ego in surrender to God. And constantly singing His Name and His praises further centers the mind and heart on Him. For the devotee the mere repetition of the Name of God brings His Presence. Then, with firm faith, one crosses the ocean of desire in the boat of the Name.

—K.K. Sah

Christ was lost in love.

—Maharaj-ji (Neem Karoli Baba)

True devotion is for itself; not to desire heaven or to fear hell.

—Rabia el-Adawia

And thou shalt love the Lord thy God with all thy heart, and with all thy soul, and with all thy mind, and with all thy strength: this is the first commandment.

—Mark 12:30

The New Testament

The Names of God or praises of God can be sung as well as spoken. Often when your heart wells up, singing alone expresses the fullness of your love for God. As you sing the Name repeatedly, the rhythm and melody fan your emotions. If this ecstasy is heightened, distinctions begin to fall away until only love, only the beloved, remain.

Kirtan, the singing of mantra, is an old and revered technique used in India and other parts of Asia. While kirtan uses music as a vehicle, aesthetics or musical ability are not the main concern. The ability to sing beautifully is enjoyable but not necessary. What matters is singing from the heart. In India often it is the old man who sings last, with no teeth, a raspy voice, and hacking cough, who blows everyone away because he knows to whom he is singing, and the beauty of his contact with God is moving and powerful.

Kirtan, like any other devotional practice, can be done from any state of mind or level of evolution.

By mere persistence it leads to deeper levels of opening and understanding. Whatever space you start from, if you persist in kirtan the space will change. You may want to get high, but find yourself getting bored. You may want to "feel devotional." If you allow each experience to arise and pass, making space for new experiences to come from within, you will open to the power that comes from singing the Names of God.

If you are blissful, be blissful and sing. If you are bored, be bored and sing. Just keep offering your experiences into the fire of the Name and it will guide you through them all.

When you are in love with God, the very sound of the Name brings great joy. It is said that "in its highest aspect, Divine Love is nothing less than the immortal bliss of liberation." To open fully to kirtan, to the singing of the divine Name, is to know this sweetest form of bliss.

What follows is the musical scoring for two mantras. The first of them, Sri Ram Jai Ram Jai Jai Ram, is a mantra often sung at the request of my guru. The second is a beautiful and simple prayer. Any devotional verse or song can be repeated as a meditation.

SRI RAM

Sri Ram Ja ya Ram Ja ya Ja ya Ra-a-am

Sri Ram Ja ya Ram Ja ya Ja ya Ram

Sri Ram Ja ya Ram Ja ya Ja ya Ra-am

Sri Ram Ja ya Ram Ja ya Ja ya Ram

Pronounced: SHREE RAHM JAY RAHM JAY JAY RAHM

TWAMEVA MATA

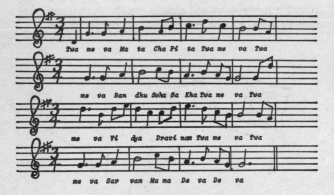

Twa me va Ma ta Cha Pi ta Twa me va Twa

me va Ban dhu Soha Sa Kha Twa me va Twa

me va Vi dya Dravi nam Twa me va Twa

me va Sar vam Ma ma De va De va

Thou art my Mother and my Father art Thou
Thou art my Friend and my Companion art Thou
Thou art my Learning, my Wealth art Thou
Thou art my ALL in ALL, My Lord of Lords.

Pronounced:

TWAH-MEY-VA MAH-TAH CHA PEE-TAH
 TWAH-MEY-VA

TWAH-MEY-VA BAN-DHU SCHA SA-KAH
 TWAH-MEY-VA

TWAH-MEY-VA VI-DHYA DRA-VEE-NAHM
 TWAH-MEY-VA

TWAH-MEY-VA SAHR-VAM MA-MA DEY-VA
 DEY-VA

*The more pure, true, and penetrating is the song
or chant, the nearer and clearer it is to His ears.
This permeates the atmosphere of the gathering
with purity, peace, love, and bliss, and all feel the
great joy of that Essence. As one becomes
absorbed and submerged in it, the chanting itself
becomes the meditation.*

—K.K. Sah

Visualization

In directed visualizations you bring to mind a mental image on which you meditate. Visualization resembles our familiar habits of fantasies, daydreams, and imaginings but brings discipline to them. Unlike ordinary daydreams, spiritual visualization exercises focus your mind on a holy image. The power of this method is that it enables you to find the qualities of the imaged beings within yourself.

You can try the following visualizations. Either read them through and then do them, or have a friend read them to you.

Sit with a straight back, eyes closed.

As if it had a nose, breathe deeply in and out of your heart center (located in the middle of your chest) for a few minutes until this area of your body feels warm and expanded. Rise up to your throat center and breathe in and out of this chakra until it feels alive. Come up to your third eye area and breathe in and out. Rise into your crown chakra on the top of your head, breathing in and out vertically. Then return your awareness and breath into your heart center. Feel the connection between your heart and your head centers. Be conscious of the energy flow that unites them.

Again, breathe into your heart, and visualize a tiny Buddha seated there, radiant, perfect. He embodies all virtues, all strengths. He radiates equanimity, compassion, all-enduring love. With each breath, the tiny Buddha glows brighter and begins to expand. Follow this expansion with your breath and flow of attention, feeding the figure until it fills your entire heart center. Keep breathing life into this Buddha-self until it overflows your heart center and slowly fills every part of your being, every cell of your body, until you and the Buddha are one. As the Buddha, there is no more striving. You are there. Just pause before the next stage.

As the Buddha, now begin to breathe into your Buddha-heart, drawing in light with each breath, converting it into love in your heart, and sending it out Buddha's third eye to the world. With each breath your heart glows brighter. Feel the love stream out of Buddha's forehead. Keep breathing in light and sending out love as the love-emanation from your third eye becomes a continuous river that flows out to cover the whole universe. Let body awareness fade and become the mighty channel for this blessing. There is no you—only a vast Buddha-heart and a spiritual eye.

Buddha's work is finished for now. Slowly, slowly start to draw into your heart center once more, until the luminous figure fills it. As the Buddha-body contracts, it becomes even more brilliant, leaving you with a fiery radiance in your heart for the rest of the day. In your dealings with the world this day, remember that part of you is still the Buddha.

—Soma Krishna

When you are composed and feel yourself in the presence of the Spirit, try this meditation. Do it slowly and with intensity.

Imagine yourself on a hilly plain. It is spring. The grass is fresh and green. The sun is warm on your skin. Feel the breath of the gentle breeze. Smell the sweet air and the new grass. A wonderful feeling of well-being flows over your body.

You are surrounded by people who are silent and waiting in prayer. Try to feel the vibrations of their devotion.

*Now look to a slightly elevated hill some
yards in front of you. A number of people on top
of the hill surround a figure whose presence you
feel immediately. Look carefully with your mind
and your ear. It is Jesus, enveloped in a beautiful
white light. An intense light shines from each of
His wounds. Gaze upon Him and feel the warmth
of His love. Whisper His name.*

*From the heart of Jesus, a ray of light bursts
forth and enters into your heart. See Him looking at you, white light joining you heart to heart.
He approaches you and slowly enters the center
of your heart. See Him there. Feel Him, feel your
heart, warm with His love and brilliant with His
light. Your mind stops, overwhelmed with God's
love. Stay there awhile. Surrender to the presence
of God.*

*Now, imagine that you are going up with
Jesus. Cast up your awareness to the center of
your head. Concentrate and go through the top of
your head, you and Jesus, going up and up through
the sky.*

*Above you is a vast ball of pulsating intense
light. Go into this light with Jesus. Let it penetrate
each cell of your body. Again, surrender yourself.
Open to your true being. Rest in the heart of God.*

*At any time during a meditation you may be
taken over by God. Everything stops. The mind
stops, the body seems to stop and you enter into
an ineffable quiet—an intense quiet of love. Just
rest in it. Be bathed in God.*

*The peace and love of Jesus be with you al-
ways.*

—*Father Ed Lavin*

At times you will think of your Guru.
Whenever such yearning arises
Visualize him upon your head
And for his blessing pray.
Visualize him sitting in the center of your heart
And forget him never.
But you should know that even your Guru
Is delusory and dreamlike;
That all things are unreal and magical.

> —Milarepa
>
> The Hundred Thousand
> Songs of Milarepa

Worship me in the symbols and images which re-
mind thee of me.

> —Srimad Bhagavatam
>
> The Wisdom of God

Movement

Every move is a prayer.

> —Man of the Crow Dog
> Family
>
> Akwesasne Notes

Though most meditation is done sitting still, you can also meditate as you move. The flow of energy in your body, its stance and positions, the way you walk, all can be meditation. In hatha yoga, for example, there is a set of postures, called asanas, each of which embodies a specific attitude and relationship to the universe. It's as if you're changing the receiving channel of your body by changing positions. If at this moment you put your hands together in prayer, you can feel as you hold them there the quality of a prayerful attitude. Or on the other hand, if you make a fist and hold it out menacingly, you can feel the way the fist accentuates a threatening attitude. So it is that each body position makes a statement of one kind or another. Just in the arching of your back, you change the movements of energy throughout the body. Hatha yoga postures open the energies of the body; each position becomes a meditative posture that allows you to tune in to a different space.

There are also hand positions, called mudras, that reflect various states of consciousness. If you study statues of the Buddha you will notice that his hands take various positions. Each of these is a mudra. In t'ai chi a flow of mudras develops into a moving meditation. While t'ai chi appears to be a continuous movement, it is actually a series of tiny stops—like a movie in slow motion.

T'ai chi, like all Oriental martial arts, is a spiritual path in itself. Indeed, Bodhidharma, who brought Buddhism to China from India, is credited with inventing karate (kung fu in Chinese). When the way of the martial arts is pursued to its highest point, the practitioner loses all trace of his ego in the perfection of his movements. To reach this point requires as intense a self-discipline as any sitting meditation.

Still another tradition that uses movement to develop a meditative awareness is Sufi dancing. The Dervishes are fabled for their whirls, but there are many other kinds of dances and walks the Sufis use. In most of these the movement is keyed to a chant, the combination of motion and prayer focusing the dancer's mind and body on God.

For a master of hatha yoga, t'ai chi, or Sufi dancing, movement is stillness.

Asanas should preferably be done in the morning or afternoon before sitting for meditation. Do not hurry through the postures. It is better to do just a few asanas in a relaxed manner than to speed through them all. Use a flat surface—a mat or a well-padded rug—and wear comfortable, loose clothing. Do not do asanas if you are sick or during menstruation unless you are being instructed by a teacher. Wait for two or three hours after eating before doing asanas and do not eat for at least twenty minutes afterwards.

If asanas are not practiced too fast, the breath will remain even. Always breathe through the nose. As you bend forward, let the breath be exhaled. As you bend backward, let the breath be inhaled. As you stretch farther into an asana, take a little breath. Inhale if you stretch backward, exhale if you bend forward. Hold the breath for a few seconds when exerting force to balance the body. By practice your body gradually will become loose. Again, go easy; do not use much force in stretching.

Each asana may be done two or three times if possible. But always take at least a fifteen- to twenty-second rest lying flat on your back (corpse pose) after each asana—letting your breath come back to normal. Or after a standing asana you may rest standing.

The following asana, Surya Namaskar— the salute to the sun—integrates several yoga positions into a flow of movement that balances and tones the body. It is in itself a meditation as well as a good prelude to sitting. As you do this asana you can concentrate on the morning sun. Let yourself become one with it. Begin by doing this exercise three times and gradually build up to six or so.

1. Stand relaxed, feet together, hands held palms together, fingers upward, at the middle of the chest. Exhale.

2. Lock thumbs and raise arms over head. Keep arms close to ears. Bend backward looking up at hands, inhaling.

3. Bend forward, head between arms, and place palms on the floor on either side of feet. Keep knees straight and try to touch head to knees, exhaling.

4. Stretch left leg back, knee to floor. Keep right foot between hands, knee to chest. Arch back, looking up, inhaling.

5. Throw right leg back to meet left foot. Raise buttocks to form a triangle with the feet, heels to floor, and the hands on floor (arms extended, head between arms), exhaling.

6. *Bring knees, chest, and chin to floor, in that order. Keep pelvis raised and palms beneath shoulders. Inhale and hold.*

7. *Bring pelvis to floor and stretch head, neck, and chest up, looking toward the ceiling, elbows alongside body, slightly bent. Hold breath.*

8. *Push up and raise the body back into the triangle in one movement, exhaling.*

9. *Thrust left leg up between hands, knee to chest. Leave right leg extended, knee to floor. Arch back, looking up, inhaling.*

10. *Bring right leg up, back into position number three, exhaling.*

11. *Stretch up and back into position number two, inhaling.*

12. *Return to beginning position, exhaling.*

—*Adapted from* Inside/Out

Learn to experience the chi, or breath energy, flowing through and moving your body. On the beach accompanied by the crash of the surf and the call of the seagull; in your own yard lit with the symphony of the rising sun, glistening dew and chirping birds; or in your room where you have the privacy and peace of familiarity— experience the chi for yourself. Try just standing quietly, arms at sides and feet at shoulder width. Let your knees be flexed. Just

*stand there relaxing your mind of all thoughts;
let yourself flow into the rhythm of your
surroundings. Your breath will become deep
and regular as you relax. Sense the energy flowing
up from the ground into your feet and through
your body. Sink into that energy. Let your arms
ride up before you on the wave of that rising
energy, slowly, effortlessly. Let them slide off the
energy wave, and slowly sink back down to your
sides. Play with this flow awhile. Perhaps at some
point you will feel the need to turn gently to one
side, your arms floating outwards. Maybe you will
need to take a step in some direction to maintain
your balance. Take your time and move slowly. Be
loose; allow the energy from within you to move
your body, instead of imposing movement through
will and muscles.*

*In t'ai chi all movements are generated
from the center of gravity within the body—the
tant'ien, just below the navel. Body and earth
and air are still one, flowing through and within
each other. Experiment with this, as a further
refinement of the earlier exercise. Again, standing
quietly, arms at side, feet at shoulder width,
knees lightly flexed, rest until your breath
becomes deep and regular. Experience the energy
flowing through your body, but instead of
moving your arms, try turning to one side from
your tant'ien. Step into the direction of that
turn. Let your shoulders follow, but don't force
them. Just experiment walking around in various
directions. Let each turn originate from your
tant'ien. Let your arms be loose, and your knees
flexed. After some time, keeping the awareness of
your tant'ien, let your arms slowly rise and
move to the flow of energy. Expanding and
contracting, rising and falling, circular flowing
nowhere going.*

—Saraswati Ransom

The following Sufi walks were developed by Murshid Samuel Lewis.

Begin by walking naturally, relaxed but alert, with back straight. Concentrate on your breath. Let your walking and breathing coordinate naturally. Count rhythmically with each two steps: 1–2. Take two steps as you inhale, then two steps as you exhale.

To create a balance of the elements earth, air, fire and water in yourself, you can develop whichever element is weak through specific walks. For example, if you are feeling flighty or unstable the earth walk would ground you.

Or you may try the walks that express the qualities of love or of strength and courage. Continue each of these walks until you feel as if you have become its essence.

Earth: Good for stabilizing emotions and grounding, balancing energy. Walk with a simple drumbeat if possible. Bend your knees slightly and walk with hands at sides, palms facing the earth. Look down; feel gravity pulling your palms and weighing down your body. Feel your connection with the earth. Breathe in heavily and exhale lightly. Coordinate your steps and breath to the drumbeat 2 counts in and 2 counts out.

Air: Light, good for a free joyful mind. Not grounded, no rhythm. Flow as you walk in erratic directions. Feel light and airy. Move in a manner that expresses what you imagine this quality to be. The breath is refined and light.

Water: Sensitive, flowing, emotional, imbalanced. Walk like dancing to a waltz— Step 2–3, Step 2–3. Sway from side to side. Without holding the nose breathe in the right nostril and out the left.

Fire: Inspirational, courageous, great desire to reach one's goal. Unstable. Walk quickly and every few steps hop on your right foot stretching your body as you reach up and clap your hands like a spark. Breathe heavily through the right nostril (without holding nose). Feel the energy of fire filling you.

The Quality of Loving: Step gracefully and lightly. The breath is refined. Slightly bow your head in reverence and cup your hands over your heart. Feel love pour into your hands, then offer the love to your Beloved with head and hands held upward. Do this several times until you feel love flowing. If you like you can softly repeat the Arabic phrase "ya wadood" which means "O thou loving."

The Quality of Strength and Courage: Walk proud with forceful steps, shoulders back, arms swinging, fists closed. You can chant the phrase "ya Malik"—"O King of Kings."

—Tara Bennett

Mindfulness

Perhaps at some time you have sat quietly by the side of an ocean or river. At first there is one big rush of sound. Listening quietly, you begin to hear a multitude of subtle sounds: the waves hitting the shore, the rushing current of the river. In that peacefulness and silence of mind you experience precisely what is happening. It is the same when you listen to yourself. At first all you can hear is one "self" or "I," but slowly this self is revealed as a mass of changing elements, thoughts, feelings, emotions, and images, all illuminated simply by listening, by paying attention.

In mindfulness you are aware of what happens in each moment. You remain alert, not allowing yourself to become forgetful. When you develop mindfulness and concentration together, you achieve a balance of mind. As this penetrating awareness develops it reveals many aspects of the world and of who you are. You see with a clear and direct vision that everything, including yourself, is flowing, in flux, in transformation. There is not a single element of your mind or body that is stable. This wisdom comes not from any particular state, but from close observation of your own mind.

Joseph Goldstein gives the following instructions for developing mindfulness by meditating on one's thoughts, on eating, and on walking.

MEDITATION ON THE MIND

*To meditate upon thoughts is simply to be aware,
as thoughts arise, that the mind is thinking,
without getting involved in the content: not going
off on a train of association, not analyzing the
thought and why it came, but merely to be aware
that at the particular moment "thinking" is happening. It is helpful to make a mental note of
"thinking, thinking" every time a thought arises;
observe the thought without judgment, without
reaction to the content, without identifying with
it, without taking the thought to be I, or self, or
mine. The thought is the thinker. There is no
one behind it. The thought is thinking itself. It
comes uninvited. You will see that when there is
a strong detachment from the thought process,
thoughts don't last long. As soon as you are
mindful of a thought, it disappears. Some people
may find it helpful to label the thinking process
in a more precise way, to note different kinds of
thoughts, whether "planning" or "imagining" or
"remembering." This sharpens the focus of
attention. Otherwise, the simple note of "thinking,
thinking" will serve the purpose. Try to be
aware of the thought as soon as it arises, rather
than some minutes afterward. When they are
noticed with precision and balance they have
no power to disturb the mind.*

*Thoughts should not be treated as obstacles
or hindrances. They are just another object of
mindfulness, another object of meditation. Don't
let the mind become lazy and drift along. Make
the effort for a great deal of clarity with respect
to what's happening in the moment.*

Suzuki Roshi in Zen Mind, Beginner's Mind
writes: "*When you are practicing Zazen
meditation do not try to stop your thinking. Let
it stop by itself. If something comes into your
mind, let it come in and let it go out. It will not*

stay long. When you try to stop your thinking, it means you are bothered by it. Do not be bothered by anything. It appears that the something comes from outside your mind, but actually it is only the waves of your mind and if you are not bothered by the waves, gradually they will become calmer and calmer. . . . Many sensations come, many thoughts or images arise but they are just waves from your own mind. Nothing comes from outside your mind. . . . If you leave your mind as it is, it will become calm. This mind is called big mind."

Just let things happen as they do. Let all images and thoughts and sensations arise and pass away without being bothered, without reacting, without judging, without clinging, without identifying with them. Become one with the big mind, observing carefully, microscopically, all the waves coming and going. This attitude will quickly bring about a state of balance and calm. Don't let the mind get out of focus. Keep the mind sharply aware, moment to moment, of what is happening, whether the in-out breath, sensations, or thoughts. In each instant be focused on the object with a balanced and relaxed mind.

MINDFUL EATING

There are many different processes of mind and body which go on while we eat. It is important to become mindful of the sequence of the *processes; otherwise, there is a great likelihood of greed and desire arising with regard to food. And when we are not aware, we do not fully enjoy the experience. We take a bite or two and our thoughts wander.*

The first process involved when you have your food is that you see it. Notice "seeing, seeing." Then there is an intention to take the food, a mental process. That intention should be noticed. "Intending, intending." The mental intention becomes the cause of the arm moving. "Moving, moving." When the hand or spoon touches the food there is the sensation of touch, contact. Feel the sensations. Then the intention to lift the arm, and the lifting. Notice carefully all these processes.

Opening the mouth. Putting in the food. Closing the mouth. The intention to lower the arm, and then the movement. One thing at a time. Feeling the food in the mouth, the texture. Chewing. Experience the movement. As you begin chewing, there will be taste sensation arising. Be mindful of the tasting. As you keep on chewing, the taste disappears. Swallowing. Be aware of the whole sequence involved. There is no one behind it, no one who is eating. It's merely the sequence of intentions, movements, tastes, touch sensations. That's what we are—a sequence of happenings, of processes, and by being very mindful of the sequence, of the flow, we get free of the concept of self.

MINDFUL WALKING

The walking meditation is done by noticing the lifting, forward and placing movement of the foot in each step. It is helpful to finish one step completely before lifting the other foot. "Lifting, moving, placing, lifting, moving, placing." It is very simple. Again it is not an exercise in movement. It is an exercise in mindfulness. Use the movement to develop a careful awareness. In the course of the day, you can expect many changes. Sometimes you may feel like walking more quickly, sometimes very slowly. You can take the steps as a single unit, "stepping, stepping." Or you may start out walking quickly and, in that same walking meditation, slow down until you are dividing it again into the three parts. Experiment. The essential thing is to be mindful, to be aware of what's happening.

In walking, the hands should remain stationary either behind the back, at the sides, or in front. It's better to look a little ahead, and not at your feet, in order to avoid being involved in the concept of "foot" arising from the visual contact. All of the attention should be on experiencing the movement, feeling the sensations of the lifting, forward, placing motions.

—Joseph Goldstein

The Experience of Insight

Meditation in Action

The final step in integrating meditation into your awareness is to use the stuff of daily life as part of meditation. There are ways of perceiving the world and the way you live in it such that each experience brings you more deeply into the meditative space. At the same time, however, this kind of meditation requires firm grounding: you must continue to function effectively in the world as you meditate on it. This is meditation in action. It finally becomes the core of a consciously lived life, a meditative space within you. This space stands between each thing you notice and each response you make, allowing a peaceful, quiet, and spacious view of the universe.

I find that even an act as stimulating as walking through New York City can be a profound meditative experience. For as I walk down the street, if I stay quiet inside—either through mantra or watching my breath—I can see my consciousness being pulled this way and that by the things along the street. Each time my consciousness is pulled, it reflects some desire system, such as desires for power or sex, to which I am still attached. Each time I notice this, I let it be, let it stay or leave as it chooses. As I do, I remain in the meditative space, not getting lost in the desire. In this way I can walk through the city, staying quiet inside, despite the incredible panoply of stimuli that impinges upon my every sense.

There are techniques that help you see moment-to-moment experiences in such a way that everything serves to awaken you. The Bhagavad Gita describes karma yoga as the path of awakening through ordinary activities. You see every action, be it eating, sleeping, marrying, or earning a living, as an act offered to God. Your every act becomes a meditation on your relation to God. If your path is through the guru, then you see each daily life experience as part of a dialogue in which the guru keeps facing you with experience after experience, each one designed for your awakening.

When you finally develop the capacity to meditate from the moment of awakening to the moment of sleep, and yet stay perfectly at ease in the world, moment to moment living becomes a totally delightful and freeing experience.

> *Zen is not some kind of excitement, but concentration on our usual everyday routine.*
>
> —*Shunryu Suzuki*
>
> Zen Mind, Beginner's Mind

> *Let me explain to you the function of Kavvanah. Kavvanah means intention. Our intention is always free. There is nothing that can obstruct your intending. Even if the whole world coerces*

you into a pattern of actions, you can always "intend" whatever you want. For instance, you sit in the dentist's chair. He drills and you feel a sting of pain, but you can "intend" this pain as an offering of love. You offer to God the moment of pain, intending to suffer it for Him. You might put it somewhat in this way: "Ribbono Shel Olam!—You are good and Your universe is good. The all is filled with Your mercy and goodness, as is the pain I feel. I cannot bring You any other sacrifice. Please accept this moment of pain as a love offering from me." Or you work in your day by day endeavor. You do whatever you must do, and you intend: "God of Law and Order, You have ordained work for man. In doing . . . I intend to do Your Will. I wish to cleave to You in this action." Or you travel and time is taken up by it. You lean back and wink at Him in your mind as if to say, "Sweet Father, I enjoy Your presence: the rhythm of the wheels, the fleeting scenery, are all nothing but You. You contain me and my vehicle. I will be careful in travel, for this is Your Will. Guard my going out and my coming back. I am secure in You."

You see these "arrows of awareness" are rather simple to practice. You will soon find that placing yourself in His Presence will come with some practice.

—Rabbi Zalman Schachter

The First Step

*It is easier for me to tell you about non-meditation
than about meditation. I sit or walk looking at
myself non-meditating—absorbed in dramas
and melodramas, heart-gripping tragedies,
loneliness, shabbiness, delights. As from another
planet I look at them, through a telescope. Then
there is a little space between me and my
all-pervasive feelings. Nevertheless, I still feel
I am my feelings, as well as whatever it is that
elicits them, plus a third entity looking at the
drama of separation between subject and object.
Is that the Eternal Triangle? After a short while
of looking at the show I take off to a more distant
planet and with a more powerful telescope I
look at myself diligently looking at myself.
Surely this self-fascination is not meditation. I
get up and do something pleasant, useful or
beautiful.*

*Then once again the voyeuse, I go back to
peering at my consciousness. It is garbage!
Garbage!? The word inspires me because I use
my kitchen garbage aesthetically and usefully by
putting peelings of fruits and vegetables in tall
colorless glass containers, semi-filled with water.
Floating in it these organic elements become
very lively, their ever-changing essence creating
forms and colors at times vivid and defined—
other times extraordinarily ethereal—a
fascinating, on-going transformation. In a week
or two when the exotic submarine bouquet
becomes too alive I put it in the compost heap
where nature's cycle continues. What about
applying the same principle to the content of my
consciousness? I decide to recycle every bit of
it into a thought of goodwill for anyone or
anything which presents itself.*

*It becomes a fun game to look at a
thought-feeling and convert it into a blessing for
the subject (person, animal, thing—whatever) of*

*the thought-feeling. Even science agrees now
that "thoughts are things." Surely if random
thoughts are consciously converted into a
message of goodwill, only something worthwhile
can result.*

*But wait a moment! At times it also
happens that when we decide to do something
constructive, all the destructive devils within arise
and form a powerful coalition. They hurl at us
the most toxic feelings and thoughts imaginable
—events bearing sadness, resentment and
injustice, a sense of uselessness, years of physical
pain and mental anguish—all of it parading,
mocking us with a challenge to be converted
to "choiceless goodwill." Ah ah ah! If this should
happen, be sure to salute all little and big devils
and acknowledge their irrefutable logic, their
astounding skill. Then either say, "We will
wrestle later," and give them a definite rendezvous
which you will keep (they will, too!) or if devils
or toxic feelings are adamant in asking now for
attention, then now is the time to exorcise by
exercise. Run, shout, breathe fast and deeply,
dance naked to music, push with all your might
against the wall, swim, jump, write a letter not
to be mailed, walk on all fours, etc. Whatever
you do, go back to the garbage recycling game
afterwards.*

*I understand that meditation is to be
undertaken in purity of intention and not for
results. If viewed as an utilitarian project like the
one I propose, then meditation becomes but
another, although higher, achievement of that
ego about which so many seem to be so worried.
The garbage recycling game, then, is not
meditation because it is ambitious and it has
goals and results: the improvement of
relationships, ambience, digestion, wrinkles,
etc. It is not meditation but, by playing it lightly
and constantly, and if "as luck would have it*

*that God is on our side," it could happen (why
not?) that one day garbage, recycling, thought,
thinker, devils, blessings—all of it becomes one,
all separation vanishing in a moment.*

> *Then there is Silence.
> Luminous Silence.
> Silence.*

—Laura Huxley

*Ch'ui the draftsman
Could draw more perfect circles freehand
Than with a compass.*

*His fingers brought forth
Spontaneous forms from nowhere. His mind
Was meanwhile free and without concern
With what he was doing.*

*No application was needed
His mind was perfectly simple
And knew no obstacle . . .*

*No drives, no compulsions,
No needs, no attractions:
Then your affairs
Are under control.
You are a free man.*

—Thomas Merton

The Way of Chuang Tzu

If you know how to do one thing well, you can do everything.

—*Gurdjieff*
Our Life with Mr. Gurdjieff

Meditation Without Form

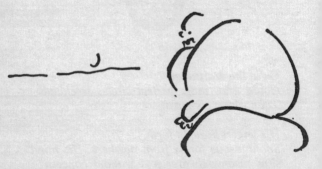

Most meditative practices give very specific instructions as to what to focus on, what to think, or what to do. But in the last analysis, the meditative state goes beyond practices. Such methods are but stepping off points to this state, but they aren't always needed. There are ways to perceive yourself and the world, right from the outset, that catapult you into the meditative state without the necessity of practices. These ways of perceiving allow you to be keenly alert, to be choiceless awareness, to have clarity. These methodless methods are found in the writings of all traditions. The following writings reflect this pathless path. One of the most beautiful statements of this non-technique is found in the Song of Mahamudra by Tilopa.

excerpts from
THE SONG OF MAHAMUDRA

Mahamudra is beyond all words
And symbols, but for you, Naropa,
Earnest and loyal, must this be said.

The Void needs no reliance,
Mahamudra rests on nought.
Without making an effort,
But remaining loose and natural,
One can break the yoke
Thus gaining Liberation.

If one sees nought when staring into space,
If with the mind one then observes the mind,
One destroys distinctions
And reaches Buddhahood.

The clouds that wander through the sky
Have no roots, no home; nor do the distinctive
Thoughts floating through the mind.
Once the Self-mind is seen,
Discrimination stops.

Do nought with the body but relax,
Shut firm the mouth and silent remain,
Empty your mind and think of nought.
Like a hollow bamboo

Rest at ease your body.
Giving not nor taking,
Put your mind at rest.
Mahamudra is like a mind that clings to nought.
Thus practicing, in time you will reach
    Buddhahood.

Cease all activity, abandon
All desire, let thoughts rise and fall
As they will like the ocean waves.

He who abandons craving
And clings not to this or that,
Perceives the real meaning
Given in the Scriptures.

Transient is this world;
Like phantoms and dreams,
Substance it has none.
Renounce it and forsake your kin,
Cut the strings of lust and hatred,
Meditate in woods and mountains.
If without effort you remain
Loosely in the "natural state,"
Soon Mahamudra you will win
And attain the Non-attainment.

Cut the root of a tree
And the leaves will wither;
Cut the root of your mind
And Samsara falls.

Whoever clings to mind sees not
The truth of what's Beyond the mind.
Whoever strives to practice Dharma
Finds not the truth of Beyond-practice.
To know what is Beyond both mind and practice,
One should cut cleanly through the root of mind
And stare naked. One should thus break away
From all distinctions and remain at ease.

One should not give or take
But remain natural,
For Mahamudra is beyond
All acceptance and rejection.

The supreme Understanding transcends
All this and that. The supreme Action
Embraces great resourcefulness
Without attachment. The supreme
Accomplishment is to realize
Immanence without hope.

At first a yogi feels his mind
Is tumbling like a waterfall;
In mid-course, like the Ganges
It flows on slow and gentle;
In the end, it is a great
Vast ocean, where the Lights
Of Son and Mother merge in one.

—*Tilopa*

Teachings of Tibetan Yoga

Meditation is a never-ending movement. You can
never say that you are meditating or set aside
a period for meditation. It isn't at your
command. Its benediction doesn't come to you
because you lead a systematized life or follow
a particular routine or morality. It comes only
when your heart is really open. Not opened by
the key of thought, not made safe by the intellect,
but when it is as open as the skies without a
cloud; then it comes without your knowing,
without your invitation. But you can never guard
it, keep it, worship it. If you try, it will never
come again: do what you will, it will avoid you.
In meditation, you are not important, you have
no place in it; the beauty of it is not you, but in
itself. And to this you can add nothing. Don't
look out of the window hoping to catch it
unawares, or sit in a darkened room waiting for
it; it comes only when you are not there at all,
and its bliss has no continuity.

—*Krishnamurti*

The Second Penguin
Krishnamurti Reader

*And look that nothing remain in thy working
mind but a naked intent stretching unto God—
not clothed in any special thought of God in
himself or any of his works, but only that He is
as He is. . . .*

—The Cloud of Unknowing

*In its true state, mind is naked, immaculate; not
made of anything, being of the Voidness; clear,
vacuous, without duality, transparent; timeless,
uncompounded, unimpeded, colourless; not
realizable as a separate thing, but as the unity of
all things, yet not composed of them; of one
taste, and transcendent over differentiation.*

—Padmasambhava

The Tibetan Book of
the Great Liberation

*There is no place to seek the mind;
It is like the footprints of the birds in the sky.*

—Zenrin

The Gospel According to Zen

*All is calm. How can we describe the indescrible?
Can we say like this, like that? Things are or
are not. There is an unreality, an emptiness, a
Maya of everything that is, like the sky that*

*covers all. Past, present and future are the same,
beyond thought. How can we explain? Is or is
not? Not like this nor like anything else. Away
even from transcendency. Emptiness and the
Dharma nature are not different. Beyond all
signs whatsoever. Beyond communication.
Different. Nameless. Sudden like lightning. With
a meaning beyond thought. Therefore there is no
meaning. Now it's all finished. Words are liars.*

—The Fifteenth Gyalwa
Karmapa
Samata Magazine

*Words!
The Way is beyond language,
for in it there is*

> *no yesterday
> no tomorrow
> no today,*

—*Sengstan*

Hsin Hsin Ming

4

FINDING
YOUR
WAY

Let It Change

Though you can start meditation any time, it's harder if your life is chaotic, if you're feeling paranoid, if you're overwhelmed with responsibilities, or if you're sick. But even starting under these conditions, meditation will help you to clear things up a bit. Slowly you reorganize your life to support your spiritual journey. At each stage there will be something you can do to create a supportive space. It may mean changing your diet, who you're with, how you spend your time, what's on your walls, what books you read, what you fill your consciousness with, how you care for your body, or where and how you sit to meditate. All these factors contribute to the depth and freedom that you can know through meditation.

You are under no pressure to rush these changes. You need not fear that because of meditation you are going to lose control and get swept away by a new way of life. As you gradually develop a quiet and clear awareness, your living habits will naturally come into harmony with your total environment, with your past involvements, present interests, and future concerns. There need be no sudden ending of relationships in order to prove your holiness. Such frantic changes only show your own lack of faith. When you are one in truth, in the flow, the changes in your life will come naturally.

After you have practiced for a while, you will realize that it is not possible to make rapid, extraordinary progress. Even though you try very hard, the progress you make is always little by little.

—Shunryu Suzuki
Zen Mind, Beginner's Mind

By the late sixties and early seventies many Americans had seen the limitations of seeking finite pleasures, and began looking for ways to break the cycle of wants. Western models no longer held; Eastern models very quickly became the fashion. But the Eastern systems weren't entirely harmonious. We in the West were used to an education that imposed systems of belief from the outside rather than letting them grow from within. We adopted the outer forms, but not the inner teachings. Wearing beads and white clothes gave the semblance of the East, but was hollow.

There are hundreds of thousands of beings for whom spiritual awakening is a reality. I can go to Omaha, Idaho City, Seattle, Buffalo, or Tuscaloosa, and everywhere thousands of people are ready to hear. They are growing spiritually in their own daily lives, without putting on far-out clothes and wearing beads around their necks. Their spiritual awakening grows from within.

Mention is made of two classes of yogis: the hidden and the known. Those who have renounced the world are "known" yogis: all recognize them. But the "hidden" yogis live in the world. They are not known.

—Sri Ramakrishna

The Gospel of
Sri Ramakrishna

It would be a mistake to think that any Tibetan would see any incongruity or harm in going from a service in Lhasa Temple to the nearest house where there was a chang-drinking party being given. Nor would it be unusual to see a pleasure-seeker in a boatful of revelers, quietly counting the beads on his rosary. . . . Religious activity is as much a part of our life as any other activity, and religious belief and thought is as much a part of our thinking as is our concern for where our next meal is coming from.

—Thubten Jigme Norbu

Tibet

It is not to be learned by world-flight, running away from things, turning solitary and going apart from the world. Rather, one must learn an inner solitude, wherever or with whomsoever he may be.

—Eckhart

Meister Eckhart: A
Modern Translation

You start cleaning up your life when you feel that you can't go on until you do. Cleaning up your life means extricating yourself from those things which are obstacles to your liberation. But keep in mind that nothing in and of itself is an obstacle; it's your attachment to it or your motive for doing it that is the obstacle. It's not an issue of eating meat or not eating meat; it's who's eating it and why.

If your senses can be caught and held by something, you are still chained to the world. It's your attachment to the objects of your senses that imprisons you. Failing to break off the attachment of the senses ultimately holds you back. The minute you aren't preoccupied with what's out there, then that pull is lost. You are free to go deep in meditation.

It's not easy. It's a stinker to get to that level of purity. You start out with things like what you eat, who you sleep with, what you watch on TV, what you do with your time. Many people fool themselves and imitate someone else's purity. They do it in an imitative way, one of fear of being unholy. Abstaining from something for the wrong reasons is no better than doing it. You can't pretend to be pure; you can only go at your own speed.

As changes occur through meditation you find yourself attracted to things that are inconsistent with your old model of who you are. Usually, for example, after having meditated in a rigorous (and somewhat righteous) fashion, I have then taken time off to wallow in television, go to movies, take baths and relax. Then, to my surprise, I found myself not being attracted as much as before to these diversions, but being pulled toward just sitting quietly. This new way of being didn't fit with my model of who I was. It was as if I were living with somebody I didn't know very well. My models of myself hadn't changed fast enough to keep up with who I was becoming.

> *Inside yourself or outside, you never have to change what you see, only the way you see it.*
>
> —*Thaddeus Golas*
>
> The Lazy Man's Guide
> to Enlightenment

The Buddhists see the meditative path as the balanced intensification of three mental traits: punya, sila, and samadhi. Punya is wisdom, or understanding. Sila is purification, or simplifying your life. Samadhi is concentration or one-pointedness. As you meditate and start to calm your mind a bit, that's the beginning of samadhi. This taste of clarity shows you how agitated your mind and body are, and how complicated your life is. So you start to simplify your life, clean up your game—the beginning of sila. The more you simplify your life, the better your meditations become. More samadhi. Stronger samadhi tunes you into more profound wisdom—more sila. More sila, more samadhi; more samadhi, more punya; more punya, more sila. Each feeds and balances the others.

Make It Simple

Meditation helps other parts of your life become more simple. As you enter quieter spaces you will see how clinging to desires has made your life complicated. Your clinging drags you from desire to desire, whim to whim, creating more and more complex entanglements. Meditation helps you cut through this clinging.

If, for example, you run around filling your mind with this and that, you will discover that your entire meditation is spent in letting go of the stuff you just finished collecting in the past few hours. You also notice that your meditations are clearer when you come into them from a simpler space. This encourages you to simplify your life.

As you observe the patterns of your thoughts during meditation, notice which areas of your life keep cropping up as distracting thoughts and pulling on you. You will easily see what you must clean out of your closet in order to proceed more smoothly. For example, if you have heavy debts, and thoughts about these debts intrude when you meditate, rather than accrue more and more debts as our society urges, you will find yourself wanting to lessen them. As you simplify things like your finances, you see more clearly the way the laws of cause and effect work in your life. You will want to get your life lighter and clearer, so that there are fewer expectations upon you from all quarters. Later, when your meditative center is strong, you can carry many responsibilities without clinging to thoughts about them.

Each time you lighten your life, you are less at the whim of thought forms, both your own and others'. It's as if you have built a world based on the thoughts of who you seem to be. As you meditate you become aware that these models are merely thoughts, not really who you are at all. Each time you give up an attachment to a thought form, your world becomes that much lighter and clearer.

<u>Meditation affects your life and your life shapes your meditation.</u> It goes both ways. Less busyness in life brings greater richness in meditation. This richness makes you content with less of the trimmings of outer life. As this process continues, less is more.

Silence is the garden of meditation.

—Ali

Maxims of Ali

I recall that as a Harvard professor I had FM in my car and stereo in my office and home; I was constantly surrounded by music—even with a speaker in my bathroom. In addition there were paintings on all the walls and decorations in my car.

Slowly, as meditation changed my perception of the universe, I started to crave simplicity. I placed objects on the walls that reminded me of higher possibilities: pictures of beings who were in higher consciousness, symbols of this consciousness, and art that represented it. I found that I was beginning to appreciate the silence and was content to enjoy a few pieces of music or art thoroughly rather than fill every space with sound and with imagery.

At times, I even felt the total contentment that comes from sitting in silence in a purely white room

He who with little is well content is rich indeed as a king; and a king, in his greatness, is poor as the pedlar, when his kingdom sufficeth him not.

—*Shekel Hakodesh*

The Holy Shekel

He who knows that enough is enough will always have enough.

—*Lao Tze*

Tao Te Ching

When my guru Maharaji instructed Hari Dass Baba to train me, Hari Dass had been silent for many years. He communicated with a chalk board on which he wrote simple phrases. He instructed me to be silent also and prepared a chalk board for me.

At first it seemed like a game, but its depth and beauty became apparent in time. First of all I got tired writing long answers, so I started to find simpler ways of saying things, which in turn simplified my thoughts. A dialogue via chalk boards slows down communication sufficiently to see individual thought forms and the space that surrounds them. This space between statement and reaction considerably deepened the quietness within me. There is a great loss of energy in our normal chatter. Silence brought me great energy and clarity. As Hari Dass wrote, "Nothing is better than something."

Unless a man is simple, he cannot recognize God, the Simple One.

—*Bengali Song*

The Gospel of
Sri Ramakrishna

*Stop talking, stop thinking, and there is nothing
    you will not understand.*
Return to the Root and you will find the Meaning;
Pursue the Light, and you will lose its source. . . .
*There is no need to seek Truth; only stop having
    views.*

—*Sengstan*

Buddhist Texts

To Everything There Is a Season

The transformation that comes through meditation is not a straight-line progression. It's a spiral, a cycle. My own life is very much a series of spirals in which at times I am pulled toward some particular form of sadhana or lifestyle and make a commitment to it for maybe six months or a year. After this time I assess its effects. At times I work with external methods such as service. At other times the pull is inward, and I retreat from society to spend more time alone.

The timing for these phases in the spiral must be in tune with your inner voice and your outer life. Don't get too rigidly attached to any one method—turn to others when their time comes, when you are ripe for them.

I first became involved in the journey through study, intellectual analysis and service. I found it difficult to work with methods of the heart. I would try to open my heart, but the methods seemed absurd. I recall going to the Avalon Ballroom in the early 1960s to hear Allen Ginsberg introduce Swami Bhaktivedanta, who led a Hare Krishna chant. This chant seemed weird to me. It left me cold and cynical. I recall thinking, "It's too bad—Allen's really gone over the edge. This chant just doesn't make it." In the years since, I've had moments of ecstasy with the Hare Krishna chant. My heart has opened wide to the beauty of the blue Krishna and the radiant Ram, and I've laughed at my own changes and growth.

A student once came to me and told me that he felt turned off by devotional practices. His practice was Buddhist; his meditation was on the dharma, the laws of the universe. Yet he felt troubled that his heart was closed. So I started him on the practice of the mantra "I love you dharma," breathing in and out of the heart saying, "I love you dharma." He loved it.

It's not an all-or-nothing game. You're not totally out of one phase before you start the next—there's a gradual shift.

> To everything there is a season,
> and a time to every purpose
> under the heaven:
> A time to be born, and a time to die;
> a time to plant, and a time to pluck up that
> which is planted;
>
> A time to kill, and a time to heal;
> a time to break down, and a time to build up;

A time to weep, and a time to laugh;
a time to mourn, and a time to dance;

A time to cast away stones, and
a time to gather stones together; a time to
embrace, and a time to refrain from embracing;

A time to get, and a time to lose;
a time to keep, and a time to cast away;

A time to rend, and a time to sew;
a time to keep silence, and a time to speak;

A time to love, and a time to hate;
a time of war, and a time of peace.

—*Ecclesiastes 3:1–8*

The Old Testament

To a sincere student, every day is a fortunate
day.

—*Zengetso*

Friends

As your meditation practice deepens, your attitudes toward other people change. The desires for gratification that make you turn to others out of need fall away. You may increasingly prefer to be alone—or with only a few people who share your interest in meditation. Let these changes happen gently.

As you grow, your friends change. Unlike your family, to whom you stay connected despite changing interests, you no longer need continue a friendship when the reasons for it no longer exist. At first it may bother you if close friends do not share your pull toward meditation. But leave judgment aside, for people develop in different ways and at their own rate. Your old friends cannot convince you meditation is wrong, nor can you convince them it is right. Simply respect the different paths that you are taking. Above all, do not proselytize. Your own quiet changes are the most convincing statement.

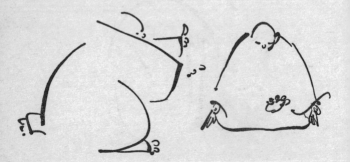

Minimize the drama that you attach to spiritual practices. When your faith is weak, you reinforce the weakness by trying to convince your friends to meditate also. Such efforts are only an attempt to reassure yourself. The fanaticism of large, popular movements often springs from this lack of faith on the part of its followers. The need to proselytize, the need to cling to and talk about your experiences, the need to dramatize them by turning simple acts of meditation into spiritual melodrama, all will fall away in time, leaving meditation a normal daily affair—nothing special.

The melodrama of fanaticism is a form of spiritual materialism: you make spiritual life into something else to acquire, like a new car or television set. Just do your practices; don't make a big deal of them. The less you dramatize, the fewer obstacles you create. Romanticism on the spiritual path is just another attachment that will have to go sooner or later.

If you meditate alone and maintain your old social relationships, you often find yourself among people who don't understand what's happening to you If so, be discrete. Keep your thoughts about meditation and its effect on your life to yourself unless others ask. Other people's doubts weaken your faith before it has had the opportunity to mature. This is one reason a mantra is often given secretly. It is not that a mantra requires secrecy to be effective, but rather it is important to concentrate singlemindedly on a mantra without entertaining the doubts or ridicule of others.

As meditation affects your life more completely, your desire for satsang, other beings who share similar spiritual interests, may lead you to seek out other spiritual aspirants to live with, either in a community or in a communal arrangement in a single house. Just because a community or commune is "spiritual" does not guarantee any less of the intense psychological melodramas usually found in group living situations. The fact that you meditate together, have a more or less shared outlook, and perhaps have the same teacher will all help you cut through some of the drama. But given human propensities, these factors will not likely cut through all of it. Living in satsang does not change the attachments with which you must work, but it changes your perspective on them. This new perspective brings a newfound sense of joy to daily activities that before seemed tedious and repetitive.

The point of satsang is not to become a meditation freak or cultist, but rather to let a new sense of things permeate your life. The more advanced your meditative practice becomes, the less it matters whether you meditate with others or alone—you need fewer supports. Satsang finally takes you beyond the need for satsang. When your life is fully inner-directed you need nobody's reassurance or help; then you can help others. Until that day, it's useful to have people around to point or share the way.

> *Who are these by whom you wish to be admired? Are not these the men whom you generally describe as mad? What do you want then? Do you want to be admired by madmen?*
>
> —*Epictetus*
>
> Arrian's Discourses of Epictetus

> *Your kinsmen are often farther from you than strangers.*
>
> —*Ali*
>
> Maxims of Ali

> *Let (the student of our Art) carry on his operations with great secrecy in order that no scornful or scurrilous person may know of them; for nothing discourages the beginner so much as the mockery, taunts, and well-meant advice of foolish outsiders.*
>
> —*Philalethes*
>
> The Hermetic Museum

Groups

Come, come, whoever you are,
Wanderer, worshipper, lover of leaving—it
doesn't matter.
Ours is not a caravan of despair.
Come, even if you have broken your vow
a hundred times
Come, come again, come.

—Jelal-ud Din Rumi

Perhaps you are concerned about which of the many meditative programs to join. You may wonder about the purity or validity of the numerous kinds of meditation flourishing on the American scene these days. Here are some points to consider.

The first is that you get what you want. You progress at the rate you are ready to. Your true desires will draw from any of these programs what you seek. Be open to groups that teach meditation and sense whether their practices feel harmonious to you. If so, go ahead, learn from them. The drawback is that their goals may be far short of liberation and you may end up despairing at their limited vision.

Some programs are purer than others. Most are sincere efforts to teach meditation; only a very few are cynical exploitations of the marketplace. In general, their impurities will primarily affect them and only incidentally affect you. If you are pure in your desire greed will not touch you.

Most people act out of very strong attachments and clingings, and the mass movements cater to their disillusionments or enthusiasms. The large, public programs make their appeal to many different motives. The best-known, the TM program, has set as its goal initiating one percent of the world's population. I share with them the feeling that if more people would meditate, social decisions would be more harmonious. And certainly, to meditate using a mantra can take you very far along the path. TM gives many people their first taste of stillness, but some eventually find it is not enough and they move on. The TM technique is a pleasant experience, and most certainly will give you some self-control and calm. For those who would go deeper, it is not that the mantra would not take them, but that the TM organization itself is limited. The people who teach the method, except perhaps at its very top levels, like Maharishi Mahesh, do not seem to be the most advanced spiritual beings.

Many people complain about paying for a mantra. There is really nothing wrong with an organization asking people to pay to support its efforts, if its wish to spread meditation is purely motivated. But the going rates of some groups seem excessive. The temptations of wealth are great; gold has been the downfall of many yogis. My guru often warned me against "women and gold," the lures of sex and money. Meditation is a very precious vehicle. It is sad that some teachers—who could know better—seek only wealth or power. They reap what they sow. For example, if you pay to learn meditation and the teacher charges unfairly, he or she is left with the money and you with the vehicle for liberation. If you use the method well, you end up free, your teacher trapped.

In general I find the large meditation organizations offensive, for they tend to attract people who want power. There are many slots in these large organizations for power players who become overbearing in their fraudulent holiness. If your desire is pure—if it is not power you're after—you can reach toward the source of these organizations. Drink from that source and let the impurities pass you by.

Suppose, for example, a group's initiation offers sound traditional techniques, but the organization itself is an obstacle in the long run. If your motive is to be part of a group of like-minded seekers, then you may be attracted to such an organization. Use such a group until your inner discipline is strong enough, then go it alone.

Many meditation groups seek to avoid any spiritual identity. TM, for example, has shed its spiritual side as fast as it can so that it will be more acceptable to the American masses, including the military and the public schools. Some programs—not at all spiritual in outlook—offer only therapeutic changes. They do a lot of good by offering mass psychotherapy that gives people a new feeling of self-worth. For that they're worth the money. They're useful, not a rip-off. Their limit is that they touch on methods that offer people much more than psychological betterment, but define their goals only in psychological terms, and thereby mislead people about the greater possibilities. For some who go these routes it will be enough, for others it won't. Those who want something more will move on. Such movements talk about higher states but actually teach ordinary effectiveness and stay within the bounds of the realities of this world. It is one thing to keep one's ground when one has never flown and quite another to fly and then return to the ground. My criticism of most mass spiritual movements is that they are not directed by people who have first flown and are now living on the ground. Someone who is lost in illusion, no matter how nice his or her words, cannot free another. The lack of freedom in those who guide others creates the most subtle suffering for everyone.

When you are just beginning your journey, almost any method will help. As you get to the more advanced stages you will find that certain guides have aspirations lower than your own. Then you must seek elsewhere for the proper teaching, one that will free you rather than entrap you.

The mass programs offer useful psychological housecleaning. They probably will make you more effective in the world. But for me the most attractive training programs are those which aim for the highest aspirations of humanity. Toward the Living Spirit. Toward knowing, or becoming God. These programs with higher aspirations are also serving humanity. In fact they serve humanity even more, for they create a space of liberation from which you can pursue your involvement in the world with inner freedom. It takes a free being to free another.

There is a story that as God and Satan were walking down the street one day, the Lord bent down and picked something up. He gazed at it glowing radiantly in His hand. Satan, curious, asked, "What's that?" "This," answered the Lord, "is Truth." "Here," replied Satan as he reached for it, "let me have that— I'll organize it for you."

> *Beware of false prophets, which come to you in sheep's clothing, but inwardly they are ravening wolves.*
>
> —Matthew 7:15
>
> The New Testament

Benares is to the East, Mecca to the West; but explore your own heart, for there are both Rama and Allah.

—*Kabir*

One Hundred Poems of Kabir

Teachers

If several teachers are available in your area, how do you select one? I say in your area, because you needn't go far afield to begin meditation. To travel all over looking for the perfect teacher adds more to your melodrama than to your liberation. Virtually any teacher is suitable simply to begin, and if no teacher is available, you can do much on your own. In the end, you are your own best teacher.

Later on you may feel drawn to a specific teacher. As you look about for teachers, be open. Listen, tune, feel. Sense whether the teacher, teachings, and practices are harmonious with your needs.

You may meet a teacher whom everyone else respects, loves, and honors, but in your heart nothing happens. There's no reason to judge this person, nor to persuade or argue with others. Simply decide what's right for you at the moment. Move on if you must. This does not deny the possibility that at some later date the same teacher may be perfect for you, or that he may be perfect for others. It's tempting to sit around and judge teachers rather than use their teachings and get on with it. There's no need for spiritual gossip.

When you take teachings you have certain obligations to your teacher and the lineage from which the teachings come. Surrender. Open yourself to the instructions. Don't hold back, saying, "I'll take just a little teaching from you, but no more." To get the most from a teacher you must dive in and immerse yourself fully. Risk getting wet. Trust that you will be able to get out of the water when you've had enough.

In one meditation course I took, on the first day the teacher said, "During these ten days you must take a vow to surrender to me, to do just as I tell you." This was a limited contract and I had no trouble with it. I understood that this surrender was necessary for the proper transmission of his teaching.

When the teaching is over, what are your obligations? Sometimes a teacher says, "Now that you have taken teachings from me, you must serve me and proselytize on my behalf." Or, "You can't leave now, you're not ready: you need more teachings." Yet you know in your heart that your business together is finished. When you have finished with a teacher, your only debt to that teacher is your own liberation. As Shakespeare said, "This above all—to thine own self be true, . . . Thou canst not then be false to any man."

All a teacher offers really is his or her own being. For example, there are many stories of enlightened teachers who by merely repeating a mantra once could change a devotee's entire life. The devotee might have been very worldly, but the spirit with which the mantra was invested evoked a deep response. Beyond the mantra, what the teacher transmitted was not only the mantra, but the ability to use it properly. If a teacher is trying to transmit what he or she has not fully received, the spirit will be lacking and the transmission will be incomplete. The student's disillusionment upon finding out that the teacher was not qualified to invest the mantra, unfortunately, may make the student averse to continuing the use of a perfectly good mantra.

Some people fear becoming involved with a teacher. They fear the possible impurities in the teacher, fear being exploited, used, or entrapped. In truth we are only ever entrapped by our own desires and clings. If you want only liberation, then all teachers will be useful vehicles for you. They cannot hurt you at all. If, on the other hand, you want power, a teacher may come along who talks about liberation but subtly attracts you by your desire for power. If you get caught and become a disciple of such a teacher, you may feel angry when this teacher turns out to be on a power trip, not leading you to enlightenment. But remember: At some level inside yourself you already knew. Your attraction to this teacher was your desire for power. Your anger is nothing more than anger toward yourself.

Some say that you should do nothing without the help of a teacher, that to do anything without guidance is dangerous. Others say that a teacher is not necessary, that you can only do it yourself. Of course, people have awakened and come to full realization without any teacher. On the other hand, most people at some point along the path need teachers. For example, if you seek to quiet your mind, at first learning to meditate is enough. Later you might need a teacher to show you how you have misused even the simplest meditation in the service of your ego rather than having used it for your liberation.

Whether teachings experienced along the way are beautiful and pleasant, or unpleasant and harsh, or even bland, all are grist for the mill of awakening. The slightest reaction reflects the subtlest clinging. It is a meaningful clue to where you are still holding on. Simply watching your reaction makes anything a teaching.

Teachers and teachings are forms, and ultimately you must go beyond forms. If you are true to your own inner voice, as it gets subtler and subtler it brings you to the moment beyond separateness of seeker and guide. Then you have served your teacher well.

When Mrs. Albert Einstein was asked if she understood her husband's Theory of Relativity, she replied, "No . . . But I know my husband and he can be trusted."

If you wish to know the road
  up the mountain,
Ask the man who goes back and
  forth on it.

—*Zenrin*

The Gospel According to Zen

A man does not seek to see himself in running
water, but in still water. For only what is itself
still can impart stillness into others.

—*Chuang-tse*

The Wisdom of China
and India

When you forget all your dualistic ideas,
everything becomes your teacher, and everything
can be the object of worship.

—*Shunryu Suzuki*

Zen Mind, Beginner's Mind

Retreats

There is an ancient and unbroken tradition of people who withdraw from the marketplace for meditation. This withdrawal can range from a day of solitude to the dedication of one's entire life as a recluse or a member of a religious order. You will benefit by devoting at least a few days or weeks to intense inner work. You needn't become a monk, but an occasional retreat accelerates your progress.

I often tell my students to take one day a month or set aside a weekend for solitude. Should you try it, the directions are simple. Go into an empty room, if you have one, or a large closet, if it gets enough fresh air. Don't see or speak to anyone. Don't read or study. Simply sit quietly, aware of yourself and the world around you. Do some formal meditation practices if you wish. Solitude shows you the way your mind creates your universe.

For longer retreats you can go to one of the centers listed in the back of this book, or go out in a tent or a cabin. Go anywhere you can be completely alone for a week, a few weeks, a month or more. During this time, follow your own schedule of methods, such as formal meditation, hatha yoga, chanting and mantra. But also spend time just sitting quietly. Sit near a tree, a brook, a rock. Set aside your intellect. Let the natural flow of the universe course through your being and harmonize your soul. Let it draw you into an eternal sense of time, of flow. While sitting quietly you may get depressed from rerunning the old movies of your life. Your fantasies and plans may plague you. But eventually a deep quietness will pervade your being, connecting you with profound aspects of yourself and of the universe. It will open you to deeper guidance from within, guidance that brings you closer to God.

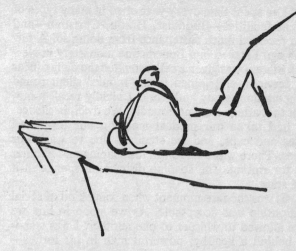

There is a pleasure in the pathless woods,
  There is a rapture on the lonely shore,

There is society, where none intrudes
  By the deep sea, and music in its roar.

—Lord Byron

Childe Harold's Pilgrimage

The homes of householders who have
well-governed minds and have banished their
sense of egoism are as good as solitary forests,
cool caves or peaceful woods.

—*Yoga-Vasishtha*

The World Within the Mind

The mind is all. If the mind is active even solitude
becomes like a market place.

—*Sri Ramana Maharshi*

Talks with Sri
Ramana Maharshi

I've spent time every year or so in many types of retreat facilities—Buddhist, Hindu, Christian—and have received much sustenance from doing so. A few years ago I stayed in a Benedictine monastery in New York State. I was given a cell, attended the daily offices and services, and joined in the monks' silent round of meditation, study and work. I vividly recall a moment that affected me profoundly. We dwelt in silence. We had taken our modest meal on our tin-plated plates and cups, and we stood in line to wash our dishes. There was a large tub for soaping and another one for rinsing. The soaping dish had a sponge in it on a stick.

It was the rare moment when some kind of social relationship was acceptable. As we stood in line we were allowed to whisper to one another. I was standing behind a healthy, powerful man in his forties—very radiant. I was watching the sponge go around on the plate he was washing as I asked, "How long have you been at this monastery?" His answer came back—"Sixteen years."

The image of that sponge going around on that plate and the words "sixteen years" were imprinted in my mind. For the way in which he said "sixteen years" had neither pride nor pity nor any other noticeable emotional quality to it. It was merely a statement of fact. That moment captured for me the equanimity, patience, and depth of meditative life.

At a lecture one of the brothers said, "Here at the monastery, we take away all freedom of choice about matters such as clothing, food, and what to do with time. This frees us to go within." There's a critical difference between external and internal freedom. The image "Stone walls do not a prison make" is apt, for monastic life is very much like imprisonment. You are totally controlled in terms of time and space. Yet within these limits you are free from the need to think so much about externals, freeing you to explore yourself.

↳ Comitment to Place, job, person

Take advantage of the excellent retreat facilities available in this country. Many are listed in the directory at the back of this book. Some allow you to be on your own, so it can be like being alone in the wilds. Others offer structured retreats where meditation is taught and strengthened through an intensive training. I have found both kinds of retreats extremely useful. Time to yourself helps you simplify your life. A ten days' sitting with fifty other people and a meditation teacher inspires you and advances your meditation dramatically.

Some religious organizations and growth centers offer such retreats. Many Christian churches and monasteries have retreat facilities open to the lay public. In Burma, retreats are a national pastime. Rather than going on vacation to the seaside or the mountains, the Burmese often use their vacation time for meditative retreats. They renew themselves and return to the world. This is starting to happen in the West.

Retreat centers offer you a totally controlled space with minimal distractions. There are no televisions, radios, newspapers, few chances for idle hanging out, and fewer still for fulfilling most of the desires that interfere with meditation. We normally can't hear the still small voice within because of the blaring trumpets of our desires. In such a setting, where there is nothing to make the trumpet sound, you can more easily hear the still small voice.

As one changes one's goals, much that was once seen as abhorrent becomes very functional—indeed, valued. Once I met a Black Panther. I was impressed with the clarity of his eyes. I said to him, "How did you become so clear?" His answer was, "It was solitary, man." He had been in solitary confinement for a long time and had used that punishment as a chance to deepen his own being.

My life was very simple in my guru's temple in the Himalayas. I slept on a mat, washed from a bucket, ate one meal a day, and sat for long hours looking out the window or studying the Gita. At one point as I was sitting there, I recalled a *Life* magazine article I had once read about some prisoners of war, captured U.S. pilots. Some photographs had leaked out depicting their life. I recalled one major's description of his life as a war prisoner: "I sit in a room all day. I am sleeping on a mat. I am washing from a bucket and eating one meal a day." The article meant to depict the horror of his life, under such dread conditions. I looked at my own life. I had voluntarily chosen to live in exactly the same conditions, and most of the time I was in ecstasy at my situation.

Each day a bus would go by outside the temple. It was my lifeline back to the world. Often when the time came for the bus in the afternoon, I found myself standing at the window watching for it. I would take out my return airplane ticket and hold it as I watched the bus go by. In this way I examined my longing to return to the world. I would fantasize getting onto that bus; then after maybe thirty or forty hours in buses and airports and planes I'd arrive in the United States, where I would jump right back into all the things I had left behind.

At that time the particular image that drew me was dancing to the Grateful Dead in San Francisco's Fillmore Auditorium. I imagined all the things I would do—eating, sex, entertainment, social relationships, visiting with the family, and so on. I could cast myself into any of these roles, run them through in detail and finally get to the point of imagining myself saying, "You know what I would really like? To be living in a temple in India where I could just sit all day." At that point I would put away my ticket and resume my practices.

Sitting quietly, doing nothing,
Spring comes and the grass grows by itself.

—Zenrin

The Gospel According to Zen

Is Meditation a Cop-out?

Better to be temporarily selfish than never just.

—*Gurdjieff*

In Search of the Miraculous,
P. D. Ouspensky

Some people do use meditation as a cop-out. For them meditation is a defense against facing the problems of life. They devote themselves wholeheartedly to meditation as an escape from responsibility. But they defeat their purpose, for you have to be somebody to become nobody. And if you're not somebody enough, you'd better become somebody first. The spiritual path is not a cop-out from life. You need to clean up your life before you attempt to give it up.

The popular image is of the meditator sitting with eyes closed, immersed in himself. Many in the West see meditation as a withdrawal from the world, an avoidance of social responsibility. Such withdrawal may occur temporarily, as when the meditator has periods of retreat. But it is not necessary, nor does it reflect the essence of the meditative state. Rather than make him withdraw from the world, meditation naturally leads the seeker to a deeper appreciation of the interrelatedness of things, of his relation to his family, friends, nation, and the world.

The meditator also comes to honor the individual differences that make up the fabric of society. Within the harmonious flow of the universe each person's part plays its role. For example, because I live in a country that allows me the freedom to meditate, I feel a duty to reciprocate by paying taxes and voting, so as to maintain the whole that allows me that freedom. At the same time, I don't have to go to Washington to protest. That isn't my particular role to play, but I don't object to anyone else doing it. Social action, if done compassionately, also betters society.

Consider compassion and protest. Each of us is predisposed to fill different social roles. One person feels harmony as a mother who keeps a loving home for her family. Another feels that same harmony only when actively protesting social injustice. No role in itself is more conscious than another. A person's consciousness is reflected in the way the role is played. If someone who has a heightened meditative awareness feels drawn to protest against social injustice, such protest would come from a more compassionate sense of the rightness of the action. His meditative awareness allows greater clarity so he can view the social predicament from all sides. This lets the protester act more effectively, since he is not so attached to his own view of how things should be. Gandhi brought together spiritual life and social action in this way. He tried to meditate and always remembered God, even in the thick of a crisis. When he was assassinated, his last words were the name of God.

Meditation changes how you do whatever you do. Look at competitive sports. Two tennis players, for example, may compete fiercely, each preoccupied with winning. Yet if at the same time they appreciate the beauty of the moment—including the fact that they are two human beings collaborating to compete—it changes the nature of the game. Their expanded awareness may also let them appreciate the beauty of the day, and their good fortune in being able to play. This added appreciation enhances the sense of playful competition and frees them of attachment to winning at all costs, an attitude we call poor sportsmanship. They can simply enjoy the moment.

The secret behind successfully performing any act, be it meditation, motherhood, social protest, or tennis, lies in the attitude of the performer, not in the particular act.

St. Abba Dorotheus, a sixth-century monk, said:

Over whatever you have to do, even if it be very urgent and demands great care, I would not have you argue or be agitated. For rest assured, everything you do, be it great or small, is but one-eighth of the problem, whereas to keep one's state undisturbed even if thereby one should fail to accomplish the task, is the other seven-eighths. So if you are busy at some task and wish to do it perfectly, try to accomplish it—which, as I said would be one-eighth of the problem, and at the same time to preserve your state unharmed —which constitutes seven-eighths. If, however, in order to accomplish your task you would

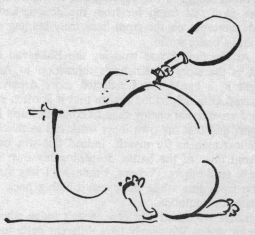

*inevitably be carried away and harm yourself
or another by arguing with him, you should not
lose seven for the sake of preserving one-eighth.*

——Early Fathers from
the Philokalia

In 1967 I spent many months in my guru's
temple in India. I recall receiving a letter from Allen
Ginsberg, describing the Chicago convention and the
revolutionary protest of many people whom I knew.
For a moment, I felt as if I were escaping from the
world by sitting in this temple in India, leading a simple

quiet life. I thought I was copping out. It was as though I were at a rest camp far from the action, and my friends were out on the front lines truly helping mankind find a better world.

At the time I was studying the Bhagavad Gita, which is the story of Krishna's injunction to Arjuna to fight in a battle. As I reflected more deeply, the Bhagavad Gita helped me realize that it is often easier to fight an external enemy than to confront one's inner demons, and that my own inner work did as much for my fellow man as for myself. Indeed this was one of the front lines of the battle, deepening my own inner being to feed others. Perhaps, I thought, I was the one on the front line while they were holding back from ultimate confrontation.

Later I realized that one needn't judge who was better or worse. We simply have different parts to play in the drama.

Calmness of mind does not mean you should stop your activity. Real calmness should be found in activity itself.

—*Shunryu Suzuki*
Zen Mind, Beginner's Mind

Many Stages, Many Paths

There are countless paths, each with its own landmarks, its own route. Meditation unfolds in a sequence, but the specific experiences and their order vary from person to person and from method to method. In devotional meditation or prayer you may be filled with intense love, or with the great pain of separation, or with the presence of the Living Spirit. If on the other hand you meditate using a one-pointedness technique, such as concentration on the breath, you may first experience agitation, then quietness, a deepening silence, more immediate awareness of smaller units of thought, and finally the silent space and emptiness that exists beyond form. In still another approach to meditation, say a movement method like t'ai chi, your first experiences might be of balance, harmony, or flow with the earth, the air, and the surroundings. It is not possible to chart a single path, or to say that every individual will have the same experience. The paths of the heart, the mind, and the body each traverse different terrain to the same goal.

Don't get attached to your way of meditation. Keep in mind that the goal is liberation and that all meditations can be used as you need them to help you in the journey. You can sit and follow your breath to bring your mind to quiet one-pointedness which loosens the hold of all your worldly thoughts. Once the basic tool of one-pointedness is forged, you can use it for any of a number of ends. If you use it to gain insight into the workings of your mind, you ultimately enter the state of Nirvana. Or you might use your one-pointedness to contemplate beings who embody spiritual qualities and develop these qualities in yourself. Or it might work another way: you can begin with prayer, and through the love of Jesus simplify your life to the point that you create no new karma. What may draw you on then is the need for silence, so you seek a simpler meditation, such as following your breath.

I've found that each meditation technique I've ever pursued seriously has helped me by touching another space in my being. Somehow I've danced through them without getting caught in a value system that would say that a single meditative technique is the only way.

You cannot, however, keep collecting methods all the way to enlightenment. Sooner or later you will be drawn to one path or another which is for you the eye of the needle, the doorway to the inner temple. The journey passes from eclectic sampling to a single path. Finally, you recognize the unity of your own way and that of other seekers who followed other paths. At the peak, all the paths come together.

The Indian saints Kabir and Tulsi Dass, as well as St. Theresa, showed an incredibly intense yearning and love for God. Ramana Maharshi, on the other hand, showed the path in which the discriminative mind, through the method of self-inquiry, extricates one from clinging even to the concept of "I." Others, such as the Tibetan sages Padmasambhava and Milarepa, embodied the skillful use of tremendous powers in the service of humanity. Jesus reflected the purest love, compassion, and sacrifice. Buddha showed the path of insight. All these are different routes to a single goal, liberation.

Many, many paths to the mountain top. Each has its own sights, experiences, hazards. Don't get stranded along the way.

> *In any way that men love me in that same way they find my love: for many are the paths of men, but they all in the end come to me.*
>
> —Bhagavad Gita 4:11

> *Water is for fish*
> *And air for men.*
> *Natures differ, and needs with them.*
>
> *Hence the wise men of old*
> *Did not lay down*
> *One measure for all.*
>
> —*Thomas Merton*
> The Way of Chuang Tzu

> *There is no particular way in true practice.*
>
> —*Shunryu Suzuki*
> Zen Mind, Beginner's Mind

When you start you most likely won't know which method will be your final one. In the beginning your view of the path is hazy, for you are still caught in your own expectations and models of reality. As your meditation advances you become attuned to your own particular route through. Then as you finish the journey you open to the universality of all lineages.

The best description of that ultimate openness is the life of the Indian saint Ramakrishna. After having followed his own lineage, which honored, worshipped, and loved Mother Kali, he transcended it and went through Moslem, Christian, and a variety of other traditions. Today in the West some people are drawn to fundamental Christianity because of an intense emotional relationship with Jesus, others are drawn to the simple austerity of Zen Buddhism, and some to the intermingling of energy and love in Sufi dancing. When you work with a particular lineage, commit yourself totally to it. Hear it, see it, smell it, taste it, totally surrender into it. Don't worry about your final path. Let the inner guru call you. Through meditation you learn to listen quietly, until the call comes, clear and unmistakable.

> *From of old there were not two paths.*
> *"Those who have arrived" all walked the same road.*
>
> —Zenrin
>
> The Gospel According to Zen

5

LOSING
YOUR
WAY

Method

It is a rare being who can cross the ocean of existence without a boat. Few of us are ready to see completely through ego's illusion and thereby achieve instant liberation. So we use methods, we use a boat, with the understanding that when we get to the other shore, we'll leave the boat. We're not going to portage; we needn't carry the boat on our heads. We'll be finished with boats.

But the boat can entrap or liberate. Whether you end up as a boatman or as one liberated depends on your original motive for spiritual work. You can become a connoisseur of boats, collecting the very best. Or you can go to the far shore, beyond beyond: "Gate, gate, paragate, parasamgate, bodhi svaha," beyond even the concept of beyond.

Whatever you seek—spiritual realization, liberation, enlightenment, merging with God, or however you describe it—don't cling to meditation as a method. At the same time, leave yourself open to any possibilities that come your way. To stand back from any method for fear of entrapment leaves you standing on this side yearning for the far shore. Jump in and trust your inner guide. The purity of your own yearning and of the methods you follow will show you the way.

Methods differ in how big, fancy, or ornate a boat they are. How dependent you become on a method depends on your degree of attachment to stuff, including your method of meditation. You can be attached to meditating on Krishna, chanting to fill your heart with love as the Hare Krishna devotees do. Or you can be attached to the ecstasy that sometimes comes from following your breath with exquisite one-pointedness.

All methods are traps. But for a method to work you must go deeply into it, deep enough to be entrapped. At the same time, trust that your yearning for spiritual self-realization and the nature of the method will ultimately free you from the method itself. For example, a pure guru exists only for your liberation. The guru has no desire to entrap you as a follower or disciple. Yet for your relationship to be productive, it demands your total involvement and surrender. If a teacher is impure, he may want to hold you as a disciple beyond the time you are ready to leave. Then it will be your purity of purpose that turns you away from the teacher.

It's the same with your relationship to meditation. As you reach each new stage, you cling to new highs. Or you may fear not getting enough after investing much of your time and effort. Or you may make the benefits of meditation, such as greater efficiency at work, ends in themselves. These are dead ends on the path.

How you use a method determines whether it

entraps or liberates you. The game isn't to become a method groupie, but to transcend method. To say I'm a meditator—or I'm an anything—is just another trap.

Some, such as Krishnamurti, question whether meditation actually does lead to liberation. They point out that all methods are just more ways of entrapping awareness. Rather than springing us from the traps of ego, they add yet another bar to our freedom. Proponents, such as Patanjali and the Buddha, say these are tools to be used until there is no longer any need for them. My feeling is that it would be best to bypass methods, but there are few of us capable of such a leap of consciousness. The rest of us need methods. These are traps through which we set ourselves free.

A good traveler leaves no track.

—*Lao Tse*

Tao Te Ching

Experience

As your mind quiets more and more in meditation your consciousness may shift radically. With quietness can come waves of bliss and rapture. You may feel the presence of astral beings; you may feel yourself leaving your body and rising into realms above your head; you may feel energy pouring up your spine. You may

have visions, burning sensations, a sharp pain in your
heart, deep stillness, stiffening of your body. You may
hear voices or inner sounds such as the flute of Krishna,
a waterfall, thunder, or a bell. You may smell strange
scents or your mouth may be filled with strange tastes.
Your body may tingle or shake. As you go deeper you
may enter what the southern Buddhists call jhanas,
trance states marked by ecstasy, rapture, bliss, and
clarity of perception. You may have visions of distant
places or find you somehow know things though
you can't explain how.

    These experiences may seduce you. If you cling
to them, fascinated—whether the fascination be out of
attraction or repulsion—you invest them with undue
importance. When you've had this kind of seductive
experience, its memory can be an obstacle to meditation, especially if you try to recreate the experience.
To keep going in meditation, you've got to give up
your attachment to these states and go beyond. If these

experiences come spontaneously, fine. But don't seek them.

I remember taking a fifteen-day insight meditation course. On the twelfth day I experienced a peace that I had never known in my life. It was so deep that I rushed to my teacher and said, "This peace is what I have always wanted all my life. Everything else I was doing was just to find this peace." Yet a month later I was off pursuing other spiritual practices. That experience of peace wasn't enough. It was limited. Any experiential state, anything we can label, isn't it.

My intense experiences with psychedelics led to very powerful attachments to the memories of those trips. I tried to recreate them through yogic practices. It took some years before I stopped comparing meditative spaces with those of my psychedelic days. Only when I stopped clinging to those past experiences did I see that the present ones had a fullness, immediacy, and richness that was enough—I didn't need the memories. Later, during intensive study of pranayama and kundalini, my breath stopped and I felt moments of great rapture. Once again, the intensity of the experience hooked me and I was held back for a time by my attempts to recreate those moments. When I saw that I was closest to God in the moment itself, these past experiences stopped having such a great pull. Again I saw my clinging to memories as an obstacle.

You come to see through your attachment to such experiences and find yourself less interested in striving for them. The despair and frustration that come from desiring a fascinating state and not getting it becomes grist for the mill of insight. It's an irritating process, in a way. You may see things clearly or have a breakthrough into another state for a second or so. But like psychedelics, it leaves you starving. You can grasp it for a moment, but you can't eat the fruit of the garden.

Meditation is not a matter of trying to achieve ecstasy, spiritual bliss or tranquility, nor is it attempting to become a better person. It is simply the creation of a space in which we are able to expose and undo our neurotic games, our self-deceptions, our hidden fears and hopes.

—Chogyam Trungpa

The Myth of Freedom

In Brindavana, the sacred city where Krishna dances with the gopis, there is a dudhwalla, a milk seller. He's a true devotee of Krishna. Once he was selling milk, and because of his purity, Krishna with his shakti Radha came right up to the stand, there on the street in Brindavana, and bought some milk. He actually saw them. His eyes are as though they had been burned out by a brilliant bulb. He can talk about nothing but the moment that Krishna and Radha came to his dudhstand. He's not worried about how much milk he sells any more. He's had the ecstasy of seeing God in the form of light. And that's who he is this lifetime. It's a high place to be.

Shouldn't that be enough? Won't you settle for ecstasy? Bliss? Rapture? Hanging out with the gods? Flying? Bet you always wanted to fly. Reading other people's minds? What power would you settle for? said the devil to Jesus in the desert. You must want something. Whatever you want you get, sooner or later. And there you are. As long as you are not finished with that desire, you are entrapped.

When you are attracted to powers and seduced by pleasures, what had been a vertical path turns horizontal. As long as your goal falls short of full liberation, you will be trapped by these experiences. If you know you want the long-range goal, that knowledge will help you give up the desires for the states along the way. As each desire arises there will be a struggle with your ego. Part of you wants to enjoy the seductive pleasures, part wants to give them up and push on.

One way to handle extraordinary experiences is to be neither horrified nor intrigued by them. The Tibetan Book of the Dead refers to the ten thousand horrible and the ten thousand beautiful visions. In the course of meditation you may meet them all: powers, great beauty, deaths, grotesqueries, angels, demons, all of it. These are just forms, the stuff of the universe. You confront them on the path just as you meet all manner of people when you walk a busy street. Notice them, acknowledge them—don't deny them—and then let them go. To cling to these heavens and hells, no matter how beautiful, slows your progress. Not to acknowledge them, or to push them away, is just a more subtle form of clinging. Follow the middle way. As stuff arises in your mind, let it arise, notice it, let it go. No clinging.

Many sensations come, many thoughts or images arise, but they are just waves of your own mind. Nothing comes from outside your mind.

To realize pure mind in your delusion is practice. If you try to expel the delusion it will only persist the more. Just say, "Oh, this is just delusion." And do not be bothered by it.

—*Shunryu Suzuki*

Zen Mind, Beginner's Mind

That thou mayest have pleasure in everything,
seek pleasure in nothing.
That thou mayest know everything,
seek to know nothing.
That thou mayest possess all things,
seek to possess nothing.
That thou mayest be everything,
seek to be nothing.

—*St. John of the Cross*

The Ascent of Mount Carmel

Planes

Our senses and thinking mind keep our awareness aligned with the physical plane. But there are planes where beings exist other than the physical. If in meditation you enter other states of consciousness, you may meet such beings who seemingly come to instruct or guide you. At first, they are awesome. They seem to exist either in disembodied states or with luminous or transparent bodies that appear and disappear at will. They do not exist for normal vision.

Because of the uniqueness of these beings you might put more value on their teachings than is merited. Beings on other planes are not necessarily wiser than those on this plane They may be well-meaning, but they may not know any more than you. Because of the way in which you met them, you are filled with awe and reverence, and you might treat their teaching as truth. All they may have to teach you is their existence itself, which shows you the relative nature of reality.

Some whom you meet on planes other than the physical may indeed come from higher, more conscious realms. They may be masters who exist in order to guide you and come forth at critical moments to instruct you. You needn't meet such masters to become liberated. They come to you only if your particular path requires their manifestation.

Just as with teachers on the physical planes, be open. Experience each being you meet and sense in your heart—do we have work to do together or not? If that teacher feels relevant to your spiritual journey, work with him or her until you have fully grasped the teaching. Then thank the teacher and proceed. This is true on every plane of existence.

Power

Even the beginnings of an inner quiet and calm allow you to see much more. You get a new sense of how you create and control your universe. You stop reacting to events simply with blind patterns and habits of thought. Your life becomes more creative. Other powers follow this new creativity as your meditation deepens. They become more and more dramatic, and can include psychic powers, astral travel, and even powers on other planes.

These are traps. They are seductive, especially for people who have felt impotent, inadequate, or weak. Because of their attractiveness these powers tend to make you slow down in your journey in order to enjoy them. This is especially likely when they offer more sensual gratification, for example, if you use the powers to attract new lovers for sexual conquests.

Power entraps even when it is used to do good. Even if you couch the exercise of power in righteous terms, it still involves you more deeply in ego, since you as a separate entity are trying to manipulate your environment. So it is that powers, just like any of the other seductions along the path, are best noted and let go of, rather than acted upon. It's better to go for broke than to take a small profit and run with it.

Meditation may attract those who seek worldly influence because of the psychic powers they can develop. Generals take it up to improve their military efficiency, and so meditation becomes part of the Cold War. Some try to develop telepathic powers or the ability to change things at a distance to win wars or control other people or things with the mind. Meditation might bring you this. So what? With the despair that comes from knowing that the worldly dance, including the greatest powers, is not sufficiently fullfilling, you recognize the deeper potential of meditation: nothing short of, not my, but Thy Will, the Will of God, out of which it all came in the first place. Why settle for less?

> *If you continue this simple practice every day you will obtain a wonderful power. Before you attain it, it is something wonderful, but after you obtain it, it is nothing special.*
>
> —*Shunryu Suzuki*
>
> **Zen Mind, Beginner's Mind**

Spiritual Pride

A persistent trap all along the path is pride in one's spiritual purity. It's a form of one-upmanship in which you judge others out of a feeling of superiority. This ultimately limits your spiritual awakening. You can see many people who are caught in this trap of virtue —for example, in the self-righteousness of some churchgoers. In the yoga scene in America there are many groups of people who dress in a certain way, eat in a certain way, are special in some way that gives them an ego-enhancing feeling of purity.

The harmful effect of this trap is not so much to one's social relationships—though they may become strained from this display of subtle arrogance—but rather the effect on oneself. This feeling of specialness or superiority inflates the ego and feeds it with pride. The best antidote to pride is humility, which leads to compassion. The sooner one develops compassion in this journey, the better. Compassion lets us appreciate that each individual is doing what he or she must do, and that there is no reason to judge another person or oneself. Merely to do what you can to further your own awakening.

> *Mad with joy, life and death dance*
> *to the rhythm of this music. The*
> *hills and the sea and the earth*
> *dance. The world of man dances*
> *in laughter and tears.*
>
> *Why put on the robe of the monk, and*
> *live aloof from the world in lonely*
> *pride?*
>
> — *Kabir*
>
> One Hundred Poems of
> Kabir
>
> *The worst man is the one who sees himself as*
> *the best.*
>
> — *Ali*
>
> Maxims of Ali

Whoever has in his heart even so much as a rice-grain of pride, cannot enter into Paradise.

—*Muhammad*

Perspectives spirituelles
et Faits humains

We are to practice virtue, not possess it.

—*Eckhart*

Meister Eckhart: A
Modern Translation

Highs

For many of us who have come into meditation through psychedelics, the model we have had for changing consciousness has been of "getting high." We pushed away our normal waking state in order to embrace a state of euphoria, harmony, bliss, peace, or ecstasy. Many of us spent long periods of time getting high and coming down. It was like the Biblical story of the wedding guest who came to the wedding but was not wearing the proper wedding garments, so he got thrown out. My guru, in speaking about psychedelics, said, "These medicines will allow you to come and visit Christ, but you can only stay two hours. Then you have to leave again. This is not the true samadhi. It's better to become Christ than to visit him—but even the visit of a saint for a moment is useful." Then he added, "But love is the most powerful medicine." For love slowly transforms you into what the psychedelics only let you glimpse.

In view of his words, when I reflected on my trips with LSD and other psychedelics, I saw that after a glimpse of the possibility of transcendence, I continued tripping only to reassure myself that the possibility was still there. Seeing the possibility is indeed different from being the possibility. Sooner or later you must purify and alter your mind, heart, and body so that the things which bring you down from your experiences lose their power over you. Psychedelics could chemically override the thought patterns in your brain so that you are open to the moment, but once the chemical loses its power the old habit patterns take over again. With them comes a subtle despair that without chemicals you are a prisoner of your thoughts.

I recall vividly a very powerful experience in 1962 in the meditation room of our house in Newton. For several hours I sat quiescent in a state of ecstatic transcendence merging into the universe. As the chemical began to wear off, I saw a blood-red wave rolling down the room toward me. In it were thousands of images of me—all of my social and psychological definitions of self. Me on a tricycle, giving a lecture, making love, and so forth. It was as if this wave was about to overrun me and carry me back into myself. I recall putting up my hands, trying to push away the oncoming wave and desperately searching my mind for some mantra or technique that would hold off this incredible force bearing down upon me. But I had no such charm or spell. The wave poured back over me and I came back into my old familiar self. In recent years I have learned how, when the thoughts arise that were contained within that wave, to use a meditative stance to witness them. This gently loosens their hold and brings me back into the moment. Then I see there's nothing special about the high, nothing dreadful about the thoughts in the wave. Just stuff.

The trap of high experiences, however they occur, is that you become attached to their memory and so you try to recreate them. These memories compel you to try to reproduce the high. Ultimately they trap you, because they interfere with your experience of the present moment. In meditation you must be in the moment, letting go of comparisons and memories. If the high was too powerful in comparison to the rest of your life, it overrides the present and keeps you focused on the past. The paradox, of course, is that were you to let go of the past, you would find in the present moment the same quality that you once had. But because you're trying to repeat the past, you lose the moment.

How many times have you felt a moment of perfection—only to have it torn away the next moment by the awareness that it will pass? How many times will you try to get high hoping that this time you won't come down—until you already know as you start to go up that you will come down? The down is part of the high. When in meditation you are tempted by another taste of honey, your memory of the finiteness of those moments tempers your desire. More bliss, more rapture, more ecstasy—just part of the passing show. The moment in its fullness includes both high and low and yet it is beyond both.

> *Paradise is the prison of the sage as the world*
> *is the prison of the believer.*
>
> —*Yahja b. Mu'adh al-Razi*
>
> De l'Unité Transcendante
> des Religions

Success

Though the numbers are proportionally few, many thousands of us have, through discipline and persistence, arrived at a view of our lives that is open, clear, and detached. In this new space we have a lightness, an ease in carrying out our daily lives, an ability to keep a certain sense of humor about our predicaments. We find that because of the quietness of our minds it's easier to relate to acquaintances, to family, to employers, to friends. It's also easier to bring together our economic scene and the other aspects of our lives.

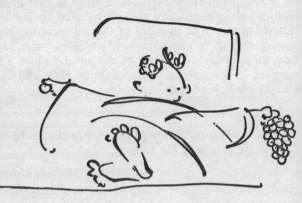

We begin to feel a little bit like gods on earth, for where we see sadness and suffering around us, we are able to empathize and still feel lightness and joy. It's as if the world is made for our delight, and even our own troubles become a source of amusement. When we look one another in the eye there is clarity and honesty. We have a certain degree of inner peace. Many of us never thought possible this feeling of equanimity, fullness, and delight in life. We have a sense of self-acceptance, spaciousness, and fullness in the moment that makes each day enough. In many ways it seems like liberation.

As I look around at people I know who have been working intensely on themselves for some time, there is a dramatic change. I see beings who were initially preoccupied with their melodramas, whose bodies were their enemies and who were attached to spiritual melodrama, now bright, clear, and strong. Their lives have come together, they have relationships that are fulfilling, moments that are enough, a lightness in their faces. To see them this way fills me with happiness.

Yet I see that this stage is but a preparation for the ultimate climb that leads in the end to total liberation. This stage has a danger: It is too comfortable. It's like a beautiful mountain pasture: there are tents in the pine grove and streams to sit by and plenty of fuel and food. The air is clear, the view is grand. There are birds and wildflowers. These pleasures are a trap.

Many beings tarry here in this role of God on earth for many lifetimes. But ultimately even this heaven is not enough. For there is another path that leads from this pleasant pasture to still higher slopes. There is the final journey.

You should feel no guilt about where you are in your spiritual path. Wherever you are, be it at the beginning of the journey, well on your way, or resting comfortably at some height, you must acknowledge where you are, for that is the key to further growth. You should keep some perspective about the entire journey so that you will not sink into complacency, feeling you have finished the journey when you have not even begun to approach liberation.

The Sage does not talk, the Talented Ones talk, and the stupid ones argue.

—*Kung Tingan*

Judging

Our deep conditioning from school exams, grades, and the like gives us the habit of looking at every achievement competitively, in terms of where we stand. How are we doing: Are we better, equal, or worse than others on the same journey? Such evaluation of our position becomes a real obstacle in spiritual life, for it constantly leads us to look at spiritual evolution in comparative terms. Someone tells you they have visions of lights when they meditate. You never have had such a vision. This fills you with feelings of inadequacy and jealousy. On the other hand, you may sometimes feel yourself leaving your body when you meditate. Your friends don't experience this. This fills you with a subtle spiritual pride that feeds your ego.

Losing Your Way • 163

In 1970 I traveled around the world on a lecture tour with Swami Muktananda. In his teaching he transmits shakti, or energy, to his students. I recall vividly a living room in Melbourne, Australia, where twenty people were gathered in meditation before him. It was late in the afternoon and he sat crosslegged on a love seat at the end of the room, with eyes closed behind sunglasses, a knit hat on his head, idly strumming a one-stringed instrument. The room was quiet.

Slowly, one by one, the people in the room started to behave bizarrely. One portly gentleman in a dark-blue suit with a watch fob suddenly began to do mudras, traditional Indian hand positions. I recall the look on his face of consternation and perplexity—it was apparent that he knew nothing of these mudras, and was certainly not doing them intentionally. Next to him a gentleman dressed in a tweed jacket and gray flannels with a pipe in his pocket, obviously the perfect professor, suddenly got up and started to do formal Indian dance. Again the look of perplexity, for in no way was he responsible for what he did. Near me was a girl who had come not to see Swami Muktananda, but to be with her boyfriend, who was interested. Suddenly she began to do intense, automatic breathing. Her rapid breathing got to such a height that she literally bounced across the floor of the room with the breaths. Again I saw the look of perplexity.

I watched more and more people experience the touch of Swami Muktananda's shakti, but never felt it myself. None of these things happened to me. I was concerned. After all, if I was "evolved enough" to lecture with Swami Muktananda, why shouldn't I have these dramatic signs of spiritual awakening? The seed of jealousy sprouted in me. Though I didn't admit it, I did my best to induce these symptoms of awakening.

Later I learned that these sometimes bizarre manifestations of shakti were the result of various blockages in people and were in no way necessary on the spiritual path. As time has gone on, I have learned that there is no experience, no symptom, no sign of spiritual growth that is absolutely necessary. Each of us has a unique predicament that stretches back over many lifetimes. Each person is drawn to a different set of practices and responds in his or her own way.

Individual differences are not better or worse, merely different. If we forgo judging, we come to understand that each of us has a unique predicament that requires a unique journey. While we share the overall journey, everyone's particular experiences are his or her own. No set of experiences is a prerequisite for enlightenment. People have become enlightened in all ways. Just be what you are.

The experiences along the way are not enlightenment. So if you don't see lights or meet remarkable beings on other planes, or if your body doesn't shake, or if you don't feel the greatest peace, or even if nothing seems to happen in meditation, don't compare or judge. Just keep going. To compare yourself with others is to forget the uniqueness of your own journey.

Always repenting of wrongs done
Will never bring my heart to rest.

—*Chi K'ang*

170 Chinese Poems

He who realizes the Lord God, the Atman, the one existence, the Self of the universe, neither praises nor dispraises any man. Like the sun shining impartially upon all things, he looks with an equal eye upon all beings. He moves about in the world a free soul, released from all attachment.

—*Srimad Bhagavatam*

The Wisdom of God

Love it the way it is.

—*Thaddeus Golas*

The Lazy Man's Guide
to Enlightenment

6

GETTING STUCK

The Body Reacts

The minute that even the most gentle attempt is made to quiet the mind, to go within, to loosen the hold of one's overlearned way of thinking and being, new experiences occur. Many people, after their first hours of meditation, feel unusual patterns or rushes of energy. There is no cause to fear. Merely watch and open to these changing energy patterns. Don't resist them. Where there is fear, there are blocks in the body, and energy cannot flow.

Each person has his or her own special weak spot where tension first manifests. For some it is stomach

upset, for others pain in the neck or in the small of the back, for others headaches. Just sitting quietly for twenty minutes often creates tensions in a body that is used to being constantly on the move.

Sleep habits may also change. You may need more sleep or less sleep. Even the tiniest quieting of the mind releases energy. If it is able to flow through you freely, you will probably feel energized and sleep less. On the other hand, if your old habits hold on strongly and you struggle against the energy, you get fatigued.

Don't get lost in overreacting to the pains or tiredness. Just make yourself as comfortable as possible and proceed with the meditation. For the most part they are only distractions, not symptoms of a real illness. In each case, gently adapt in whatever way is required. Don't be afraid or exaggerate these things into a melodrama. Don't obsess. These physical symptoms come and go during meditation.

If you treat each such manifestation as real, you'll spend thousands on doctor bills. Once when I was meditating intensely for several months, I began to feel very ill. I went to a doctor who kept making me come back for more tests. He charged me outrageous fees, until I had run up a six-hundred-dollar bill on tests alone, none of which showed anything. I got so frustrated that I just decided to get better. I stopped worrying about my symptoms, and they went away.

This is not to say that you should not treat illness. Remember, your body is your temple—you must take care of it properly. Just give up your melodrama about being sick. If you're ill, get whatever treatment you need. But do so matter-of-factly, and don't use illness as a cop-out to stop meditating.

The body constantly tries to draw attention to itself by its shiverings, its breathlessness, its palpitations, its shudders and sweats and cramps; but it reacts quickly to any scorn and indifference in its master. Once it senses that he is not taken in by its jeremiads, once it understands that it will inspire no pity that way, then it comes into line and obediently accomplishes its task.

—René Daumal

Mount Analogue

Do not try to drive pain away by pretending that it is not real;
Pain, if you seek serenity in Oneness, will vanish of its own accord.

—Sengstan

Buddhist Texts

The way that will relieve your woes on the physical plane will also take you to the highest spiritual realizations. And the way is simple. No resistance.

—Thaddeus Golas

The Lazy Man's Guide
to Enlightenment

The Mind Reacts

Over the years we develop strong habits of perceiving the universe, and we come to be very secure within these habits. We selectively perceive our environment in ways that reinforce them. This collection of habits is what we call ego. But meditation breaks the ego down. As we begin to see through it we can become confused as to what reality is. What once seemed absolute now begins to seem relative. When this happens, some people get confused; others fear they may be going insane.

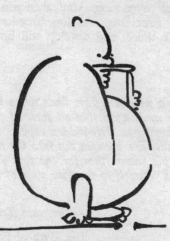

You must expect that growth requires change. A child's structure of reality alters as his or her endocrine system starts to change in puberty, leading sometimes to confusion and emotional upset. So it is with meditation that as you grow into a more conscious being, your old realities crumble and there will be moments of disorientation. The best strategy for dealing with this disorientation is to note it and let it be. Don't try to push it away and retreat into familiar habits. Most people need not fear this disruption. Although you may feel some anxiety, the ego's defense mechanisms usually give way no faster than you can handle it. But if you find these reactions too disturbing you can cut back on the amount of meditation you do, or even stop altogether for a while. When you feel more calm and relaxed, ease back into meditation.

The path to freedom is through detachment from your old habits of ego. Slowly you will arrive at a new and more profound integration of your experiences in a more evolved structure of the universe. That is, you will flow beyond the boundaries of your ego until ultimately you merge into the universe. At that point you have gone beyond ego. Until then you must break through old structures, develop broader structures, break through those, and develop still broader structures.

> *In fact, a person always finds when he begins to practice meditation that all sorts of problems are brought out. Any hidden aspects of your personality are brought out into the open, for the simple reason that for the first time you are allowing yourself to see your state of mind as it is.*
>
> —Chogyam Trungpa
>
> The Myth of Freedom

Recently a woman came to see me who considered herself very close to having a nervous breakdown. One of her symptoms was unpredictable amounts of energy, so great at times that though she would ride her bicycle for three or four hours, afterward she would have more energy than when she began. She also cried unpredictably, for no apparent reason. She would sometimes look at some of her clients—she was a therapist—and feel such love for them that she wanted to kiss their feet or worship them. She would wake up at night with visions of beings talking to her, and feel presences in the room. Her vision would keep shifting so that what seemed a reality at one moment would be a dream a moment later. Sometimes she wasn't sure whether something that happened the night before was real or a dream. A constriction in her throat kept rising upward, and she felt energy racing through her spine.

Most of these symptoms, if presented to a traditional psychotherapist, would be treated as pathology. When I heard her description I recognized at once that what was happening to her was the awakening of the kundalini, the energy that resides in the psychic tube in the spine known as the shushumna. I rummaged through my papers and found a list of the symptoms that occur when kundalini awakens. I read her the list, and over 80 percent of her symptoms were on the list. As I read, her anxiety subsided, for suddenly she felt she was no longer crazy. She could now understand that she was in the midst of a spiritual process and there were clear steps for her to take to work with these energies. Just the reduction in anxiety was enough to change the nature of the entire experience for her. She could let the changes happen.

In the initial stages of meditation it is unlikely that you will have any such severe symptoms. But as your meditations get deeper, the ego will cling by whatever means it knows. Very often that clinging will take its form in physical symptoms or intensely negative psychological states. It's as if something that has remained quiescent for a long time is suddenly stirred up and rises to the surface. These long-latent impurities must be skimmed off.

Each of us has psychological weak points. Our weakness may be paranoia, depression, lassitude, confusion, or indecisiveness. I've had clear, decisive people come to me who, after meditating for some time, found themselves becoming less and less certain. Close examination revealed that their previous decisiveness came from being locked into rigid models of reality. As these models crumbled and they began to see the relative nature of the world they once thought they knew, it became more difficult to make decisions. This was only a stage. Later they quieted enough to hear the entire domain of possibilities, not just a narrow slice as before. Their decision-making became even better than before. As each such reaction occurs, merely allow it, sit with it.

> *(Krishnakishore) passed through a God-intoxicated state, when he would repeat only the word "Om" and shut himself up alone in his room. His relatives thought he was actually mad, and called in a physician. Ram Kaviraj of Natagore came to see him. Krishnakishore said to the physician, "Cure me, sir, of my malady, if you please, but not of my Om."*
>
> —*Sri Ramakrishna*
>
> The Gospel of
> Sri Ramakrishna

Distractions

Meditation texts name certain mental states that are hindrances. Try to be aware and work to overcome them in your meditation. The major unhelpful states are: tiredness and torpor; strong desires; distractedness, agitation and worry; and anger, depression, and doubt. Each of these is bound to occur from time to time, and each represents a special danger to meditation practice, because they are so compelling.

Should any of these states of mind arise—e.g., a sexual fantasy, or the thought "I'm too tired to keep meditating, I'll go to sleep instead," or ruminations over some pressing problem—they should be treated like any other distraction. Simply return your full attention to the meditation. These hindering states demand that you exert greater effort to get your mind back to meditation than do most of the other random thoughts that cross your mind. Making this effort is the essence of meditation.

I've meditated hours and hours where nothing at all seemed to happen. I became increasingly bored and disgusted. Every tactic I could think of for cutting through these emotional states was useless. I had to examine my inadequacies, my doubts about my practice, my belief that it would lead me to God. I had to confront my reactions to meditation. Take fatigue, for example. It was a chronic problem for me. I remember propping myself up with piles of cushions so that I would not fall over into sleep. I often went to meditation courses because I was afraid that alone I would drift off into sleep. I've since learned to handle drowsy states with breathing techniques. What I experienced as fatigue often was actually a state of deep stillness that I misinterpreted. Instead of taking the feeling of fatigue as an invitation for a nap, I now regard it as a passing state, and keep sitting.

By letting go of whatever thoughts may come, no matter how powerful or fascinating they may be, and constantly returning to the meditation, our mental habits lose their hold over us. We create space for new possibilities, new realities, new being.

In Bodhgaya, where Buddha was enlightened, perhaps a hundred of us gathered at a monastery for meditation training. For ten days at a time we meditated intensively from five-thirty in the morning until ten at night. During these ten-day periods on about the eighth day the teacher would instruct us to spend a sixty-minute period in the hall without moving at all. I recall vividly one such period. The room was crowded, it was darkened—a gentle night. Outside I could hear the sound of the village, the creaking of the wooden wheels of the oxcarts, drivers yelling at their water buffalo, the laughter of children at play. I sensed a gentle, timeless civilization close to the earth.

Inside the teacher was reminding us, "Be aware of your breath. Do not move." From the distance I became aware of the buzz of a mosquito, the sound becoming louder. The horrible thought arose in my mind, "I hope the mosquito lands on someone else if he must land at all." Then there was guilt, and then with the next following of the breath, the thought of guilt faded. The mosquito approached. My consciousness once again was entrapped by the sound of the mosquito. It landed on my cheek. "Do not move," the teacher intoned.

I could feel the mosquito walking over my skin looking for an appropriate place to feed. My automatic impulse to brush away or kill mosquitoes came to mind. I wrestled with my mind to bring it back to my breath. Then I felt the mosquito inserting its proboscis into my skin. Slowly I felt it getting heavier as it filled with my blood. I wrestled to bring my mind back to my breath, but it kept being caught by the drama that was unfolding on the surface of my skin. Slowly the mosquito withdrew, was still for a moment, and then staggered across my skin preparing for takeoff with its new burden—my blood. I felt the fullness of the engorged mosquito. It flew away.

Just beneath the surface of my skin there came a sensation. Itching, itching. I wrestled to bring the mind back to my breath. Itching, itching. I watched the itch arise, become overwhelmingly insistent, and then slowly subside, as the alien fluids were absorbed into my system.

How much I learned in that tiny bit of suffering! By holding back my reaction I saw the entire sequence clearly. What grace that mosquito provided in allowing me to examine the passing nature of phenomena.

If at prayer we do nothing but drive away temptations and distractions, our prayer is well made.

—St. Francis de Sales

Conformity to the
Will of God

We must do our business faithfully, without trouble or disquiet, recalling our mind to God mildly, and with tranquillity, as often as we find it wandering from Him.

—Brother Lawrence

The Practice of the
Presence of God

When you are practicing zazen, do not try to stop your thinking. Let it stop by itself. If something comes into your mind, let it come in, and let it go out. It will not stay long. When you try to stop your thinking, it means you are bothered by it. Do not be bothered by anything.

—Shunryu Suzuki

Zen Mind, Beginner's Mind

The man of wandering mind lies between the fangs of the Passions.

—Santi-deva

The Path of Light

*Constantly struggle with your thought and
whenever it is carried hither and thither, collect
it together. God does not require from novices
prayer completely free from distractions. Do
not despond when your thought is distracted, but
remain calm, and unceasingly restore your
mind to itself.*

—*St. John of the Ladder*

On the Prayer of Jesus

*A wandering thought is itself the essence
of Wisdom—
Immanent and intrinsic.*

—*Milarepa*

The Hundred Thousand
Songs of Milarepa

Doubt

You can't expect that your ego is going to lie down
and stop resisting immediately. It finds new and more
subtle ways to use your every weakness. At many
points in your spiritual journey your faith may be
tenuous and your commitment minimal, and your zeal
may evaporate.

One of the ego's favorite paths of resistance is to
fill you with doubt. When you want to sleep late, you'll
find reasons not to get up to do your sadhana. You

won't see the usefulness of meditation any more. You'll doubt your teacher, yourself, and the Spirit. You'll doubt God. And on and on and on.

These doubts have to be dealt with, for some may be valid. For example, you may be right to doubt your teacher. Your teacher may not be worthy of his or her following. On the other hand, this very doubt may be a mind game to keep you from a deeper commitment. In truth, only you know which it is. There is a place in you that knows whether you are conning yourself in order to cop-out, or whether you're indeed dealing with a legitimate awareness of limitations.

Doubt demands you examine what you are doing with a critical eye. In this examination, include the doubt itself. If the doubt seems just another dodge of your ego, suspend it and proceed. The antidote to doubt is faith, but it should be an informed faith, not blind.

> *Let go the things in which you are in doubt for the things in which there is no doubt.*
>
> —*Mohammed*
>
> The Forty-Two Traditions of An-Nawawi

> *It is when your practice is rather greedy that you become discouraged with it. So you should be grateful that you have a sign or warning*

signal to show you the weak point in your practice.

—*Shunryu Suzuki*

Zen Mind, Beginner's Mind

Once a man was about to cross the sea. Bibhishana wrote Rama's name on a leaf, tied it in a corner of the man's wearing-cloth, and said to him: "Don't be afraid. Have faith and walk on the water. But look here—the moment you lose faith you will be drowned." The man was walking easily on the water. Suddenly he had an intense desire to see what was tied in his cloth. He opened it and found only a leaf with the name of Rama written on it. "What is this?" he thought, "Just the name of Rama!" As soon as doubt entered his mind he sank under the water.

—*Sri Ramakrishna*

The Gospel of
Sri Ramakrishna

Fear

Some people from time to time feel fear during meditation. Fear takes all kinds of objects. Fear of hypnosis, faddism, insanity, losing control, irresponsibility, losing friends, loss of identity or of will, apathy, or passivity. Fear of being lost in the void or the emptiness. Nameless fear, of nothing particular. Fear that nothing will happen. Fear that something really will happen that will change you.

Such fears will grab at you and influence you to stop meditation. Examine these fears; be open to them. But don't worry; they will pass. The changes that meditation brings will not be such that there is anything to fear. Roosevelt was right: "We have nothing to fear but fear itself." For the defenses of your ego are sturdy enough that you have ample opportunity to offset any negative effects of meditation.

My suggestion is to relax and enjoy the journey. As fears arise, allow them their space. Understand that, like all the other feelings meditation brings you —confusion, pleasure, pain, excitement, boredom— your fears, too, will pass.

It was a dark night, early summer, finally turning warm. As Grandpa Joe slipped out of the car, I called to him to ask for his advice. I had been warned that the bears of the mountains were now active especially at night. It was dangerous to walk in the woods in the dark. And furthermore, last summer a bear had actually come and circled the very tipi where I was now living, for it is pitched a good twenty minutes' walk further up the mountain from the other Lama dwellings.

"Grandpa," I asked, "tonight I must walk alone in the dark a long way to get to my tipi. Perhaps I will meet a bear. What should I do? Should I talk to the bear? Should I send it love?"

Grandpa leaned back and we shared a gentle space of silence together. Then he gave me this advice. "No talk to bear. Talk to God!"

—Saraswati

It is not that you must be free from fear. The moment you try to free yourself from fear, you create a resistance against fear. Resistance, in any form, does not end fear. What is needed, rather than running away or controlling or suppressing or any other resistance, is understanding fear; that means, watch it, learn about it, come directly into contact with it. We are to learn about fear, not how to escape from it, not how to resist it through courage and so on.

—Krishnamurti

Loss of Meaning

Very often people report to me that meditation has brought an emptiness into their life. Everything seems meaningless. It takes great faith to ride through such heavy periods of spiritual transformation.

I recall the near anger I had towards spirituality as I saw my favorite rushes fall away. Things I had previously gotten great thrills from became empty. For example, many years back one of my aesthetic highs was to visit Tanglewood, the music festival where the Boston Symphony played. I recall in particular a beautiful evening when I lay under the elm trees on a blanket with wine and cheese and listened to the symphony in the outdoor shell play Berlioz' *Requiem*. I was in ecstasy.

A few years ago, some twenty years later, I was passing by Tanglewood and remembered that moment. I decided to drop by to attend an evening concert. Much to my delight, I found they were to play the Berlioz *Requiem* that evening. I immediately got some wine and cheese, took a blanket, and arrived very early so I would have a choice elm to lie under. The evening was beautiful, soft and warm. The music began to play.

Much as I tried, I could not recapture the ecstasy. The experience was incredibly beautiful, delightful and enjoyable. But it wasn't as I remembered it. I had to realize that my memory of that moment was so high because by comparison the rest of my life was much lower. But now things had changed and each moment of every day had started to have a quality of newness and radiance and intensity. The driving to the concert, the buying of the wine, the lying under the elm were equally as high as the concert. Instead of peaks and valleys, I had a plateau.

Meditation brings this change. Each moment starts to have a richness or thickness of its own. Fewer moments are special as more of them become richer. This lessens the rushes, the highs and lows. As they disappear we sometimes feel a sadness and depression, a sense of having lost the richness and the romance of life. Indeed, an awakened being is not romantic, for nothing is special any more. Every moment is all of it. No romance. Just the coming and the going. Coming and going.

In a way it is sad to see one's story line turn into empty form. The dark night of the soul is when you have lost the flavor of life but have not yet gained the fullness of divinity. So it is that we must weather that dark time, the period of transformation when what is familiar has been taken away and the new richness is not yet ours.

"*Perhaps your Reverence has met a certain lady?*"
Mahatissa the Elder replied:
"*I know not whether a man or woman passed.
A certain lump of bones went by this way.*"

—*Buddhaghosa*

The Path of Purity

*He who contemplates the Lotus Feet of God
looks on even the most beautiful woman as
mere ash from the cremation ground.*

—*Sri Ramakrishna*

The Gospel of
Sri Ramakrishna

*Before a man can find God, . . . all his likings
and desires have to be utterly changed . . . All
things must become as bitter to thee as their
enjoyment was sweet unto thee.*

—*John Tauler*

Life and Sermons of
Dr. John Tauler

*The attainment of enlightenment from ego's
point of view is extreme death, the death of self,
the death of me and mine, the death of the
watcher. It is the ultimate and final
disappointment.*

—*Chogyam Trungpa*

The Myth of Freedom

On Not Finding Your Guru

Seeking one's guru is like going on pilgrimage. It is a useful journey, but you don't have to take it to finish the path. There is a good possibility you will never meet your guru. But because you do not meet your guru does not mean you do not have one. Any person that reaches toward God, toward liberation, toward the spirit, is noticed, and a contact is made with the vehicle or form that will ultimately draw you home.

You needn't know your guru. It is only necessary that your guru know you. Only your need to maintain control compels you to try to know your guru. Your journey is one of purification, and you can proceed whether you know your guru or not. Don't worry about it. Your guru will become known to you, if and when necessary. If the guru were to manifest too soon, you might get lost in an interpersonal devotion that would just be another trap for you. You must trust that the process is benevolent. When needed, the guru appears. It's a benign conspiracy.

I once asked my guru, "How do you know if a person is your guru?" He answered that it is simply whether this person can take you all the way. Taking you all the way does not mean that the guru does it for you. Rather the guru *is* the way. The guru's very being creates a space that is the doorway to your freedom.

Along the way you may meet your guru and feel overwhelming love for him or her. This makes you cling to the guru. In the end you must go beyond the separateness of the forms you have loved. To go all the way is to go beyond the concept of guru. Ramana Maharshi said it: God, Guru, Self—all the same thing.

> *For thirty years I went in search of God, and when I opened my eyes at the end of this time, I discovered that it was really He who sought for me.*
>
> —*Bayazid al-Bistami*
>
> Translations of Eastern Poetry and Prose

> *I had heard about a superior type of man, possessing the keys to everything which is a mystery to us. This idea of a higher and unknown strain within the human race was not something I could take simply as an allegory. Experience has proved, I told myself, that a man cannot reach truth directly, nor all by himself. An intermediary has to be present, a force still human in certain respects, yet transcending humanity in others. Somewhere on our Earth this superior form of humanity must exist, and not utterly out of our reach. In that case shouldn't all my efforts be directed toward discovering it? Even if, in spite of my certainty, I were the victim of a monstrous illusion, I should lose nothing in the attempt. For, apart from this hope, all life lacked meaning for me.*
>
> —*René Daumal*
>
> Mount Analogue

In time, and always just at the right moment, a teacher or maggid arrives. He may manifest in many ways, as old Kabbalistic documents indicate. One may not see him more than once, or realize one has known him all his life. It can be one's grandfather or a fellow student, the man crossing the sea with you on a boat, or someone you thought a fool. He may arrive at your front door or already be in the house.

—*Z'evben Shimon Halevi*

The Way of Kaballah

7

GETTING FREE

Keep Your Ground

If you feel free only when you meditate, you're not really free. Freedom does not come from turning your back on your responsibilities. The game is to be in the world but not of it. Even when you find yourself feeling spaced out, disoriented, or untogether, you can make an extra effort to meet the needs of the moment, whether it's the baby's diapers that need changing or your income tax that is due. Don't make meditation a cop-out from life.

You can allow yourself adjustment periods when

you don't have to function quite as well as at other times, especially just after periods of intense retreat. Eventually you learn to function in the world even right after the deepest meditation. That's the goal: balancing inner and outer. You're part of society, you're part of a family, you're part of all sorts of groups. Do what you must to meet your responsibilities, but do it as an exercise that furthers your own liberation as well. The true freedom of awareness that you seek is possible only when you acknowledge and fulfill honorably all aspects of the dance of life. It is in the perfection of form that we are free.

The time of business does not with me differ from the time of prayer, and in the noise and clatter of my kitchen, while several persons are at the same time calling for different things, I possess God in as great tranquillity as if I were upon my knees at the blessed sacrament.

—*Brother Lawrence*

The Practice of the Presence of God

Do not permit the events of your daily lives to bind you, but never withdraw yourselves from them. Only by acting thus can you earn the title of "A Liberated One."

—*Huang Po*

The Zen Teaching of Huang Po

The true saint goes in and out amongst the people and eats and sleeps with them and buys and sells in the market and marries and takes part in social intercourse, and never forgets God for a single moment.

—Abu Sa'id ibn Abi
l-Tkayr

Studies

I did not go to the "Maggid" of Meseritz to learn Torah from him but to watch him tie his boot-laces.

—A Hassidic saint

Major Trends in
Jewish Mysticism

Facing Weaknesses

We have all been enchanted with getting high, having a free awareness, and so we have tried to repress or deny lows when our awareness once again gets caught in this or that. We love the illusion of being high but are afraid of coming down. As your journey proceeds, you realize that you can't hold on to your highs and deny your lows. Your lows are created by the remaining attachments that blind your awareness. Facing your lows—your anger, loneliness, greed, fears, depressions, and conflicts—is the most productive fire of purification you can find.

As your connection with the spirit deepens, you might even choose to seek out those things that bring your attachments to the surface, so that you might confront them and free your awareness from them. It's a tricky business—playing with fire. You must feel your own way, unless you have a guide to say when to go and when to stop. If you don't have a guide, trust your own judgment. For example, if anger still traps your awareness, you might put yourself in situations which usually elicit anger and then attempt to maintain clear awareness.

If you confront your attachments out of guilt, out of "oughts" or "shoulds," or through some externally imposed discipline, it won't work. For these confrontations are difficult and your motives to confront them must come from deep within. It takes the innermost resolve to resist your powerful temptations, or separate your awareness from your strong desires, be they lust, anger, or whatever. Your gains through meditation give you the enthusiasm that can bring a breakthrough into another plane, or the heartfelt desire to go in deeper, or the hunger to change your life. But it still takes much courage and fortitude to face the deepest attachments head on.

When you feel that your life is committed to the spirit you can no longer avoid confronting these weaknesses. Your strategy changes, you seek to move faster, wishing to confront head-on the things that bring down your awareness. You can no longer let them have their way. So you ask for a hotter fire, a fiercer confrontation. Even though this is often painful rather than pleasurable, it's all right, for you are reaching toward that freedom which lies beyond pleasure and pain. When you want to burn away the grip of your ego on your awareness you'll endure whatever is needed to clean up your life.

Truth alone is the austerity of the Kali Yuga.

—*Sri Ramakrishna*

Women Saints of
East and West

Handling Energy

Meditation is like diving deep in the ocean. To allow you to go to the depths and come back up smoothly your body must acclimate at each stage. As you adjust to each new level, you are filled with a greater energy.

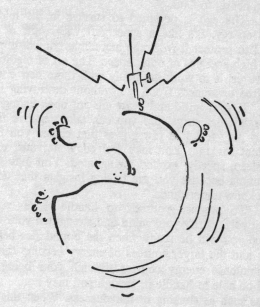

The predicament is that as you receive greater energy during meditation, it carries over to the times you are not meditating, when your old habits of mind to which you are still attached hold sway. The temptation is to use these new energies to strengthen your old habits, to use the meditative energy in the service of your ego. For example, you may find that these new energies enhance your sexual excitement, enthusiasm, and proficiency or your social power or charisma. This undoubtedly is one of the attractions of meditation.

But if your yearning is to go to the depths of your own soul—if your journey is to seek what Buddha had, what Christ had, what Ramakrishna had, what Abraham had, what Mohammed had—then you must beware of dissipating these energies through your old habits. You must channel them to go deeper. The energies that come from going near God can take you even nearer to God.

The ego is designed to survive in the midst of this energy. It's like a spacecraft with walls of thick steel to protect it from the incredible bombardment of the high energies of outer space. The art of meditation, however, is to work gradually with these new energies to free awareness from ego without destroying it.

If your mind and heart are not open enough, the energies that surge into you can take negative forms. They may feel like raw power that causes you fits of violent shaking. You may feel edgy, nervous, unable to sleep, speedy, excited, or agitated. You may feel a paranoia because you are having insights that no one you know understands.

To prepare yourself to handle these energies positively, purify your mind and strengthen your body. Then you will be ready when the boundaries between you and the larger sources of energy become thin. As this intense energy courses through your being, you will be able to handle it, though you may notice symptoms such as shaking or nervousness. When this happens to me, I focus on my heart, breathe in and out of it, filling with love on each breath. Great force can come to you, but when it is balanced with love you won't feel overwhelmed. With love, you are more open to the energy. Then you will grow in power—the power of love. You are on the way home.

Live as quiet a life as you can during intense periods of meditative practice. Get enough rest. You may encounter new spaces that will consume or create huge amounts of energy. Your body one moment may be totally exhausted and the next moment full of energy and refreshed. Your behavior may become erratic. Sometimes when I'm in intense spaces, my body is just barely strong enough to stand what it undergoes. Then I'll suddenly fall into a sound sleep that lasts maybe fifteen minutes. When I come out of it my whole body is vibrant with energy, fully re-vitalized.

Some people feel the need for a guide who senses when they are getting more energy than they can balance. Such a guide sees what they need to do to acclimate to new levels of energy. For most of us, our intuitive common sense will handle the moderate changes that we face.

The practice of meditation will open us gradually to more and more of the energy of the universe. If we remember the highest wisdom—that energy and love are one—this journey will be without fear.

Faith and Persistence

Many times in the course of meditation you will think of things you'd rather be doing. There may be moments of boredom, of sexual desire, doubt, or fatigue. At these moments you must call upon your faith. Faith in what? Faith in the power of meditation to change your awareness and your perspective about reality.

It is to strengthen this faith that you study books such as this rather than simply do your practices. Study brings you a deeper understanding of why you meditate and what to expect. When you read other people's stories of a meditative life you get a sense of the possibilities for your own. These inspirations can generate sufficient faith to override the difficult moments in meditation. Understanding feeds your faith.

Along with faith comes the requirement for dogged persistence. At first meditation may bring you mild highs or some relief from suffering. But there may come a time—just as there does in the development of any skill—when there will be a plateau. You may be bored, discouraged, or even negative and cynical. This is when you will need not only faith, but persistence. Often you will find yourself in training that forces you to sit when you wish you didn't have to. You subject yourself to this because something deeper within tells you to go on. It forces you to persist despite your abhorrence of the process. This persistent effort brings greater faith.

Even to the end of the journey faith is vulnerable. For example, though your faith may be strong enough to sit in meditation, if you mix with people who sneer at it, their skepticism may weaken your resolve. But if you stay with meditation, faith in your path will strengthen until you can withstand any criticism, even your own doubt and dark night of the soul.

When meditation works as it should, it will be a natural part of your being. There will no longer be anything apart from you to have faith in. Hope starts the journey, faith sustains it, but it ends beyond both hope and faith.

A young lad was sent to school. He began his lessons with the other children, and the first lesson the teacher set him was the straight line, the figure "one." But whereas the others went on progressing, this child continued writing the same figure. After two or three days the teacher came up to him and said, "Have you finished your lesson?" He said, "No, I'm still writing 'one.'" He went on doing the same thing, and when at the end of the week the teacher asked him again he said, "I have not yet finished it." The teacher thought he was an idiot and should be sent away, as he could not or did not want to learn. At home the child continued with the same exercise and the parents also became tired and disgusted. He simply said, "I have not yet learned it, I am learning it. When I have finished I shall take the other lessons." The parents said, "The other children are going on further, school has given you up, and you do not show any progress; we are tired of you." And the lad thought with sad heart that as he had displeased his parents too he had better leave home. So he went into the wilderness and lived on fruits and nuts. After a long time he returned to his old school. And when he saw the teacher he said to him, "I think I have learned it. See if I have. Shall I write on this wall?" And when he made his sign the wall split in two.

—Hazrat Inayat Khan

The Sufi Message of
Hazrat Inayat Khan

A group of us were in a sauna bath—just hanging out, going out into the sun, coming back into the bath—and a telegram arrived for me saying, "Rohatsu Dai Seshin is being held at Mt. Baldy in Los Angeles. We are holding a space for you." This is the most difficult of the zen sittings each year. It was to start the next day. So I got on a plane and went to Los Angeles.

I arrive at the zen monastery having sacrificed a sauna bath in the warm desert for this cold mountain outside of Los Angeles. I expect a greeting like, "Oh, Ram Dass, we're so happy you could come!"—a little bit of ego feeding. Instead I'm met by a guy in a black outfit with a clipboard and a shaved head who says, "Dass, Ram; you will be in bunk six. Here is your robe. Brother John will show you how to put it on and you are to be in the zendo in six minutes."

So I think, OK, baby, I'll play. I go in and I set up my bunk. You're not supposed to look at anybody or talk to anybody for nine days. Nine days. Every morning it's pitch black and all these people in black outfits are rushing to toilets, toothpaste, zendo at two in the morning and it's freezing. If you don't sit straight they beat you with a stick. There's snow all around and I had a cold. I'm getting sicker and sicker and plotting how to get out of this. Should I have a telegram sent saying I have been called away on an emergency, or remember I had a lecture or something?

Four times a day you go in to visit Joshu Sasaki Roshi, a tough, squat Japanese of about sixty-five. It's called dokusan. He had given us the koan "How do you know your Buddha nature through the sound of a cricket?" When it comes my turn, I go in, bow the proper number of times, and sit down. He's got a bell and a stick, and he says, "Ah, Doc-tor. How you know your Buddha nature through sound of cricket?" I had been sitting out there waiting my turn, thinking, now how would you know . . . You're not supposed to do that but I figured, what the hell, here is a Jewish Hindu in a Zen Buddhist scene—I'll give him a

Tibetan Buddhist answer. So I concluded that the best thing to do when he asked me was to hold my hand up to my ear, like the Tibetan Milarepa listening to the sounds of the universe outside his cave. The Roshi says only, "sixty percent," and rings the bell that means I should leave.

It goes on like this for days. I'm getting sicker and sicker and madder and madder and just bored and disgusted. Even though my sitting is stronger, I can't solve the damned koan. Finally about the fourth or fifth day, I walk up to see the Roshi. I still haven't solved the koan. I stand up there and think, "I don't give a damn what the answer to that koan is. Screw this whole scene. I've had enough."

I walk in and he says, "Ah, Doc-tor, how you know your Buddha nature through sound of cricket?"

And I say, "Good morning, Roshi." Like, let's cut the crap. Good morning, enough already.

"Ah, Doc-tor. Finally you are becoming a beginning student of zen."

Grace is proportionate to exertion.

—*Sathya Sai Baba*

Do not do things off and on. Have your sadhana every day with greater and greater intensity.

—*Swami Ramdas*

Guide to Aspirants

> *The result is not the point; it is the effort to improve ourselves that is valuable. There is no end to this practice.*
>
> —*Shunryu Suzuki*
> Zen Mind, Beginner's Mind

> *To endure is the disposition of the sage.*
>
> —The I Ching

Trust Your Heart

In the first part of your journey you may be quite eclectic, trying out many methods. Don't consider these changes from one method to another a weakness. Nor is it a weakness to stay with one method if it feels right to you. But it is a weakness to stay with a method that doesn't feel right, or to shift methods to avoid going too far with any one of them. How do you know when to shift, when to stay? Listen to your inner voice, your heart, and be truthful with yourself. This self-reliance and honesty will guide you not only in these early stages, but all the way to enlightenment. Each person has to be very honest and honor his or her stage of evolution. Nobody can live another's life. You've got to live your own.

When I went to Bodhgaya in India I took course after course in meditation. After a while I started to eat more and more, get up later and later, and waste more time each day, until the message was clear. This was no longer the time for intense meditation. It was time for me to take it easy. To try to meditate too intensely before you are ready will bring you similar tensions and difficulties. On the other hand, not meditating when the pull to do so is strong may raise the same difficulties.

Be prepared for the possibility that what seemed to be the right practice or strategy at one moment may not feel so a moment later. The process is dynamic and changing. Sometimes, for example, you may feel a very deep pull toward meditation. You may join a spiritual group only to find that the group's goals are far more limited than your own. As your practice takes on a dimension beyond that of the group's you will have to seek more profound methods and teachers.

Be prepared to give up your models of the path as you travel it. There is no shame in admitting your mistakes. Mahatma Gandhi once led a protest march in which many thousands of people left their jobs and homes to endure great hardship. As the march was well underway, Gandhi called a halt and disbanded it. His lieutenants came to him and said, "Mahatma-ji, you can't do this; the march has been planned for a long time and there are so many people involved." Gandhi's answer was, "My commitment is to truth as I see it each day, not to consistency."

All that you seek is already within you. In Hinduism it is called the Atman; in Buddhism, the pure Buddha-mind. Christ said, "The Kingdom of Heaven is within you." Quakers call it the "still, small voice within." This is the space of full awareness that is in harmony with all the universe, and thus is wisdom itself. Every new level of meditation, every new understanding of who you really are, attunes you more delicately to this space so that you can hear and be guided by your inner voice more clearly. Time and time again your attachments may veil this truth from you. Your attachments lead you to seek outside of yourself for answers that can only come from your own heart. Each time you lose contact with that inner awareness, you need only meditate. For through meditation you will hear that inner "click," that sense of rightness about what you are doing. Your answers are unique. Listen with your heart.

> *We have what we seek. It is there all the time, and if we give it time it will make itself known to us.*
>
> —*Thomas Merton*

> *If you do not get it from yourself
> Where will you go for it?*
>
> —*Zenrin*
>
> The Gospel According to Zen

Humor

Have you ever had a bad day? Everything seems to go wrong and you are completely lost in anger, frustration, and self-pity. It gets worse and worse, until the final moment when, say, you have just missed the last bus. There is some critical point where it gets so bad the absurdity of it all overwhelms you and you can do nothing but laugh. At that moment you uplevel your predicament, you see the cosmic joke in your own suffering.

Meditation, because of the space it allows around events, gives you the chance to see the humor of your predicament. Awareness of the passing show of one's own life allows a lightness to enter in where only a moment before there was heaviness.

Humor puts things in perspective. There are many levels of humor—there is a humor of survival, a humor of sex and gratification, a humor connected with power. Beyond all these there is a humor that is filled with compassion. It is reflected in the tiny upturn in the mouth of the Buddha, for he sees the humor in the universal predicament: all beings are lost in illusion, yet he knows that they will awaken from that illusion for they are, at heart, already enlightened. He knows that what seems so hard to them is from another perspective their own path to liberation.

Often the perspectives about yourself and the universe that you arrive at through meditation make you want to giggle or laugh. This giggle is without malice. It's a cosmic giggle, one that I identify with my guru, Maharaji. For his giggle was not of this world. It was not a social or personality giggle, but rather a cosmic chuckle, the delight in the fun of it all. His giggle was from the place that gives us the term "lila," the divine dance of life.

If it were not laughed at, it would not be sufficient to be Tao.

—Lao Tse

Tao Te Ching

Maharaj-ji was sitting with a group of devotees when suddenly he asked, "Who's coming, who's coming?" No one could be seen. Just then the servant of one of his devotees came. The minute Maharaj-ji saw him he yelled, "I won't go. I know he's dying. I won't go." The servant was surprised because no one knew that his employer had just had a heart attack and had called for Maharaj-ji. Everyone pleaded with Maharaj-ji to go, but he continued to refuse. Finally he picked up a banana and said, "Here, give him this, he'll be all right." The servant rushed home with the banana. It was mashed up and fed to the dying man, and as he took the last bite he died.

c devotee

The monks of a large Gelugpa monastery were appalled one morning to find a man on top of the prayerflag pole in their main courtyard. Since this was considered a very bad omen they determined at once to hold a ceremony to exorcise this apparition. Five thousand monks gathered that afternoon in the courtyard and en masse chanted the Heart Sutra. At the end of the recitation, in accordance with tradition they proclaimed two verses to accomplish the exorcism.

> *By the power of our words may this evil being come down.*
> *By the power of our contemplation of these words may this evil being come down.*

As they chanted the first verse, the man on the flagpole (who was the Mad Yogi of Bhutan) slid halfway down. As they chanted the second, he went back to the top.

—Chogyam Trungpa

Visual Dharma: The
Buddhist Art of Tibet

A certain Bektashi dervish was respected for his piety and appearance of virtue. Whenever anyone asked him how he had become so holy, he always answered: "I know what is in the Koran."

One day he had just given this reply to an enquirer in a coffee-house, when an imbecile asked: "Well, what is in the Koran?"

"In the Koran," said the Bektashi, "there are two pressed flowers and a letter from my friend Abdullah."

—Idries Shah

A rabbi visited a village reputed to have a miracle-working tzaddik, and asked: "What miracles has your tzaddik actually performed?"

"Our tzaddik has fasted every day for three whole years now!"

"Three years?! But that's impossible. He'd be dead by now!"

"Certainly he would! But our tzaddik knows that if he fasted every day that demonstration of saintliness would put everyone else to shame; so he eats only to spare everyone's feelings—and conceals the fact that privately he's fasting."

—Leo Rosten

The Joys of Yiddish

Anyone walking about Chinatown in America will observe statues of a stout fellow carrying a linen sack. Chinese merchants call him Happy Chinaman or Laughing Buddha.

This Hotei lived in the T'ang dynasty. He had no desire to call himself a Zen master or to gather many disciples about him. Instead he walked the streets with a big sack into which he would put gifts of candy, fruit, or doughnuts. These he would give to children who gathered around him in play. He established a kindergarten of the streets.

Whenever he met a Zen devotee he would extend his hand and say: "Give me one penny."

Once as he was about his play-work another Zen master happened along and inquired: "What is the significance of Zen?"

Hotei immediately plopped his sack down on the ground in silent answer.

"Then," asked the other, "what is the actualization of Zen?"

At once the Happy Chinaman swung the sack over his shoulder and continued on his way.

—Paul Reps

Zen Flesh, Zen Bones

8

THE JOURNEY OF CONSCIOUSNESS

We are departing for the skies. Who has a mind for sightseeing?

—Rumi

Picture a beautiful warm summer day. A group of people has decided to climb a nearby mountain. The going is easy, the day gentle. After several hours they reach a plateau with a rest station. Here they find a

restaurant, comfortable chairs, rest rooms, telescopes —all the conveniences. The view is inspiring. The air is cooler and clearer than down below. A sense of well-being, of health and energy, animates the climbers body and soul. For many in the group this is enough. They return home refreshed and satisfied. They are Sunday climbers.

A few remain, having discovered another path. Or perhaps it is the same path that began far down in the valley. Impelled by the need to explore, they thrust forward onto it. After a while the air grows cooler still. The trees thin out. Clouds obscure the sun from time to time. The path keeps rising, getting steeper and steeper. It is not yet beyond the skill of those who are determined to go on.

They reach a second rest area, with no conveniences other than an outhouse and an outdoor fire-place. The comraderie is now deeper. Their eyes feast on a grander view. The villages in which they grew up nestle tiny and remote from this new distance. It is their past they see in a new perspective. They see the limits of their lives in the valley far below. Few people

leave this station to travel higher. Most stay for awhile, then go back down.

Some remain—a handful. They seek and find a hidden path disappearing above. Are they ready to ascend the flat faces of rocks, to creep along narrow ledges, to explore caves high above, to crawl up to the snow line and beyond?

They feel some fear and loneliness now, some confusion. They ask themselves why they left the conviviality of the rest stop to tackle this painful, dangerous journey—or is it a pilgrimage? Their physical hardships reflect their spiritual struggle. The obstacles of rock and cliff mirror the possibility of great injury, worse than before because the openness and risk are greater.

Added now is an inner battle. The climbers feel they have taken on an adversary. The mountain has become something to be mastered and controlled. Of the handful of people that climbs to this height, only one or two can reach the top. Those few who go for broke, who want to reach the top, will use their every tool to its utmost. They want all of it, the top of the mountain, the mystic experience every great climber has known.

We have in America little appreciation, less experience, and no models for this ultimate journey. This final path is reflected in Christ's forty days in the desert, by the many years of intense spiritual work which Gautama Buddha underwent before enlightenment, by the years in which the great saint Swami Nityananda sat in a tree like a monkey, living close to the edge of insanity, or by Ananda Mayee Ma, who roamed about lost to self and family in trance. Asia has innumerable stories of these few beings who made such a fierce journey—a journey that can only be made if you are propelled by an inner fire, a yearning and pull for liberation that is so powerful there is no way to deny it.

After one arrives at the summit, after going through the total transformation of being, after becoming free of fear, doubt, confusion, and self-consciousness, there is yet one more step to the completion of that journey: the return to the valley below, to the everyday world. Who it is that returns is not who began the climb in the first place. The being that comes back is quietness itself, is compassion and wisdom, is the truth of the ages. Whatever humble or elevated position that being holds within the community, he or she becomes a light for others on the way, a statement of the freedom that comes from having touched the top of the mountain.

The return completes the cycle. It is this cycle which brings the spirit to earth and allows the divine to feed once again the hopes and aspirations, the barely sensed possibility, that exists in each human being. This is the way of the bodhisattva, the maggid, the shayk, the enlightened soul, the saint.

You cannot stay on the summit for ever; you have to come down again . . . So why bother in the first place? Just this: what is above knows what is below, but what is below does not know what is above.

One climbs, one sees. One descends, one sees no longer but one has seen. There is an art to conducting oneself in the lower regions by the memory of what one saw higher up. When one can no longer see, one can at least still know.

—René Daumal

Mount Analogue

There is no real coming and going.
For what is going but coming?

—Shabistari

The Secret Rose Garden of
Sa'd Ud Din
Mahmud Shabistari

Keeping Still is the mountain.

—The I Ching

But can one say that such a being has returned from beyond? In truth, he or she is beyond return. The one who arrives at the top is not the being who set out at the bottom. One who arrives at the top goes through the fear of death, and sees what only a few ever see, knows what only a few ever know. Such a being returns to the world to live in humility and simplicity. For to have faced the forces of the universe and found a way to harmonize with them is to find one's true place, to be in the flow. This is the achievement which is no achievement. <u>This very special journey allows such a being to be nothing special.</u>

Up to the very end of the climb up the mountain of liberation the most subtle suffering still remains, for there is still an individual who identifies with his or her own separateness. There is still clinging. There is still a final bond to break. At the moment of scaling the highest peak or walking the narrowest ledge the climber must let go of everything, even self-consciousness, in order to become the perfect instrument of the climb. In the ultimate moments of the climb, he or she transcends even the identity of climber. As Christ said, one must truly die and be born again.

The absence of identity with personal ego means that the being is free, is pure compassion, pure love, pure awareness. For such a being, everything is in the moment. There is a richness in which past, present, and future all co-exist. You cannot say of a moment of full awareness that something is not present, nor can you say that something stands out. You can focus on one thing or another, or on the emptiness of the form, or on the many planes within the form. The focus of a totally free being is guided by the need of the moment, by the karma of the individual he or she is with. For such a being, life is a constant unfolding. No need to think about what to do. It's all intuitive. It's as simple as the innocence and freshness that a young child experiences. Only in this silence—the silence that lies behind thought—can one hear the symphony of the universe, can one hear the whisper of the Word, can one approach the inner temple wherein dwells the soul.

The moment is timeless. But within timelessness there is time. The moment is spaceless. But within the undifferentiated boundaries of infinite space lies form, with its demarcations. There is clarity, so that everything is discrete and can be seen clearly if one focuses. There is liberation; there is perfect faith; no fear of change, no clinging to the moment. The moment is enough. The next moment is enough also. And the judgment of "enough" is gone—choiceless awareness.

Grown men may learn from very little children, for the hearts of little children are pure, and, therefore, the Great Spirit may show to them many things which older people miss.

—*Black Elk*

The Sacred Pipe

It is all an open secret.

—*Ramana Maharshi*

Talks with Sri
Ramana Maharshi

Such unbounded spacious awareness contains an intense love of God, equanimity, compassion, and wisdom. In it there is openness and harmony with the whole universe. Beings whose awareness is free enter into the ocean of love that has no beginning or end—love that is clear like a diamond, flowing like the ocean, passionate as the height of the sexual act, and soft like the caress of the wind.

This is the all and everything. It is the love that includes hate, for it is beyond polarity. It is the love that loves all beings.

There is a universal tradition of people who complete the path of meditation, who transcend their intellects, open their hearts, and come into tune with that from which the universe flows. Such beings are sages, enlightened, realized, free, children of God. They are God people.

One day I was sitting in the courtyard across from my guru, Maharaji. Many people were sitting around him, joking and talking with him, rubbing his feet, giving him apples and flowers. He was giving things right back and I could see the love flow back and forth. But I sat across the courtyard, in a very impersonal state.

I thought, "That's all well and good, but it is just attachment to form. I've done that. I must go beyond that. He is nothing special, although he is everything. I can be at his feet anywhere in the universe. The way in which he and I are connected has nothing to do with form. We are one in awareness."

At that moment I saw Maharaji whispering to an old devotee who came running across the courtyard and touched my feet. I asked, "Why did you do that?" He replied, "Maharaji said, 'Touch Ram Dass' feet. He and I understand each other perfectly.' "

From having met Maharaji I have a sense of what a free being is like, what a pure awareness is like that does not cling to time, to space, to identity. I sense what it is to live so totally in the moment, that you do not cling at all.

Anjani says of him:

There can be no biography of Maharaji. Facts are few, stories many. He seems to have been known by different names in many parts of India, appearing and disappearing through the years. His Western devotees of recent years knew him as Neem Karoli Baba, but mostly as "Maharaj-ji" —a nickname (meaning "great king") so commonplace in India that one often can hear a tea vendor addressed thus. Just as he said, he was "nobody."

He gave no discourses; the briefest, simplest stories were his teaching. Usually he sat or lay on a bench wrapped in a plaid blanket while a few devotees sat around him. Visitors came and went, food was given them and a few words, a nod, a slap on the head or back, and they were sent away. There was gossip, laughter—he loved to joke. Orders for running the ashram were given, usually in a piercing yell across the compound. Sometimes he sat in silence, absorbed in another world to which we could not follow, but bliss and peace poured down on us.

Who he was was no more than the experience of him, the nectar of his presence, the totality of his absence—enveloping us now like his plaid blanket.

—*Anjani*

The true men of old
Knew no lust for life,
No dread of death.
Their entrance was without gladness,
Their exit, yonder,
Without resistance.
Easy come, easy go.
They did not forget where from,
Nor ask where to,
Nor drive grimly forward
Fighting their way through life.
They took life as it came, gladly;
Took death as it came, without care;
And went away, yonder,
Yonder!

They had no mind to fight Tao.
They did not try, by their own contriving,
To help Tao along.
These are the ones we call true men.

Minds free, thoughts gone
Brows clear, faces serene.
Were they cool? Only cool as autumn.
Were they hot? No hotter than spring.
All that came out of them
Came quiet, like the four seasons.

—*Thomas Merton*

The Way of Chuang Tzu

THE DIRECTORY

1

INTRODUCTION

*Though the sages speak in divers ways, they
express one and the same Truth.*
                              —*Srimad Bhagavatam*

This directory is an endeavor to provide at least some
access to the spiritual resources that exist within our
communities. What a wealth of opportunities it reflects!
From the most pristine Buddhists to the visionary New
Agers, from Vipassana techniques to visualization approaches, from groups that have been practicing together for years to groups that are just beginning to find
themselves in satsang . . . each has something unique
to offer.

The directory consists of two parts: a guide to
groups that teach meditation, and a list of retreat
facilities. Many groups of meditators meet, many teachers
instruct, and many organizations offer opportunities for
retreats; not all are listed here. This is an incomplete
list, compiled from information given by the groups
themselves, from other lists, from advertisements, from
research by friends.

There has been no effort to judge the many
resources in the United States and Canada in selecting
these listings, nor in presenting them. Usually the de-

scriptions are those offered by the groups themselves. Some groups which might seem to be emphasized are not well esteemed by the compilers; others, which are well regarded, might be found described just once, and very briefly. This is done in the faith that each of us can best judge for himself or herself. So dive in—and trust yourself to know how to swim.

Beyond the use of this directory, you may find that friends, local churches, newspapers and magazines, and bulletin boards at schools or health food stores will offer something to meet your interest. The Yellow Pages contain useful information too—under such headings as Camps; Churches; Meditation Instruction; Metaphysicians; Religious Organizations; Retreat Houses; Yoga Instruction, etc.

A number of excellent books have been published which offer extensive listings of meditation groups and retreat facilities. There were four which proved particularly useful in the compilation of this directory:

Buddhist America: Centers, Retreats, Practices, Don Morreale, editor (John Muir Publications, Santa Fe, NM, 1988).

Directory of Retreat Ministry Centers (Retreats International, Notre Dame, IN, 1989).

Traveler's Guide to Healing Centers and Retreats in North America, Martine Rudee and Jonathan Blease (John Muir Publications, Santa Fe, NM, 1989).

The New Consciousness Sourcebook, Parmatma Singh Khalsa, executive editor (Arcline Publications, Pomona, CA, 1985).

If you are unable to find a suitable group nearby, there are many organizations which offer correspondence courses in various aspects of meditation. Here is a sampling of groups which offer such programs:

Arcana (Manhattan Beach, CA)
Astara (Upland, CA)
Collegians International (Fairbanks, AK)
Meditation Group for the New Age (Ojai, CA)
Nyingma Institute (Berkeley, CA)
The Theosophical Society in America (Wheaton, IL)
Universal Life (New Haven, CT)

All of these are included in the National and Local Listings; check there for further information about the group's orientation and address. Some other group which particularly interests you might also have correspondence courses, literature, or book lists which are not mentioned in the directory. Write and ask; most groups welcome such inquiries.

And finally there is the gift of modern technology, the "electronic sangha" of audio cassettes and videotapes. Many groups offer meditation instruction tapes; again, the best policy is to write and inquire. Two organizations which offer audiotapes on meditation techniques by teachers from varying traditions are:

Hanuman Foundation Tape Library
PO Box 2320
Delray Beach, FL 33447
(Telephone: (407) 272–9165)

Dharma Seed Tapes
Box 66
Wendell Depot, MA 01380
(Telephone: (508) 544–2653)

Either would be happy to send you a catalog.

2

GROUPS THAT TEACH MEDITATION

This list has two parts—the National Listings and the Local Listings. The National Listings include those groups that are both nationwide and quite large. They are arranged alphabetically by name. The Local Listings are made up of smaller groups, those having no more than two dozen or so centers, if that many. They are arranged alphabetically by state, city, and name, with a separate section for Canadian Listings. For the most part churches are not included here as they are too numerous to list.

National Listings

ANANDA MARGA
97–38 42nd Avenue, Suite 1F
Corona, NY 11368
Tel. (718) 898–1603

The integration of spiritual life and social philosophy is the goal of Ananda Marga's teachings. Courses are offered in Tantra Yoga meditation and postures; individual instruction and group meditations are provided.

There are nearly 100 Ananda Marga centers in North America; contact the National Headquarters for the address of a group near you.

ANANDA WORLD BROTHERHOOD VILLAGE
14618 Tyler Foote Road
Nevada City, CA 95959
Tel. (916) 292–3494; (800) 346–5350 (outside California)

Ananda Village is one of the most successful New Age intentional communities in the world. Located on over 900 acres in the Sierra Nevada foothills, Ananda was founded by Sri Kriyananda, a direct disciple of the great Paramhansa Yogananda (author of *Autobiography of a Yogi*). More than 350 adults and children live at Ananda. The Expanding Light, Ananda's year-round guest retreat, offers the teachings of Raja Yoga and many different programs called "Secrets of Living with Greater Awareness." There are more than 35 meditation groups located throughout the United States and Europe. Call Ananda Village for information about the one nearest you.

ASSOCIATION FOR RESEARCH AND ENLIGHTENMENT, INC.
PO Box 595
Virginia Beach, VA 23451
Tel. (804) 428–3588

The Association is a nonprofit organization made up of individuals interested in spiritual growth, parapsychological research, and the work of Edgar Cayce. The aim is to make available to anyone the information given by the late psychic Edgar Cayce. His gift of the spirit was his ability to enter into profoundly deep meditation and from this higher state of consciousness to give discourses. Central to the philosophy of those readings was the premise that man is a spiritual being, whose purpose on earth is to reawaken and apply this knowledge. Meditation as well as other principles of physical, mental, and spiritual attunement are studied and practiced. The Assocation offers an open meditation with the staff, daily healing prayer groups, retreats, workshops, study groups, and lectures throughout the country. Its Meditation Room is open daily for individual meditation.

BRAHMA KUMARIS
WORLD SPIRITUAL ORGANIZATION
Church Center for the United Nations
777 United Nations Plaza
New York, NY 10017
Tel. (718) 565–5133

Founded in 1937 by Prajapita Brahma, the Brahma Kumaris World Spiritual University now has 1,700 branches in over 50 countries, and serves as a nongovernmental organization of the United Nations with consultative status to the Economic and Social Development Council and UNICEF. With world headquarters at Mount Abu, Rajasthan, the University offers a variety of activities, including retreats, conferences, exhibitions, workshops, individual instruction, and group classes at all levels of spiritual practice. Through meditation, each individual learns to remove inner negativity and tension, to enhance mental alertness, and to release what is eternally present in the consciousness of every human being. Counseling and meditation therapy are made available to cancer and AIDS patients, the physically handicapped, and those who are drug- or alcohol-dependent.

HIMALAYAN INSTITUTE
RR 1, Box 400
Honesdale, PA 18431
Tel. (717) 253–5551; (800) 444-5772

Founded in 1971 by Swami Rama, the Himalayan Institute is dedicated to teaching the various aspects of yoga and meditation as a means to foster the personal growth of the individual and the betterment of society. In addition, the Institute undertakes scientific research to explore the different facets of yoga and meditation and to clarify their application in the areas of health and the evolution of consciousness. From biofeedback and the science of breath to natural health care and the positive use of emotions, the Institute offers a variety of options for personal growth and development, including seminars, workshops, and intensives in meditation, Hatha Yoga, kundalini, pranayama, vegetarian cooking, and stress management. Opportunities are also available for advanced students to undertake individual meditation retreats and self-training programs. Underlying all of the work at the Institute is the practice of the techniques of yoga and meditation as a systematic method for developing one's consciousness. By increasing self-awareness, participants are helped to regulate the various aspects of body, mind, and emotions.

INTEGRAL YOGA INSTITUTE
227 W. 13th Street
New York, NY 10011
Tel. (212) 929–0585

The Integral Yoga Institutes are founded and guided by Rev. Sri Swami Satchidananda. Integral Yoga is a synthesis of the various branches of yoga, designed to bring about the harmonious development of every aspect of the individual: physical, emotional, social, intellectual, and spiritual. The practices taught by the I.Y.I. include Hatha Yoga (physical postures, breathing techniques, and deep relaxation), Raja Yoga (concentration and meditation), Japa Yoga (mantra repetition), Karma Yoga (selfless action), Bhakti Yoga (chanting and other devotional practices), and Jnana Yoga (study of self-inquiry). Daily classes in these yogas are held at the 27 Integral Yoga Institutes and Teaching Centers, which also offer scripture study and satsang. Guests are also invited to visit the Integral Yoga Homes connected with many of the Institute branches. Check the phone book or write for the address of the nearest Institute.

A body of perfect health and strength, mind with all clarity and control, intellect sharp as a razor, will of steel, heart full of love and compassion, a life dedicated to the common welfare and realization of the true Self.

—*Swami Satchidananda*

SATHYA SAI BABA BOOK CENTER OF AMERICA
PO Box 278
Tustin, CA 92681
Tel. (714) 669–0522

Sathya Sai Baba is a world teacher with millions of followers in India and around the globe. For information about Sai Baba and his centers, write to the above address.

There is only one caste, the caste of Humanity;
There is only one religion, the religion of Love;
There is only one language, the language of the Heart.

—*Sathya Sai Baba*

SELF-REALIZATION FELLOWSHIP
3880 San Rafael Avenue
Los Angeles, CA 90065
Tel. (213) 225–2471

Self-Realization Fellowship was founded in 1920 by Paramhansa Yogananda to make known India's ancient spiritual science of direct personal communion with God, and to help unite East and West in an understanding of the fundamental harmony of all religious paths. From its headquarters in Los Angeles, the worldwide spiritual and humanitarian work he began continues today under the guidance of one of his foremost disciples, Sri Daya Mata. SRF has temples, retreats, and meditation centers around the world; monastic training programs; and a Worldwide Prayer Circle, a network of groups and individuals dedicated to serving those in need through the power of healing prayer and affirmation. A comprehensive series of lessons for home study, compiled from Sri Yogananda's lectures and writings, presents instruction in the various Yoga systems with emphasis on the science of Kriya Yoga meditation; practical methods for achieving harmony of body, mind, and spirit; and a wealth of spiritual counsel covering a broad range of topics. The life and teachings of Paramhansa Yogananda are described in his *Autobiography of a Yogi,* which is widely regarded as a classic introduction to Yoga and Eastern thought. Write or call for further information and free literature.

SIDDHA YOGA
SYDA FOUNDATION
PO Box 600
South Fallsburg, NY 12779
Tel. (914) 434–2000

Siddha Yoga begins with Shaktipat, the divine act of initiation by a Siddha Master, the descent of grace from Guru to disciple. With this initiation, the Kundalini energy is awakened and a spontaneous process of transformation begins to unfold in the seeker. The lineage of Siddhas is imperishable and timeless, handed down from Guru to disciple. Gurumayi Chidvilasananda, the current head of the Siddha lineage, was commanded and empowered by her Guru, Baba Muktananda, to bestow the grace of the lineage on seekers and to set them on the path of meditation. Gurumayi says of meditation, "It is the power of the Absolute; through meditation alone you touch eternity. Meditation is the power which attracts the mind to its source and fills the body and mind with luster." Regular programs of chanting, meditation, and instruction are offered free of charge at Siddha Meditation Centers all over the world. It is also possible to spend time with Gurumayi Chidvilasananda as she travels around the world or when she is in residence at one of her ashrams. For further information about Siddha Yoga Centers and Siddha Yoga Intensives (the program at which Shaktipat is transmitted), and for information concerning Gurumayi's current location, contact SYDA Foundation.

SILVA MIND CONTROL INTERNATIONAL, INC.
1110 Cedar
PO Box 2240
Laredo, TX 78044
Tel. (512) 722–6391

During intensive training classes, students are taught to produce and maintain tranquil, positive mental states and to develop ESP. This is done by learning to function at alpha and theta frequencies of the brain. The training is accomplished without the use of biofeedback equipment. The Silva Method is presently being taught throughout the United States, in 75 foreign countries, and in 16 different languages. Check the phone book or write for the address of the nearest office.

SIVANANDA YOGA VEDANTA CENTER
8th Avenue
Val Morin, QU JOT 2R0 Canada
Tel. (819) 322–3226

A nonsectarian organization practicing a synthesis of yoga which combines all the different paths of yoga into one homogeneous, workable pattern, as prescribed by Swami Sivananda. Swami Vishnu Devananda is the founder-president of the Center. Yoga classes, retreats, summer yoga vacations, and teacher training programs are available. There are branch centers and retreats located around the world. Write for locations.

SRI AUROBINDO ASSOCIATION
PO Box 372
High Falls, NY 12440
Tel. (914) 687–9222

Through its headquarters in High Falls, the Association

distributes books and information about Sri Aurobindo's philosophy of Integral Yoga. For information about Auroville, the spiritually based experimental community in South India based on the teachings of Aurobindo and The Mother, contact Auroville International U.S.A., PO Box 162489, Sacramento, CA 95816, or telephone (916) 452-4013.

> *Sri Aurobindo came upon earth to teach this truth to men: That man is only a transitional being living in a mental consciousness, but with the possibility of acquiring a new consciousness, the Truth-consciousness, and capable of living a life perfectly harmonious, good and beautiful, happy and fully conscious.*
>
> *—The Mother*

SUFI ORDER
National Secretariat
PO Box 85569
Seattle, WA 98145
Tel. (206) 323-2944

The Sufi Order is dedicated to the awakening of the consciousness of humanity. Pir Vilayat Inayat Khan (the successor of Hazrat Inayat Khan who founded the Sufi Order in the West in 1910) leads frequent meditation seminars, camps, and retreats in North America and Europe, giving darshan, counseling, and training in meditation. Sufi Order centers throughout the United States, Canada, and Western Europe offer programs of spiritual training, hold weekly classes in Sufi teachings and meditation, and celebrate Universal Worship paying homage to all the world's great religions and teachers.

> *Toward the One, the Perfection of Love, Harmony, and Beauty, the Only Being, united with all the Illuminated Souls who form the Embodiment of the Master, the Spirit of Guidance.*
>
> *—Sufi Invocation*

THE THEOSOPHICAL SOCIETY IN AMERICA
PO Box 270
Wheaton, IL 60187
Tel. (312) 668–1571

The Theosophical Society is a nonsectarian body of seekers after truth, promoting brotherhood and striving to serve humanity. Its declared objectives are to form a nucleus of the Universal Brotherhood of Humanity; to encourage the study of comparative religion, philosophy, and science, and to investigate unexplained laws of nature and the powers latent in all people. The society sees every religion as an expression of the Divine Wisdom. H. P. Blavatsky and Annie Besant have been among the leaders of the movement. Several correspondence courses in Theosophy are offered, such as "The Study and Practice of Meditation." There are also courses offered at the National Headquarters, frequently including one in meditation. There are over 150 branches, study centers, and camps of the Theosophical Society in America. Check the phone book or write for the address of the nearest branch.

3HO FOUNDATION
PO Box 35006
1620 Preuss Road
Los Angeles, CA 90035
Tel. (213) 550–9043

The 3HO (Healthy, Happy, Holy) Foundation, founded by Yogi Bhajan in 1969, is an international educational and spiritual organization offering instruction in Kundalini Yoga, White Tantric Yoga, meditation, and other techniques for enhancing the power of intuition and the quality of life. 3HO requires no formal initiation, but students commit themselves to a regular routine of sadhana which includes Kundalini Yoga, meditation, hard work, and sharing within the community—practices based on the Sikh Dharma of the 15th-century teacher Guru Nanak, who instructed his students to "Meditate

Work, and Share." To fulfill the requirement to do service, 3HO centers engage in a wide variety of community assistance projects such as drug rehabilitation programs and free kitchens to feed the poor. 3HO has centers in major cities in the United States and around the world.

TWIN CITIES VIPASSANA COOPERATIVE (TCVC)
1911 South 6th Street
Minneapolis, MN 55424
Tel. (612) 332-2436

TCVC is a meditation group which sponsors quarterly retreats of 2-10 days led by experienced teachers as well as twice monthly sittings of 2-10 hours. The Vipassana meditation technique is presented in an eclectic manner without dogma, ritual or cultural trappings. It entails clear, continuous observation of different aspects of the mind-body process. Through this observation insights leading to personal growth and a more deeply satsifying sense of connectedness are developed.

VAJRADHATU INTERNATIONAL/USA
1345 Spruce Street
Boulder, CO 80302
Tel. (303) 444-0190

Vajradhatu was founded by the Venerable Chogyam Trungpa, Rinpoche, a Tibetan meditation master of the Kagyu and Nyingma lineages. It has over a hundred centers around the world, offering meditation instruction and practice and programs on Buddhist philosophy. In addition, there are three retreat centers (in Colorado, Vermont, and Nova Scotia) which offer opportunities for contemplation and study in a quiet, rural environment.

VEDANTA SOCIETY OF SOUTHERN CALIFORNIA
1946 Vedanta Place
Hollywood, CA 90068
Tel. (213) 465-7114

Vedanta is the philosophy which has evolved from the Vedas, a collection of ancient Indian scriptures, perhaps the oldest religious writings in existence. The fundamental truths of Vedanta are that the Godhead, the underlying reality, is omnipresent within each of us, within every creature and object, so man in his true nature is God; it is the purpose of man's life on earth to unfold and manifest this Godhead, which is eternally existent within him, but hidden; and truth is universal in that men seek the Godhead in various ways, but what they all seek is the same. The Vedanta centers in the United States, of which the Vedanta Society of Southern California is one, are united under the spiritual guidance of the Ramakrishna Order of India. In charge of each Vedanta Center is an ordained monk of the Ramakrishna Order of India. At several of the centers, resident students live under the supervision of swamis who train them in the practice of meditation, worship, and service. Each center has a schedule of services, classes, and meditations open to the public. For the location of the nearest center write to the Vedanta Society in Hollywood.

Local Listings

ALABAMA

BRAHMA KUMARIS CENTER
2408 Charles Avenue
Tuskegee, AL 36083
Tel. (205) 727–6172

For further information, see National Listings.

ALASKA

ANCHORAGE ZEN CENTER
2401 Susitna
Anchorage, AK 99517
Tel. (907) 248–1049

The Center's teachings are in the Soto Zen tradition. It offers weekly zazen meditations, which are open to the public, and two sesshins a year.

3HO FOUNDATION
GURU RAM DAS ASHRAM
4501 Bayview Drive
Anchorage, AK 99516
Tel. (907) 345–1339

The Ashram is a center for the teachings of Yogi Bhajan, and offers ongoing classes in Kundalini Yoga and meditation.

UNITY-AND-DIVERSITY CENTER NORTH
PO Box 211155
Anchorage, AK 99521

The Center, which is a branch of the Unity-and-Diversity World Council, Inc., initiates local events bringing together people of diverse backgrounds to celebrate the essential unity of all mankind and to share ideas for ways of actualizing that unity in all human relationships. Each month there is a full moon "world healing meditation," and each year at the time of the full moon in May there is a community Wesak Festival, recognizing the work and teachings of the Buddha and the Christ.

> *We invoke for mankind the Light to see and choose the nobler way.*
>
> —*Wesak Invocation*

VIPASSANA MEDITATION GROUP
PO Box 92085
Anchorage, AK 99509
Tel. (907) 278–2910

Weekly meditation practice and occasional meditation retreats.

COLLEGIANS INTERNATIONAL CHURCH
PO Box 929
Fairbanks, AK 99707
Tel. (907) 479–8433

Collegians offers seasonal classes, full moon meditations, celebrations of the sacraments, and correspondence courses.

ARIZONA

3HO FOUNDATION
GURU NANAK DWARA ASHRAM
2302 N. 9th Street
Phoenix, AZ 85006
Tel. (602) 271–4480; (602) 256–9731

The Ashram is a center for the teachings of Yogi Bhajan, and offers ongoing classes in Kundalini Yoga and meditation. For more information, see National Listings.

KARMA THEGSUM CHOLING
6231 E. Exeter Boulevard
Scottsdale, AZ 85251
Tel. (602) 264–2930

A Tibetan Buddhist meditation center, offering sitting practice at 6:30 PM on Monday and Thursday evenings and at 6:00 AM on Wednesday mornings.

LOGOS INTERFAITH CHURCH
AND MEDITATION CENTER
6333 E. Thunderbird Road
Scottsdale, AZ 85254
Tel. (602) 438–8777

Logos offers private meditation instruction, as well as
weekly group meditation classes and monthly full moon
meditations. Day-long "Adventures in Meditation" workshops are offered periodically; call or write for dates.

THE RAINBOW CENTER
2515 N. Scottsdale Road, Suite 9
Scottsdale, AZ 85257
Tel. (602) 945–2590

The Rainbow Center offers instruction in guided meditation.

> *Be part of the Light, and learn.*
> —*Joanna Ernest*

AQUARIAN EDUCATIONAL GROUP
PO Box 2264
Sedona, AZ 86336
Tel. (602) 282–2655

Weekly meditation sessions.

DESERT ASHRAM
3403 W. Sweetwater Drive
Tucson, AZ 85745-9103
Tel. (602) 743-0384

This Ashram in the desert foothills of Tucson was
founded in 1975 by Prabhushri Swami Amar Jyoti.
Since then, Truth Consciousness Community has also
been developed at the Ashram. Pujya Swamiji teaches
no single religion or dogma, but the classical, timeless
spirituality that contains all paths. The God-centered
life of the Ashram and Community is reflected in the
beautifully tended grounds with their quiet walkways,

trees, organic gardens, and orchard. Desert wildlife abounds, and has become marvelously tame in the Ashram atmosphere. It is truly an oasis of peace and inspiration for residents and for the many seekers who come there. Desert Ashram offers weekly satsang, meditation, retreats, and opportunities for selfless service. Prabhushri Swamiji's books and tapes and many other fine spiritual publications are available through the Ashram.

> *There is joy in that ever-widening consciousness; there you will feel and see the purpose of being here. We didn't come here to rule these earthly kingdoms. The purpose of life is to be conscious, to be one with the Divine, to know.*
> —*Swami Amar Jyoti*

ARKANSAS

DEVACHAN TEMPLE
5 Dickey Street
Eurkea Springs, AR 72632

Devachan is a small meditation center in the Ozark Mountains. Ch'an meditation and Pure Land chanting practices are open to the public. There are private rooms available for solitary retreats.

SUFI ISLAMIA RUHANIAT SOCIETY
HEARTSONG FARM
Star Route
Nall, AR 72056
Tel. (501) 428–5503

The American Sufi leader, Murshid Samuel Lewis, made the Dances of Universal Peace a central feature of contemporary Sufism. Murshid Lewis's work with spiritual walk and dance is carried on by the Sufi Islamia Ruhaniat Society, which sponsors instruction and practice in the dances and in the meditative practice of zikr.

CALIFORNIA

SHANTI ANANTAM
3528 Triunfo Canyon Road
Agoura, CA 91301
Tel. (818) 706–3440

Shanti Anantam is a spiritual community which offers classes and practice in meditation.

BERKELEY BUDDHIST PRIORY
1358 Marin Avenue
Albany, CA 94706
Tel. (415) 528–2139

Founded in 1973, the Berkeley Buddhist Priory is a Buddhist church in the Serene Reflection Meditation tradition affiliated with the Order of Buddhist Contemplatives, whose headquarters is Shasta Abbey in Mt. Shasta, CA (see Local Listings). The Priory's meditation hall is open to the public for meditation between the hours of 9:00 AM and 7:00 PM, Tuesday through Saturday. Guests are also welcome to attend scheduled meditation periods, services, and lectures. One-day retreats are open to anyone who has attended an introductory meditation instruction class. In addition to the meditation hall, the Priory has a Buddhist library and bookshop.

BERKELEY ZEN CENTER
1931 Russell Street
Berkeley, CA 94703
Tel. (415) 845–2403

Established by Zen Master Suzuki Roshi, the Center is a lay community based on the teachings of the Soto Zen tradition. There is a small residential community, with limited accommodations for solitary retreats. Day-long and weekend sittings are offered each month, and sesshins are conducted three times a year.

CHAGDUD GONPA FOUNDATION, INC.
1933-D Delaware
Berkeley, CA 94709
Tel. (415) 849–3300

Both new and advanced students are taught by Chagdud Tulku, Rinpoche, a Vajrayana Buddhist meditation master. Activities include weekly group practice, weekend workshops, introductory instruction, and extended retreats.

DHAMMACHAKKA MEDITATION CENTER
2124 Kittredge Street
Box 206
Berkeley, CA 94704

The Dhammachakka Center is associated with the Venerable U Silananda, a Burmese Theravadin monk, who teaches Vipassana meditation in the tradition of Mahasi Sayadaw. U Silananda is also an expert in Abhidhamma, a system of Buddhist psychology which focuses on consciousness, mental factors, and Nibbana. The Center offers a regular program of meditations, classes, and retreats. Tapes of U Silananda's talks are available. For further information, contact Sarah Marks, (408) 258–6514.

EMPTY GATE ZEN CENTER
1800 Arch Street
Berkeley, CA 94709
Tel. (415) 548–7649

Practice at Empty Gate emphasizes regular meditation practice, work, and communal living as methods of overcoming preoccupations with "I, me, mine." Daily practice is open to the public. There are opportunities for monthly retreats, for residency, and for participation in Zen sesshins.

NYINGMA INSTITUTE
1815 Highland Place
Berkeley, CA 94709
Tel. (415) 843–6812

A large building in the Berkeley hills, with a panoramic view of the San Francisco Bay, offering meditation practice and instruction, and residential retreat and training programs of one week to six months duration. Nyingma offers both day and evening classes, weekend seminars, work-study opportunities, and a correspondence course.

RIGPA FELLOWSHIP
816 Bancroft Way
PO Box 7866
Berkeley, CA 94707
Tel. (415) 644–3922

Rigpa Fellowship is an association of people who study Tibetan Buddhism under the guidance of Venerable Lama Sogyal Rinpoche, an incarnate lama and meditation teacher from Tibet. Each year Rinpoche gives talks, weekend teachings, and retreats in the United States, Europe, and New Zealand. Ongoing teaching and practices are offered at the Fellowship's center in Berkeley, CA; other practice groups meet regularly in Santa Cruz, CA, San Diego, CA, Seattle, WA, Boston, MA, New York, NY, and Washington, DC.

SUFI ISLAMIA RUHANIAT SOCIETY
GARDEN OF BISMILLAH
851 Regal Road
Berkeley, CA 94708
Tel. (415) 527–2569

The American Sufi leader, Murshid Samuel Lewis, made the Dances of Universal Peace a central feature of contemporary Sufism. Murshid Lewis's work with spiritual walk and dance is carried on by the Sufi Islamia

Ruhaniat Society, which sponsors instruction and practice in the dances and in the meditative practice of zikr.

TAUNGPULU KABA-AYE MONASTERY
18335 Big Basin Way
Boulder Creek, CA 95006
Tel. (408) 338–9918

Established by the Ven. Taungpulu Sayadaw, TKA is a monastic meditation center, available for those who wish to learn and practice Vipassana meditation in a peaceful, natural setting. Meditation instruction, Vipassana courses, weekend sittings, and supervised solitary retreats are all available at the Monastery. There are two meditation halls, one in the Monastery and one in a Peace Pagoda, and two meditation sittings are conducted each day.

THE UNIVERSITY OF THE TREES
PO Box 347
Boulder Creek, CA 95006
Tel. (408) 338–2161

The University of the Trees community is an intense, fast-growth environment for those who want self-realization and are prepared to do the work of self-discovery. The community is founded on the three principles of meditation, creative conflict, and selfless service. Members of the community meditate and chant together each morning before beginning the day's work. Those wishing to make contact with the teachings of the community are invited to attend the public meditation and lecture programs held on Friday evenings at 7:15 PM.

SILVA METHOD
6283 Manchester Boulevard
Buena Park, CA 90621
Tel. (818) 989–5952; (714) 670–8622

Write or call for a schedule of free introductory lectures.

SUFI ISLAMIA RUHANIAT SOCIETY
NUR MANZIL
122 Central Avenue
Capitola, CA 95010
Tel. (408) 462–1512

Instruction and practice in spiritual walk and dance in the tradition of the American Sufi leader, Murshid Samuel Lewis.

TASSAJARA ZEN MOUNTAIN CENTER
Carmel Valley, CA 93924
Tel. (415) 863–3136 (students); (415) 431–3771 (guest reservations)

For information see Zen Center, San Francisco, in the Local Listings.

SIERRA CREEK CENTER
2401 Sierra Creek Road
Cornell, CA 91301
Tel. (818) 889–1052

Situated on nine acres in the Santa Monica Mountains, Sierra Creek Center is a place for spiritual unfoldment. Various teachers and groups use the facility to offer such diverse activities as hatha yoga classes, the American Indian Prayer Wheel Ceremony, and discussions of Rudolf Steiner's spiritual science. There are no overnight facilities.

THE YOGA CENTER OF MARIN
142 Redwood Avenue
Corte Madera, CA 94925
Tel. (415) 927–1850

The Yoga Center holds morning meditation sessions several days each week. Classes in hatha yoga, based on B.K.S. Iyengar's methods, are also offered. Strength and flexibility are emphasized, and special attention is given to proper alignment, breathing, and relaxation.

CHAPEL OF ST. JOHN
5550 Mesmer Avenue
Culver City, CA 90230
Tel. (213) 822-3643

The Chapel of St. John is dedicated to assisting groups and individuals in the awakening and development of the soul at a time of planetary transition. Its purpose is to enable participants to become conscious vehicles for Love, leading to healing, transformation, and a life of joyful service. Offerings include individual instruction as well as workshops and retreats and spiritual development groups.

DHAMMANANDA VIHARA
68 Woodrow Street
Daly City, CA 94014

Insight Meditation instruction by Ven. Bhikkhu U Silananda.

THERAVADA BUDDHIST SOCIETY
68 Woodrow Street
Daly City, CA 94014
Tel. (415) 994-8272

A meditation center in the tradition of the Burmese teacher, U Silananda. There are daily meditation sittings from 7:00 to 8:00 PM, and periodic one-day and weekend retreats.

THE HELIX CENTER
22821 Lake Forest Drive
El Toro, CA 92630
Tel. (714) 859-7940

Helix offers a wide spectrum of workshops and classes on meditation, and holds weekly meditation practices as well as new moon and full moon meditations.

MATRI SATSANG
PO Box 876
Encinitas, CA 92024
Tel. (619) 942-7159

Matri Satsang holds weekly kirtans, which are universal in their spiritual qualities. Serious aspirants are welcome.

SELF-REALIZATION FELLOWSHIP
215 K Street
Encinitas, CA 92024
Tel. (619) 753-2888

The seaside meditation gardens overlooking the Pacific, on the grounds where Paramhansa Yogananda lived and taught for many years, are open to the public Tuesday through Sunday, 9:00 AM to 5:00 PM. Lectures and meditation services are conducted by monks of the Self-Realization Order at the SRF Temple two blocks away. For further information see the National Listings.

THE CENTER FOR THE DANCES
OF UNIVERSAL PEACE
114 Forrest
Fairfax, CA 94930
Tel. (415) 453-8159

The Dances of Universal Peace are a form of meditative, spiritual dance, dedicated to the goal of "one world, within and without." The dances were originally created by the American mystic Samuel Lewis, under the inspiration of his spiritual teachers Hazrat Inayat Khan and Ruth St. Denis. Call for information about the Center's twice-monthly programs of dance and about retreats, workshops, and training programs.

SPRING GROVE
PO Box 807
Fairfax, CA 94930
Tel. (415) 453-7799

Spring Grove is like a monastery without walls, offering a spiritual home to people who are seeking to lead a sincere spiritual life while living very much in the world. It includes many small communities of people who help each other enjoy a richly rewarding path of spiritual growth.

SHIVA-SHAKTI ASHRAM
108 Gurudevi Lane
PO Box 1130
Groveland, CA 95321
Tel. (209) 962–6883

Her Holiness, Siddha Guru Swami Savitripriya, is the founder of Shiva-Shakti Ashram, a Kashmir Shaivite Hindu monastery located in the Sierra Mountains. Gurudevi teaches the highest nondual philosophy: that life is meant to be happy, and becomes happy through discovering that the entire universe is composed solely of Divine Consciousness; that the Godhead or Self is omnipresent within every creature and object; and that the purpose of life is to realize that one's true self is the same Divine Self that is within all forms. This awareness unfolds spontaneously due to a powerful, tangible awakening of the Kundalini initiated by the Guru. The Ashram provides various programs for lay people, including a Resident Program for training in the powerful practices of Maha Siddha Yoga. The Ashram also offers short-term Guest Programs and Maha Siddha Yoga Intensives. Some scholarships are available.

HSI-LAI TEMPLE
3456 S. Glenmark Drive
Hacienda Heights, CA 91745
Tel. (818) 961–9697

A nonsectarian Buddhist temple, offering instruction in mindfulness meditation, Rinzai and Soto practices, chanting, and mantra. There are open meditations and puja services each day, and retreats and sesshins are offered throughout the year. Accommodations are available for supervised or unsupervised solitary retreats.

LOS ANGELES BUDDHIST VIHARA
1147 N. Beechwood Drive
Hollywood, CA 90038
Tel. (213) 464–9698

Meditation classes are offered every Tuesday and Friday evening from 6:00 to 7:00 PM. Each month, on the day of the full moon, there is a special service including a sermon, discussion, and recitation of the Ten Precepts. Solitary retreat facilities are available.

VEDANTA SOCIETY OF
SOUTHERN CALIFORNIA
1946 Vedanta Place
Hollywood, CA 90068
Tel. (213) 465–7114

For further information see the National Listings.

WESTERN SON ACADEMY
2 Hopkins
Irvine, CA 92715
Tel. (714) 786–9586

The center is open daily for meditation practice and instruction.

THE DESERT VIPASSANA CENTER
Star Rt. 1, Box 250
Joshua Tree, CA 92252
Tel. (714) 362–4815

Insight Meditation classes taught by Ruth Denison.

EWAM CHODEN TIBETAN BUDDHIST CENTRE
254 Cambridge Street
Kensington, CA 94708
Tel. (415) 527–7363

Classes in meditation, the Tibetan Book of the Dead,

Buddhist Dharma, and the Tibetan language are conducted by Lama Kunga Thartse Rinpoche, the designated reincarnation of Sevan Repa, Heart Disciple of Milarepa. Treasure vases, specially empowered to attract spiritual and material wealth, are available. On Sunday there is a meditation open to everyone.

ANANDA ASHRAMA
5301 Pennsylvania Avenue
PO Box 8555
La Crescenta, CA 91224
Tel. (818) 248–1931

Srimata (Rev. Mother) Gayatri Devi is Ananda Ashrama's spiritual leader. There are two public services each week: Sunday at 11:00 AM and Thursday at 8:00 PM. The Thursday service includes group meditation and a talk on some aspect of spiritual life. Ananda Ashrama houses a community of resident monastics and householder families, which follows the teaching of Sri Ramakrishna. Their spiritual guide, Srimata Gayatri Devi, is in residence about half of each year. There is another center in Cohasset, MA.

METROPOLITAN VIPASSANA
14713 La Mesa Drive
La Mirada, CA 90638
Tel. (714) 521–3046

In the lineage of the Burmese teacher U Ba Khin, Metropolitan Vipassana offers discourses and meditation instruction one night a week in five-week-long courses. Ten-day retreats are offered periodically.

ISKCON
284 Legion Street
Laguna Beach, CA 92651
Tel. (714) 494–7029

The International Society for Krishna Consciousness

offers chanting, devotional dance, and meditation programs. All are free; everyone is welcome.

BUDDHA SASANA FOUNDATION
45 Oak Road
Larkspur, CA 94939
Tel. (415) 924–6447

Alan Clements, the Resident Director of the Foundation, offers Vipassana meditation instruction and retreats in the tradition of Mahasi Sayadaw and the Ven. U Pandita Sayadaw.

KANZEON ZEN CENTER
20 Magnolia
Larkspur, CA 94939
Tel. (415) 924–5322

Kanzeon offers daily practice in Zen meditation and Iyengar-style Hatha Yoga. One- to seven-day retreats are held during the year.

CHURCH OF THE WHITE EAGLE LODGE
3809 Pacific Avenue
Long Beach, CA 90807
Tel. (213) 424–6227

The Church of the White Eagle Lodge is a nondenominational Christian Church. The Church offers a meditation course which teaches members how to relax the physical body so that it is comfortable and to relax the outer mind so that it becomes still and quiet and can truly touch that "peace which passeth all understanding."

ZEN CENTER OF LONG BEACH
1942 Magnolia Avenue
Long Beach, CA 90806
Tel. (213) 599–3275

Daily meditation practice, with sesshins offered three or four times a year.

PALO ALTO DHARMADHATU
201 Covington Road
Los Altos, CA 94022
Tel. (415) 949–3092

Affiliated with Vajradhatu International, the Palo Alto group offers a wide range of classes and group practice opportunities. There are also day-long and weekend sittings and Shambhala training.

BRAHMA KUMARIS
WORLD SPIRITUAL ORGANIZATION
8009 Hollywood Boulevard
Los Angeles, CA 90046
Tel. (213) 876–5545

For further information, see National Listings.

CIMARRON ZEN CENTER
2505 Cimarron Street
Los Angeles, CA 90018
Tel. (213) 732–2263

Daily chanting and meditation sessions in the Rinzai tradition. The Center was founded by Joshu Sasaki Roshi, and is the headquarters of the Rinzai-Ji Organization.

COMMUNITY MEDITATION CENTER
OF LOS ANGELES
1041 Elden Avenue
Los Angeles, CA 90006
Tel. (213) 384–7817

The Center offers an introductory course in insight meditation.

DHARMA VIJAYA BUDDHIST VIHARA
1847 Crenshaw Boulevard
Los Angeles, CA 90019
Tel. (213) 737–5084

Meditation instruction and a Dharma talk are given each Friday and Sunday, 7:00 to 9:00 PM. Short Vipassana courses and weekend intensive meditation retreats are offered from time to time.

EAST-WEST CULTURAL CENTER
2865 W. 9th Street
Los Angeles, CA 90006
Tel. (213) 480–8325

The Center's goal is to integrate the cultural and spiritual values of East and West by presenting public programs on yoga, religion, philosophy, and spiritual inquiry. The teachings of Sri Aurobindo and The Mother inspire the work of the Center, and classes are offered in Sri Aurobindo's techniques of Integral Yoga. The Center's extensive oriental library is open daily, and a large hall is available for rent to spiritual groups.

GOLD WHEEL MONASTERY
1728 W. 6th Street
Los Angeles, CA 90017
Tel. (213) 483–7497

Gold Wheel is an affiliate monastery of the City of Ten Thousand Buddhas. The principal residents of Gold Wheel are Bhikshunis (nuns), who give lectures twice each day on the Buddhist Sutras. Daily sittings are open to nuns and monks only, but ceremonies and periods of meditation are also offered which are open to the public.

INTERNATIONAL BUDDHIST MEDITATION CENTER
928 S. New Hampshire Avenue
Los Angeles, CA 90006
Tel. (213) 384–0850

Founded by the Vietnamese Zen Master Thich Thien-An, the Center teaches a method of Integral Zen which incorporates koan, chanting, and visualization techniques. Both Zen and Vipassana meditation are taught, and visualization or koan practices may sometimes be recommended. Day-long retreats are offered every month, and weekend-long retreats every four months.

KANZEONJI ZEN BUDDHIST TEMPLE
944 Terrace 49
Los Angeles, CA 90042
Tel. (213) 255–5345

Kanzeonji utilizes the unique spiritual discipline of Zen Yoga, developed by Swami Premananda. Swami conducts zazen training and leads three-day sesshins several times each year.

KDC MEDITATION
12021 Wilshire Boulevard, #667
Los Angeles, CA 90049

For information, write to Ken McLeod.

LOS ANGELES CENTER FOR PLANETARY GOODWILL
4450 Beauvais Avenue
Los Angeles, CA 90065
Tel. (213) 222–6945 or (213) 829–3779

The Center for Planetary Goodwill is a small group of Alice Bailey students who have been meeting together for a number of years. The group meets once a month at the time of the full moon for meditation in service to the planet. New members who wish to participate in this service are warmly welcome.

LOS ANGELES INTERGROUP
PO Box 39385
Los Angeles, CA 90039
Tel. (213) 222–6945; (818) 353–9535

The primary purpose of the Los Angeles InterGroup is

to establish, through meditation, a conscious link with spiritual energies for the unfoldment of the Divine Plan on earth. Write or call for information about Meditation Festivals.

SAI FOUNDATION
7911 Willoughby Avenue
Los Angeles, CA 90046
Tel. (213) 656–9373

SAI, The Spiritual Advancement of the Individual, is dedicated to spreading the teachings of Sri Sathya Sai Baba, believed by his followers to be the living Avatar of this age. Activities at the Center include meditation, lectures, films, and bhajans (prayer and song meetings).

SELF-REALIZATION FELLOWSHIP
3880 San Rafael Avenue
Los Angeles, CA 90065
Tel. (213) 225–2471

For further information see the National Listings.

SELF-REALIZATION FELLOWSHIP
LAKE SHRINE
17190 Sunset Boulevard
Los Angeles, CA 90272
Tel. (213) 454–4114

The ten-acre SRF Lake Shrine, established in 1950 by Paramhansa Yogananda, is open to the public Tuesday through Sunday, 9:00 AM to 4:45 PM. This peaceful sanctuary, with its natural spring-fed lake and scenic meditation gardens, provides an ideal setting where those of all religious traditions can come for quiet reflection and communion with God. On the grounds is the Mahatma Gandhi World Peace Memorial, where a portion of Gandhi's ashes is enshrined. Lectures and meditation services are conducted by monks of the Self-Realization Order at the Lake Shrine Temple. For further information see the National Listings.

SHAMBHALA TRAINING
Los Angeles, CA
Tel. (213) 224–8061

For further information, contact Shambhala Training, Boulder, CO (see Local Listings).

SIVANANDA YOGA VEDANTA CENTER
1600 Sawtelle Boulevard
Los Angeles, CA 90025
Tel. (213) 478–7842

The Center offers classes in yoga, meditation, pranayam, and vegetarian cooking. Daily satsang is open to the public. There is a limited residential program for sincere students.

THUBTEN DHARGYE LING
2658 La Cienaga Avenue
Los Angeles, CA 90034
Tel. (213) 838–1232

A center following the Gelugpa tradition, T.D.L. conducts meditation classes, studies in Sutra and Tantra, and frequent retreats.

THE YOGA CENTER
1639 S. La Cienega Boulevard
Los Angeles, CA 90035
Tel. (213) 275–4160

The Yoga Center is a branch of the 3HO Foundation, and provides instruction in kundalini yoga as taught by Yogi Bhajan. Yoga and meditation retreats are offered from time to time.

ZEN CENTER OF LOS ANGELES, INC.
923 S. Normandie Avenue
Los Angeles, CA 90006
Tel. (213) 387–2351

Taizan Maezumi Roshi, Director of ZCLA, is a Soto

Zen priest and a master in both the Soto and Rinzai
lineages of Zen Buddhism. The influence of both traditions is reflected in the practice at the Zen Center.
There is an ongoing resident training program for intensive pratice and an extended resident training program
for those with outside employment. Families are welcome. There is a daily schedule of meditation, open to
members and nonmembers alike, which includes sitting
periods in the morning and evening; and for members
and trainees, interviews with Roshi are available. In
addition, a week-long sesshin (meditation retreat) is
held each month at the ZCLA and/or the affiliated Zen
Mountain Center. There is also a varied format of seminars, and for newcomers there are weekly meditation
instructions and introductory workshops.

CENTER FOR SPIRITUAL AWARENESS/
NORTHERN CALIFORNIA
PO Box 1454
Los Gatos, CA 95031
Tel. (408) 395–1414

The Center for Spiritual Awareness offers a unique
Sunday morning worship service which incorporates
teachings from all enlightenment traditions, including
Yoga, Zen Buddhism, Christianity, and contemporary
philosophy. Also included in the Sunday program are
opportunities for chanting and deep silent meditation. In
addition to the Sunday service, CSA offers meditation
instruction, classes on living a spiritual life, counseling,
and meditation retreats.

LOS GATOS ZEN GROUP
16200 Matilija Drive
Los Gatos, CA 95030
Attn: Arvis Joen Justi
Tel. (408) 354–7506

Meetings are held every Sunday from 8:15 AM to 10:00
AM. Instruction is offered for beginners. The meetings

consist of meditation and chanting; tea and discussion are optional.

ARCANA WORKSHOPS
PO Box 506
Manhattan Beach, CA 90277
Tel. (213) 379–9990

Arcana offers meditation training in weekly workshops and through correspondence courses, and community meditation meetings at the time of each full moon. All who are concerned for the common good are welcome.

ZEN MOUNTAIN CENTER
PO Box 43
Mountain Center, CA 92361
Tel. (714) 659–5272

Fred Jitsudo Ancheta, Instructor.

MOUNTAIN VIEW ZEN CENTER
292 College Avenue
Mountain View, CA 94040
Tel. (415) 948–5020

Mountain View Zen Center, or "Kannon Do," is a nonresidential center emphasizing the application of practice in everyday life. There are daily zazen sittings and retreats throughout the year.

MT. BALDY ZEN CENTER
PO Box 429
Mt. Baldy, CA 91759
Tel. (714) 985–6410

This Center was established in 1971 to provide a monastic setting for the training of students under the guidance of Rinzai Zen Master Joshu Sasaki Roshi. Located 35 miles east of Los Angeles in the San Gabriel National Forest, MBZC offers a rigorous daily schedule of zazen (meditation) and samu (work practice). Visitors are welcome most Saturday mornings for introductory instruction. Weekend stays are also available; reservations are required. The three-month Winter and Summer Training Periods include several week-long intensive reteats. Please contact the Center for further information.

SHASTA ABBEY
HEADQUARTERS OF THE ORDER OF
BUDDHIST CONTEMPLATIVES
3612 Summit Drive
PO Box 199
Mt. Shasta, CA 96067
Tel. (916) 926–4208

Shasta Abbey, headquarters of the Order of Buddhist Contemplatives, is a monastery and seminary in the Serene Reflection Meditation tradition of Buddhism (called in Japanese Soto Zen and in Chinese Ts'ao-tung). Founded in 1970 by Rev. Master Jiyu-Kennett, Abbess and Spiritual Director, the Abbey provides religious training for both male and female members of the priesthood, and a year-round program of retreats and residential training for laypeople of varying backgrounds and experience. Weekend and week-long retreats have a daily schedule of sitting meditation, classes, working meditation, and Buddhist services. Training at Shasta Abbey is based upon the formal practice of meditation, the keeping of the Precepts, and the integration of the Precepts into every aspect of our daily lives. There are affiliated priories in three western states and Canada, and meditation groups meet regularly in more than a dozen cities; contact Shasta Abbey for further information.

GREEN GULCH FARM ZEN CENTER
1601 Shoreline Highway
Muir Beach, CA 94965
Tel. (415) 383–3134

Green Gulch is a branch of the San Francisco Zen

Center located on a 15-acre farm, and practices emphasize the application of mindfulness to everyday activities. Daily zazen, one-day and weekend retreats, and one- to three-month practice periods are offered. The teachings at Green Gulch have been strongly influenced by the Vietnamese teacher Thich Nhat Hanh.

ANANDA WORLD BROTHERHOOD VILLAGE
14618 Tyler Foote Road
Nevada City, CA 95959
Tel. (916) 292–3464

Ananda is a spiritual community in the foothills of the Sierra Nevada Mountains, with branch communities in Palo Alto, Sacramento, Portland, Seattle, and Assisi, Italy. Sri Kriyananda, who founded the community in 1968 and lives in full-time residence, is a close, direct disciple of Paramhansa Yogananda. Ananda's more than 500 members are also disciples of Yogananda and practice the Kriya Yoga meditation technique that he taught. The community consists primarily of "householder renunciants," although there are also some monastics. Ananda is a free enterprise community, employing almost all members through community or member-owned businesses. Community children attend Ananda School. Ananda's meditation retreat, The Expanding Light (see Retreat Facilities) is a year-round, fully staffed facility offering a variety of retreat experiences, including week-long and month-long courses in Raja Yoga and Hatha Yoga, plus programs for experiencing spiritual community. A Raja Yoga home-study course called *Lessons in Yoga: 14 Steps to Higher Awareness* is also offered. Ananda is dedicated to the fulfillment of Paramhansa Yogananda's dream:

> *To spread a spirit of brotherhood among all people and to aid in establishing, in many countries, self-sustaining world brotherhood colonies for plain living and high thinking.*

TAOIST INSTITUTE
10630 Burbank Boulevard
North Hollywood, CA 91601
Tel. (818) 760–4219; (213) 271–9308

The Taoist Institute offers instruction, practice, and certification in a number of traditional Chinese Taoist and Buddhist Internal Arts, including Chi Kung (Chinese yoga and meditation).

WAT THAI OF LOS ANGELES
8225 Coldwater Canyon Avenue
North Hollywood, CA 91605
Tel. (818) 785–9552

Wat Thai is a Thai Vipassana temple. There are monthly weekend meditation retreats and all-night retreats on Buddhist holidays.

THE INNER LIGHT FOUNDATION
PO Box 761
Novato, CA 94948
Tel. (415) 382–1040

Betty Bethards's nondenominational Foundation offers ongoing programs in meditation techniques, dreamwork, affirmations, and visualizations.

SUFI ISLAMIA RUHANIAT SOCIETY
GARDEN OF INAYAT
910 Railroad Avenue
Novato, CA 94947
Tel. (415) 897–5426

Murshid Samuel Lewis's work with spiritual walk and dance is carried on by the Sufi Islamia Ruhaniat Society, which sponsors instruction and practice in the dances and in the meditative practice of zikr.

SIDDHA YOGA ASHRAM
1107 Stanford
Oakland, CA 94608
Tel. (415) 655–8677

Regular programs of chanting, meditation, and instruction are available at the Ashram. For more information, see the National Listings.

THE TAOIST CENTER
420 14th Street
Oakland, CA 94612
Tel. (415) 763–9352

The Taoist Center, founded by Master Tsuei Wei, offers acupuncture, T'ai Chi, Qi Gong, and meditation weekends.

CALIFORNIA VIPASSANA CENTER
PO Box 510
Occidental, CA 95465
Tel. (707) 874–3031

The Center offers ten-day Vipassana courses based on the teachings of S. N. Goenka.

KROTONA INSTITUTE OF THEOSOPHY
46 Krotona Hill
Ojai, CA 93023
Tel. (805) 646–1139 or 646–2653

Krotona is a theosophical educational center in a retreat setting which offers a variety of courses dealing with ancient wisdom. For more information see the National Listing for the Theosophical Society in Wheaton, IL.

MEDITATION GROUP FOR THE NEW AGE
PO Box 566
Ojai, CA 93023

Meditation Group for the New Age offers a correspondence course in techniques and aspects of meditation.

Attention is focused on service to humanity. The first year is free, and a Spanish-language version of the course is available.

OJAI FOUNDATION
PO Box 1620
Ojai, CA 93023
Tel. (805) 646-8343

Through The Foundation School, the Ojai Foundation teaches seminars and practice programs in mindfulness practice, ecology, and Native American traditions. The Ojai Foundation also offers the opportunity for students to make personal retreats on its beautiful land in the Upper Ojai Valley. There is sitting meditation twice daily and other practice opportunities with the staff. Call or write for further information.

CRYSTAL CAVE OF ORANGE
777 S. Main Street, #2
Orange, CA 92668
Tel. (714) 543-0551

Classes in meditation, chakras, visualizations, and other topics are offered regularly. Group meditations are held once a week.

THE BUILDERS
Vintage Marina
2950 S. Harbor Boulevard
Oxnard, CA 93030
Tel. (805) 985-6417

Visitors are welcome to participate in daily meditations and other events. For further information, see the Salt Lake City, UT, center in the Local Listings.

INTEGRATRON HEALING CENTER
PO Box 1022
Pacific Palisades, CA 90272
Tel. (213) 281–6114

Meditation and other powerful methods for awakening are taught at weekend workshops. Topics include inner vision, vision quests, new ways of healing, inner initiations, and sacred geometry; methods emphasize sonics, chanting, mantra, and prayer work. Workshops, facilitated by Emile Canning, are high-energy transformational experiences. Evening workshops are regularly scheduled throughout California. For further information, contact Gary Abreim.

ANANDA FELLOWSHIP OF INNER COMMUNION
299 California Avenue, #208
Palo Alto, CA 94306
Tel. (415) 323–3363

Founded by Sri Kriyananda, Ananda Fellowship offers ongoing classes in Raja Yoga (meditation, yoga, etc.) based on the teachings of Paramhansa Yogananda. Other courses are also available, in addition to Sunday Services and the Festival of Light.

INNER LIGHT FOUNDATION
PO Box 750265
Petaluma, CA 94975
Tel. (707) 765–2200

Betty Bethards, self-help author, psychic, and mystic, founded the nonprofit Inner Light Foundation in 1969. The ILF provides ongoing programs and lecture series in developing and understanding our human potential.

Through the use of dreams, meditation, and visualization, Betty teaches how each person can tap into receiving his own insights, inspiration, and guidance from the unlimited God-source. All answers truly do lie within. ILF offers a free newsletter setting out its meditation techniques; send a stamped, self-addressed envelope.

SONOMA COUNTY DHARMA STUDY GROUP
24 Western Avenue
Petaluma, CA 94952
Tel. (707) 762–0195

The Group offers meditation instruction and regular sessions of meditation practice.

ASSOCIATION FOR RESEARCH
AND ENLIGHTENMENT, INC.
348 Western Drive & Casey
Point Richmond, CA 94801
Tel. (415) 234–0415

The Association offers weekly study groups, which meet to meditate, pray, and share discussions about a series of books entitled "A Search for God." Other programs include bonfire meetings, lectures, all-day workshops, and an annual retreat. Point Richmond is also A.R.E.'s northern California regional office, and can provide information about groups meeting throughout the area. For more information about A.R.E., see the National Listings.

ATMANIKETAN ASHRAM
1291 Weber street
Pomona, CA 91768
Tel. (714) 629–8255

All seekers sincerely aspiring to become selfless instruments in the progressive manifestations of a "Divine

Life" upon the earth are invited to collaborate in the practices of Atmaniketan Ashram. The Ashram is not a meditation retreat, but a living laboratory for the practice of Sri Aurobindo's Collective Yoga of Integral Perfection—a place for those who wish to serve the Divine with dynamism and concentration. Intimate spiritual guidance is provided by Ashram founder Swami Sadhu Loncontirth during his twice-yearly visits.

SHAMAZ MEDITATION RETREAT
Potter Valley, CA 95469

For information, contact Sant Bani Ashram, Franklin, NH (see Local Listings).

FULL CIRCLE WORKSHOPS, INC.
PO Box 458
Pt. Reyes Station, CA 94956

Full Circle offers monthly meditation groups and a sacred mystery school for women called "Keepers of the Flame." The school celebrates an ancient women's lineage committed to rekindling the sacred wisdom flame in all Earth's children. Spiritual practices include sitting meditation to develop concentration, working with the breath and with the double spiral of Earth and sky energy, celebration of the seasonal ceremonial cycle, and sacred sound and movement.

JOSHU ZEN TEMPLE
2303 Harriman
Redondo Beach, CA 90278
Tel. (213) 374–2934

Morning and evening zazen sittings are open to the public. Meditation instruction is available by arrangement.

THE INTERGROUP FOR PLANETARY ONENESS
6801 Lindley
Reseda, CA 91335
Tel. (818) 343–4998

The Intergroup is a nonprofit organization dedicated to world unity. It seeks to network peoples and groups of all faiths and cultures for the purpose of expansion of consciousness, brotherhood, and world peace. Activities include weekly classes, full moon meditations, and publication of a quarterly magazine entitled *Meditation.*

FELLOWSHIP OF INNER COMMUNION
4343 Marconi Avenue, #7
Sacramento, CA 95821
Tel. (916) 484–1999

Founded by Sri Kriyananda, Ananda Fellowship offers ongoing classes in Raja Yoga (meditation, yoga, etc.) based on the teachings of Paramhansa Yogananda. Other courses are also available, in addition to Sunday Services and the Festival of Light.

THE UNICORN ASHRAM
PO Box 8495
San Diego, CA 92102
Tel. (619) 544–6461

The Unicorn Ashram's only creed is the unfolding of consciousness through meditation, study, and service.

BRAHMA KUMARIS
RAJA YOGA MEDITATION CENTER
401 Baker Street
San Francisco, CA 94117
Tel. (415) 563–4459

Raja Yoga meditation is based on an understanding of how the mind works in connection with memory, perception, feeling, and action, as well as on an understanding of the relationship between the individual being of consciousness (soul) and the Supreme. Practiced with open eyes, Raja Yoga meditation does not involve physical exercises, chanting, breath control, mantras, or any rituals of worship. Classes are taught on an individual basis by appointment, and are free of charge.

CHURCH OF AMRON
2254 Van Ness Avenue
San Francisco, CA 94109
Tel. (415) 775–0227

Meditations are held every Sunday from 10:45 to 11:15 AM, prior to morning services. On Tuesday evenings from 6:00 to 7:00 PM there is a healing meditation. About once every three months the Church sponsors a Saturday "meditation happening," which includes a half hour of meditation instruction and an afternoon of both active and passive meditation practice.

GOLD MOUNTAIN SAGELY MONASTERY
800 Sacramento Street
San Francisco, CA 94108
Tel. (415) 421–6117

The Monastery offers a rigorous daily schedule of ceremonies, lectures, and meditation. There are informal meditations daily, morning and evening; formal meditation classes on Saturday and Sunday from 7:30 to 9:30 AM; and lectures twice daily. The lectures are given in both English and Mandarin by Bhikshus (monks) and Bhikshunis (nuns) trained at the City of Ten Thousand Buddhas in Mendocino County. On Sunday mornings the Monastery conducts Dharma School classes for children ages six to fifteen.

HARTFORD STREET ZEN CENTER
57 Hartford Street
San Francisco, CA 94114
Tel. (415) 861–6779

The Center offers a schedule of morning and evening zazen practice, Buddhist study classes, and retreats, with a special focus on the needs of gay men and lesbians.

INTEGRAL YOGA INSTITUTE
770 Dolores Street
San Francisco, CA 94110
Tel. (415) 824–9600 or (415) 821–1117

Under the guidance of Sri Swami Satchidananda, Integral Yoga offers a practice combining techniques from several systems of yoga; hatha yoga (physical postures, breathing practices, and relaxation techniques); karma yoga (selfless service); raja yoga (concentration, meditation, and ethical perfection); japa yoga (repetition of a sound vibration); bhakti yoga (love of, and devotion to, God); and jnana yoga (self-inquiry). All of these practices are designed to help the student find the peace and happiness which lie within. The Integral Yoga Institute of San Francisco offers classes for the community and provides a live-in household for spiritual seekers. One-day silent retreats are held regularly.

> *The Goal of Integral Yoga is to realize the universal truth, to express the spiritual unity behind all the diversities in the entire creation, and to live harmoniously as members of one universal family.*
> —*Sri Swami Satchidananda*

KAGYU DRODEN KUNCHAB
1892 Fell Street
San Francisco, CA 94117
Tel. (415) 752–5454

Kagyu Droden Kunchab, founded by the Very Venerable Kalu Rinpoche, is a center for the study and practice of Tibetan Mahayana and Vajrayana Buddhism. Rinpoche's representative, Ven. Lama Lodru, leads meditations and answers questions during regular weekly programs; the Ngondro (Four Foundations) Meditation is conducted each Saturday at 10:00 AM, and the Green Tara Meditation each Sunday at 10:00 AM. Lama Lodru also offers weekly meditation classes in Mill Valley and in Sebastopol, and guides a two-day Nyung Nes Retreat each month at the full moon.

NAMA-RUPA
10 Arbor Street
San Francisco, CA 94131
Tel. (415) 334–4921

Weekly meditation sittings and classes in the Abhidhamma are open to the public.

SIVANANDA YOGA VEDANTA CENTER
1200 Arguello
San Francisco, CA 94122
Tel. (415) 681–2731

Meditation classes, yoga classes, vegetarian cooking classes, and a fasting clinic are among the offerings of the San Francisco Sivananda Yoga Vedanta Center. Weekly lectures and group meditations are open to all without charge.

> *To control the restless mind and bring all thoughts and cravings to a stillness and sublimation is the greatest problem of man. If he has subjugated the mind, he may be said to be, in his subjective freedom and power, the emperor of emperors.*
> —*Swami Sivananda*

SRI CHINMOY CENTRE AT
EVEREST ASPIRATION BOOKSTORE
1383-A 9th Avenue
San Francisco, CA 94112
Tel. (415) 753–3798

Under the guidance and inspiration of Sri Chinmoy, the Centre schedules weekly free classes in sitting meditation and music meditation. There are also free concerts of devotional music from time to time.

SUFI ISLAMIA RUHANIAT SOCIETY MENTORGARTEN
410 Precita Avenue
San Francisco, CA 94110
Tel. (415) 285–5208

Founded by Murshid Samuel L. Lewis, the Society's core study centers around the teachings of Hazrat Inayat Khan and Sam Lewis. Public and esoteric classes, including Dances of Universal Peace (a joyful celebration of the Divine Presence through simple but Sacred Dance), are held throughout the Bay area. All are welcome. The Society also directs the Dervish Healing Order, Universal Worship, and an annual summer camp in Mendocino.

YOGA SOCIETY OF SAN FRANCISCO
2872 Folsom Street
San Francisco, CA 94110
Tel. (415) 285–5537

Meditation training, hatha yoga, t'ai chi ch'uan, and Sanskrit classes.

THE ZEN CENTER
300 Page Street
San Francisco, CA 94102
Tel. (415) 863–3136

The Zen Center was founded by Shunryu Suzuki Roshi. The Abbots are Tenshin Reb Anderson and Sojun Mel Weitsman. It is a large, residential center, with daily zazen and services which are open to everyone. Lectures and zazen instruction are offered on Saturday mornings. See *Zen Mind, Beginner's Mind* by Suzuki Roshi for a description of the practice followed at the

Center as well as at Green Gulch Farm, Tassajara Zen Mountain Center, and Berkeley Zen Center.

> *The zazen I speak of is not learning meditation. It is simply the Dharma-gate of repose and bliss, the practice-realization of totally culminated enlightenment.*
> —Dogen Zenji

BADARIKASHRAMA
15602 Maubert Avenue
San Leandro, CA 95478
Tel. (415) 278–2444

Badarikashrama is a spiritual center which promotes a life of dedicated service based on Vedantic wisdom. Meditation, puja, yoga, social service, and kirtan are utilized as techniques to bring the individual into closer connection with the Divine. Ashram activities include festival celebrations, retreats, and Tuesday evening meditation classes, and each fall the center offers classes in Indian art, music, and languages.

SAMI MAHAL SUFI CENTER
248 Laurel Place
San Rafael, CA 94901
Tel. (415) 459–4122

The Sami Mahal Sufi Center is representative of Chisthi-descendant Sufism through the lineage of Hazrat Inayat Khan, Pir Vilayat Khan, and Murshid Samuel Lewis. The Center is committed to the evolution of a Sufism for the West, while at the same time honoring the historical and esoteric heritage to the *Silsila*, the 1400-year-old chain of masters particular to this Sufi lineage. The Center offers classes in different aspects of Sufism, always from an experiential point of view, and weekly group practice of Dhikr, the Sufi mantric ceremony of remembrance. In addition to classes, the Center stresses one-on-one work with the sheikh, and has a school for training in the work of the cherag, the ministerial function of Sufism unique to this lineage.

SUFI ISLAMIA RUHANIAT SOCIETY
PO Box 1066
San Rafael, CA 94915
Tel. (415) 499–8578

Based on the teachings of Murshid Samuel Lewis.

SANTA BARBARA BUDDHIST PRIORY
509 Casitas Road
Santa Barbara, CA 93103
Tel. (805) 962–3071

The Santa Barbara Buddhist Priory is a Zen Buddhist church and training center, established to teach and practice the Buddhist religion of the Order of Buddhist Contemplatives (whose headquarters are at Shasta Abbey in Mt. Shasta, CA (see Local Listings). This is the Serene Reflection (Soto Zen) school of practice. The Priory offers a schedule of daily meditation and religious services, periodic one-day and weekend retreats, and lectures. Spiritual counseling is available by appointment with the prior. The Priory is open to the general public; however, participants must have received meditation instruction at the Priory or at Shasta Abbey.

AVADHUT ASHRAM
PO Box 8080
Santa Cruz, CA 95061
Tel. (415) 588–7907

Meditation pactices in the tradition of Ramana Maharshi.

THE CALIFORNIA SCHOOL OF JAPANESE ARTS
526 Ashbury Avenue
Santa Rosa, CA 95404
Tel. (707) 578–8014

Modeled after the Oomoto School of Traditional Japa-

272 • *Journey of Awakening*

nese Arts, the California School emphasizes learning through actual practice of the arts. Oomoto is a Shinto religious organization that encourages the study of the arts as a basis for spiritual practice.

SONOMA MOUNTAIN ZEN CENTER
6367 Sonoma Mountain Road
Santa Rosa, CA 95404
Tel. (707) 545–8105

A Buddhist lay sangha practicing with Jakusho Kwong, Roshi. Rurally located in California's Valley of the Moon, the Sonoma Mountain Zen Center emphasizes a commitment to the practice of sitting meditation (zazen) every day as a way to deepen our true nature, and to actualize it clearly in our work and activities. We invite others to join us in this wonderful venture. Saturday community practices and extended resident training programs are also offered.

TAYU CENTER
PO Box 11554
Santa Rosa, CA 95046
Tel. (707) 829–9579

Tayu Center is a Fourth Way Spiritual School founded by Tayu Master Hassein, spiritual heir of Master E. J. Gold. The primary Tayu practice is a special form of meditation called Self-observation, which is used to focus awareness on the three major operational centers of the human organism: the motor/instinctive, the emotional, and the intellectual. An important form of Self-observation involves a two-person technique called "relational meditation." This method is designed to help those who have grown up in Western culture to cut through the sense of isolation and separateness fostered by this culture, and for whom Eastern-style solo sitting meditation might not be effective. Tayu Center is open to the public for regularly scheduled activities. Three-, seven-, and thirty-day residential training programs are available to qualified students.

BRAHMA KUMARIS CENTER
302 15th Street
Seal Beach,, CA 90740
Tel. (213) 430–4711

For further information, see National Listings.

MIDDLEBAR BUDDHIST MONASTERY
2503 Del Rio Drive
Stockton, CA 95204
Tel. (209) 462–9384

Middlebar is of the Soto Sect of Zen Buddhism. Founded in 1956 by Takashina Zenji, the temple was incorporated as a monastery in 1964. The Abbot, MacDonough Roshi, is the personal disciple of Archbishop Togen Sumi, Primate of the Soto Sect in Japan. The training given at Middlebar is under the personal supervision of the Roshi and directed by his disciple, Bro. James Percival. Traditional Zen methods and values are followed, emphasizing American life and language rather than preserving Japanese cultural practices. Applicants for admission must be high school graduates, unmarried, and in good health. At present no resident facilities are available for women. However, the monastery has a program of zazen and Buddhist studies for nonresident students of both sexes on weekdays.

CITY OF TEN THOUSAND BUDDHAS
PO Box 217
Talmage, CA 95481
Tel. (707) 462–0939

The City of Ten Thousand Buddhas, which is affiliated with the Dharma Realm Buddhist Association, is under the spiritual leadership of the Venerable Hsuan Hua. The monastery offers a rigorous schedule of practice seven days a week, from 4:00 AM to 10:00 PM. Daily practices include group meditation, group recitation, and lectures on the Buddhist scriptures. There are week-long intensive recitation and meditation sessions every other month, and a three- to ten-week meditation session in the winter. The cornerstone of all the practices is adherence to a high standard of ethics, and all residents embrace the Five Buddhist Precepts. Training is offered through a two-year Laity Training Program or a three-year Sangha Training Program; the latter is a partial fulfillment of requirements for receiving the 250 Precepts of a Bhikshu or the 348 Precepts of a Bhikshuni through traditional ordination procedures.

OPEN LOTUS CIRCLE
6404 Valmont Street
Tujunga, CA 91042
Tel. (818) 353–9535

Open Lotus Circle is a meditation group which studies the ancient wisdom teachings to understand the spiritual responsibilities of planetary citizens. Monthly meditation meetings are held at the exact time of the full moon; these meetings are open to all experienced meditators.

ASTARA
800 W. Arrow Highway
PO Box 5003
Upland, CA 91785
Tel. (714) 981–4941

Astara, founded and guided by Earlyne and Robert Chaney, is a center of all religions and philosophies, tracing its origins to the ancient mystery schools of Egypt and Greece. Instruction in meditation and other spiritual practices is available through correspondence courses, books, and on-site classes and seminars on a ten-acre campus. Sunday meetings are held at 11:00 AM. Retreat facilities are available.

HEALING ARTS CENTER
17280 Saticoy
Van Nuys, CA 91406
Tel. (818) 343–0339

Classes in meditation, yoga, t'ai chi, and acupressure.

THE INSTITUTE OF FOURTH WAY STUDIES
241A Lincoln Boulevard, #25
Venice, CA 90291
Tel. (213) 392–9555

The goal of the Institute is to provide a wide array of techniques which enable the student to explore and expand each level of consciousness in an orderly fashion. The Institute utilizes movement and dance exercises taught by Gurdjieff, spiritual systems taught by the Sufi masters, and meditative and visualization techniques developed during the Middle Ages and the Renaissance.

ORDINARY DHARMA
247 Horizon Avenue
Venice, CA 90291
Tel. (213) 396–5054

Ordinary Dharma offers workshops, weekly classes, weekend sittings, and instruction in Vipassana meditation.

JO REN ZEN CENTER OF SAN DIEGO
246 Santa Clara Avenue
Vista, CA 92083
Tel. (619) 436–5747

The Jo Ren Zen Center, a satellite of the Zen Center of Los Angeles (see Local Listings), offers a weekly zazen schedule on Tuesday from 7:30 to 9:15 PM, as well as zazen instruction, monthly talks, and one- and two-day retreats. Beginners are welcome. For further informa-

tion contact Nicolee Jikyo Miller, (619) 436–5747, or
Jake Jiyu Gage, (619) 724–9541.

MAKOM OHR SHALOM
PO Box 1066
Woodland Hills, CA 91365
Tel. (818) 344–3113

Makom Ohr Shalom is a synagogue community explor-
ing Jewish paths to holistic spiritual growth. Celebrations include stories, music, chanting, and guided
meditation (often using imagery from the Torah).

MYSTIC MERCHANT
4825-C Valley View Avenue
Yorba Linda, CA 92686
Tel. (714) 993–4788

Mystic Merchant is an enlightenment center where "the
Old World meets the New Age." Meditation classes are
offered for assistance in maintaining the flow with Self
in perfect wholeness. Guided meditation workshops focus on universal law, spiritual awareness, communication with the higher self, color healing, and meditation
interpretation. The meditation healing circle fosters spiritual growth by focusing on the soul's purpose for this
life path, on raising consciousness, and on harmonizing
love and responsibility. American Indian and Eastern
meditation healing ceremonies are offered for the four
seasons.

COLORADO

SPIRITUAL INTEGRATION CENTER
PO Box 31183
Aurora, CO 80041
Tel. (303) 366–0569

Meditation classes at SIC integrate traditional techniques
(Tantric, Taoist, Christian, Buddhist, and Yogic) with

recent advances in left-right brain synchronization to accelerate progress in meditation proficiency. Utilizing a context called the "homing process," complementary procedures drawn from the fields of meditation and psychology work to enhance the meditator's quality of life and growth. The homing process provides a unifying arena for integrating such polarities as good and bad, spiritual and material, or worthy and unworthy, thus supporting and augmenting the healing effects of meditation.

> *Find the door of your heart; you will discover it is the door of the Kingdom of God.*
> —*St. John Chrysostom*

BOULDER ZEN CENTER
PO Box 7283
Boulder, CO 80306
Tel. (303) 444–5577

A Rinzai Zen Center, offering early morning sitting and chanting sessions each weekday, zazen practice two evenings each week, and instruction twice monthly. One-day and weekend-long retreats are offered in alternate months.

CLEAR MIND/OPEN HEART
537-½ University
Boulder, CO 80302
Tel. (303) 443–5606

Under the guidance of Swami Brahmananda and Dharmavati, Clear Mind/Open Heart offers classes and seminars in meditation, yoga nidra, pranayam, and other techniques.

KARMA DZONG
1345 Spruce Street
Boulder, CO 80302
Tel. (303) 444–0190

Founded by the Ven. Chögyam Trungpa, Rinpoche,

Karma Dzong offers meditation practice and ongoing classes.

NAROPA INSTITUTE
2130 Arapahoe
Boulder, CO 80302
Tel. (303) 444–0202

Naropa is an accredited academic institution, offering B.A. degrees in such areas as Buddhist studies, contemplative psychology, and visual arts, and M.A.s in contemplative psychotherapy, dance therapy, and writing and poetics. But at Naropa, education means more than rigorous academic discipline; equal attention is placed on cultivating intuition beyond the conceptual mind. This is "contemplative education"—a program of study that links what happens in the classroom with what happens in the rest of our lives. In addition to degree offerings, Naropa presents a series of summer programs in which nationally known artists and scholars present workshops, conferences, and seminars.

NYINGMA INSTITUTE OF COLORADO
1441 Broadway
Boulder, CO 80302
Tel. (303) 443–5550

Regular weekly meditation practice and year-round facilities for solitary retreats.

SACRED MOUNTAIN ASHRAM
10668 Gold Hill Road
Boulder, CO 80302-9716
Tel. (303) 447-1637

Sacred Mountain Ashram is a haven of peace and upliftment where disciples may live in the awakening presence of the Guru, and all sincere seekers are welcome to come for guidance, service, and spiritual renewal. Founded in 1974 by Prabhushri Swami Amar

Jyoti, Sacred Mountain Ashram is one of three ashrams in the United States incorporated within Truth Consciousness, a nonprofit organization. Master's approach is universal, giving no one dogma or religion but the pure, unalloyed spirituality that unfolds the path within each seeker. The ashram is located on 65 mountaintop acres at 8600-foot elevation, blending evergreen forests, aspen groves, and flower-filled meadows. Sacred Mountain Ashram offers weekly satsang, meditation, retreats, and opportunities for selfless service. A wide selection of Pujya Swamiji's books and tapes and many other fine spiritual publications are available through the Ashram.

> *I wish to impart to you the classical foundation of genuine spirituality. This is the royal road, the eternal path. When the ground is well prepared and the foundation is solid, then the rest of the structure is really very easy and not time-consuming. Very simple and straight, this classical path needs your patience in the beginning, but it gives you sustenance and its results are abiding.*
>
> —*Swami Amar Jyoti*

SHAMBHALA TRAINING
2130 Araphahoe Avenue
Boulder, CO 80302
Tel. (303) 444-7881

Founded in 1977 by the late Venerable Chogyam Trungpa, Rinpoche, Shambhala Training presents the ancient teachings of Shambhala Warriorship, which are based on gentleness and the simplicity of mindfulness/ awareness (shamatha/vipassana) meditation. The basic message of the Shambhala teachings is that the best of human life can be realized under ordinary circumstances— that in this world, as it is, we can find a good and meaningful life that will also serve others. Meditation practice allows us to experience, without bias, all the ups and downs, hopes and fears, of our life's journey. Such experience gives rise to genuineness, and it is the warrior's discipline to be genuine in each moment of life.

3HO FOUNDATION
GURU RAM DAS ASHRAM
3460 Berkley Avenue
Boulder, CO 80303
Tel. (303) 494–4643

The Ashram is a center for the teachings of Yogi Bhajan, and offers ongoing classes in Kundalini Yoga and meditation. For more information, see National Listings.

TRUTH CONSCIOUSNESS
Gold Hill
Salina Star Route
Boulder,, CO 80302
Tel. (303) 447–1637

Truth Consciousness is a vehicle for the teachings of Swami Amar Jyoti. Satsang, meditation classes, spiritual retreats, and other programs are available.

DENVER CENTER FOR BUDDHIST STUDIES
1440 High Street
Denver, CO 80218
Tel. (303) 377–1592

Courses in Nyingma meditation and Vajrayana teachings.

THE DENVER ZEN CENTER
1233 Columbine
Denver, CO 80206
Tel. (303) 333–4844

The Center offers formal zazen sittings, special celebrations of Buddhist holidays, and introductory workshops on Zen practice.

DRIKUNG KAGYU MEDITATION CENTER
801 W. 5th Avenue
Denver, CO 80203
Tel. (303) 623–1507

In addition to offering traditional Tibetan meditation instruction, the Center offers courses in T'ai Chi Ch'uan, chanting retreats, and supervised solitary retreats.

WAT BUDDHAWARARAM
4801 Julian Street
Denver, CO 80221
Tel. (303) 433–1826

The monks at Wat Buddhawararam sit in meditation every morning and evening; anyone interested in insight meditation practices is invited to join them. Week-long meditation retreats are conducted several times a year.

THE CREATIVE LIGHT CENTER
416 Plateau Parkway
Golden, CO 80403
Tel. (303) 278–1152

The Center's weekly classes in spiritual development include instruction in meditation, the synthesis of Eastern and Western religions, and spiritual counseling. There are monthly full moon meditations for group alignment and to raise consciousness on the Earth plane.

> *Through that door [the full moon], approaches can be made to the planetary Hierarchy . . . which are at other times not possible.*
>
> —*Alice A. Bailey*

CONNECTICUT

LIVING DHARMA CENTER
PO Box 513
Bolton, CT 06043
Tel. (203) 742–7049

Richard Clarke, the founder of Living Dharma, developed his practice during 13 years of formal Zen training and additional training and experience in other spiritual traditions. The practice is self-empowering, and takes into account the particular needs of each student. Workshops, weekly zazen meditations, dokusan (private interviews on practice), and sesshin (prolonged meditation retreats) are offered regularly. Sincere participants are warmly welcomed.

NORTHEAST TRANSMISSION
MEDITATION NETWORK
PO Box 125
Canton, CT 06019
Tel. (203) 693–6201

Many people today are looking for a way to serve. One of the most potent forms of service on the planet is Transmission Meditation—a specialized form of group meditation in which the members act as positive, poised mental channels through which the energy sent by the Masters can be stepped down (transformed) and made more usable. Write or call for information.

3HO FOUNDATION
GURU HARKRISHAN ASHRAM
127 Tremont Street
Hartford, CT 06105
Tel. (203) 236–1191

The Ashram is a center for the teachings of Yogi Bhajan, and offers ongoing classes in Kundalini Yoga and meditation. For more information, see National Listings.

NEW HAVEN ZEN CENTER
193 Mansfield Street
New Haven, CT 06511
Tel. (203) 787–0912

A small meditation group, offering daily practice, monthly Dharma talks, and twice-yearly workshops. One- to three-day retreats are conducted every other month.

UNIVERSAL LIFE
PO Box 3549
New Haven, CT 06525
Tel. (203) 281–7771

At the heart of Universal Life is the Christian Mystery School, called into being by Christ in order to teach the direct and perfect inner path to God. Meditation instruction is available through two correspondence courses, called the "Path of Preparation" and the "Path of Address." Students in Universal Life, and those who are interested in learning from the revelations of the Divine Spirit and from each other, come together on the second and fourth Friday of each month in gatherings called "the Inner Spirit of Christ Church." There are also monthly international teleconferences, connecting groups of people by telephone to transmissions from the Universal Life headquarters in Wurzburg, West Germany.

SELF-ENHANCEMENT GROUP
26 Massapeag Point Road
Uncasville, CT 06382
Tel. (203) 848–3332

The Group offers instruction for beginners and intermediate students in the practice of meditation, stress management, and immunity-enhancement.

AVALONIA MEDITATION CENTER
780 Vauxhall Street Extension
Waterford, CT 06385
Tel. (203) 443–1517

Avalonia is a nonprofit organization which offers courses in yoga and meditation to interested students. For information, contact Robert or Mary Jo Crooks.

PERSONAL DEVELOPMENT CENTER
Box 251
Windham Center, CT 06280
Tel. (203) 423–4785

Advanced yoga free of charge to qualified individuals.

THE WOODBURY YOGA CENTER
122 West Side Road
Woodbury, CT 06798
Tel. (203) 263–2254

Located on 38 acres of fields, streams, and woods, the
Center offers courses in Hatha Yoga, Kundalini Yoga,
meditation, and the Yoga of Death and Dying. There
are also free meditation programs each Wednesday and
Sunday at 7:00 PM. All are welcome.

DELAWARE

CHRYSALIS CENTER
1008 Milltown Road
Wilmington, DE 19808
Tel. (302) 994–0565

The Chrysalis Center offers classes in yoga, Taoist
meditation, T'ai Chi, and inner guidance.

SIVANANDA YOGA CENTER
2307 Baynard Boulevard
Wilmington, DE 19802
Tel. (302) 733–7576

Free weekly meditation groups and hatha yoga classes.

DISTRICT OF COLUMBIA

AHIMSA ASHRAM
1704 Q Street, N.W.
Washington, DC 20009
Tel. (202) 328–7140

Through classes and workshops, techniques of yoga and meditation are taught and practiced, and specific skills for living in the natural world are presented. In addition to the classes offered at the center in downtown Washington, Ahimsa conducts rural summer retreats, called "Earth Living School," directed by Gurujiwan Singh Khalsa.

BRAHMA KUMARIS CENTER
3621 Ingomar Place
Washington, DC 20015
Tel. (202) 966–7547

For further information, see National Listings.

BUDDHIST VIHARA SOCIETY
5017 16th Street, N.W.
Washington, DC 20011
Tel. (202) 723–0773

The Vihara Society is open daily. There is a service on Sunday, and regular meditation classes are offered in the practice of mindfulness of breath as taught in Theravadin Buddhism. The teacher is the Ven. Maharagama Dhammasiri from Sri Lanka. A Buddhist library and Buddhist bookstore are open from 9 AM to 9 PM daily.

CHUA KY VIEN
1400 Madison Street, N.W.
Washington, DC 20011
Tel. (202) 882–6054

Chua Ky Vien, a Vietnamese meditation center, is open for informal sittings throughout the year. Ten-day Vipassana retreats are offered four times a year.

KA SHIN ZENDO GENZO-JI
7004 Ninth Street, N.W.
Washington, DC 20012
Tel. (202) 829–1966

Ka Shin Zendo is open to those who have had some
experience in meditation practice. There is a program of
basic instruction in zazen meditation on Wednesday
evenings, and two one-day zazen workshops each year.

PENTAGON MEDITATION CLUB
PO Box 46126
Washington, DC 20050

The Peach Shield Meditation/Prayer Campaign invites
you to center your awareness in your heart and meditate
daily; as you heal yourself, your thoughts "ripple" to
heal your family, your community, and the world.

SRI CHINMOY CENTRE
3502 Connecticut Avenue, N.W.
Washington, DC 20008
Tel. (202) 363–4797

The Centre offers weekly classes in meditation, music-
for-meditation concerts, and weekly meditations at the
U.S. Congress.

TIBETAN MEDITATION CENTER
5603 16th Street, N.W.
Washington, DC 20011
Tel. (202) 829–0005

The Center offers daily practices, lectures, special guided
visualization techniques, and weekend retreats. Meditation practitioners at any level of ability are welcome.

FLORIDA

THE BRIDGE, SOUTH
6015 Town Colony Drive, #313
Boca Raton, FL 33433
Tel. (407) 487–8961

The Bridge offers classes and workshops in methods of utilizing energy to release personal blocks and contact the God-energy within. The techniques taught are a synthesis of many methods, including insight meditation, chanting, and kundalini yoga.

SWAHA MEDITATION AND YOGA CENTER
4210 Barganza Avenue
Coconut Grove, FL 33133
Tel. (305) 662–6625

Meditation classes and group practice.

SHAKTI YOGA, Inc.
2315 S.W. 42nd Avenue
Coral Gables, FL 33134
Tel. (305) 444–4321

Shakti Yoga is a Tibetan Buddhist institution for those who are seriously interested in the science of spiritual knowledge. Master Oscar Basurto, Director, offers classes in meditation and physical exercise. Students begin on an individual basis and then are incorporated into groups.

GAINESVILLE ZEN CIRCLE
562 N.E. Second Avenue
Gainesville, FL 32601
Tel. (904) 373–7567

Weekly sittings are open to the public.

JACKSONVILLE DHARMA STUDY GROUP
7405 Arlington Expressway
Jacksonville, FL 32211
Tel. (904) 387–4925

Group meditation practice twice weekly; tranquility meditation classes are taught periodically during the year.

BODHI TREE DHAMMA CENTER
11355 Dauphin Avenue
Largo, FL 34648
Tel. (813) 392–7698

Weekly Vipassana sittings, monthly half-day retreats, and periodic longer intensives.

BRAHMA KUMARIS CENTER
5801 S.W. 42nd Terrace
Miami, FL 33155
Tel. (305) 661–0373

Raja Yoga is both a meditation and a study that examines in a practical way how to establish a clear connection with God, and how to enjoy this in daily life. Silent meditation is the core of Brahma Kumaris's teachings, and each morning students begin the day with meditation and the study of spiritual truths. For more information about Brahma Kumaris, see the National Listings.

YOGASHAKTI MISSION, INC.
3895 Hield Road, N.W.
Palm Bay, FL 32907
Tel. (407) 725–4024

Yoga-oriented teaching inspired by Ma Yogashakti Saraswati.

THE YOGA INSTITUTE OF MIAMI
PO Box 431201
South Miami, FL 33143
Tel. (305) 661–9558

Based on the methods of B.K.S. Iyengar, the Yoga Institute teaches hatha yoga as meditation in action, focused on precision in body awareness.

BRAHMA KUMARIS CENTER
2207 E. Busch Boulevard
Tampa, FL 33612
Tel. (813) 935–0736

For further information, see National Listings.

INTERNATIONAL SOCIETY
FOR KRISHNA CONSCIOUSNESS
13821 N. 37th Street
Tampa, FL 33613
Tel. (813) 977–0026

Regular free programs of meditation and bhakti yoga are offered. There is a free program and vegetarian feast every Sunday at 6:30 PM. Call or write for further information.

TAMPA KARMA TRIYANA DHARMACHAKRA
820 S. MacGill
Tampa, FL 33609
Tel. (813) 870–2904

Members meet weekly throughout the year; weekend and 30-day retreats are scheduled from time to time. Activities are open to the public, but visitors are asked to telephone in advance.

GEORGIA

ATLANTA SOTO ZEN CENTER
1404 McLendon Avenue, N.E.
Atlanta, GA 30307
Tel. (404) 659–4749

The Center has a daily schedule of meditation, and

offers an introductory program on Sunday mornings. Two-day intensive retreats are conducted six times a year.

DHARMADHATU OF ATLANTA
1458 Highland Road
Atlanta, GA 30306
Tel. (404) 885–9637

Affiliated with Vajradhatu International, the center offers tranquility meditation instruction and regularly scheduled practice periods twice weekly.

SHAMBHALA TRAINING
Atlanta, GA
Tel. (404) 876–3139

For further information, contact Shambhala Training, Boulder, CO (see Local Listings).

3HO FOUNDATOIN
GURU RAM DAS ASHRAM
112 Millbrook Circle
Roswell, GA 30075
Tel. (404) 993–6633

The Ashram is a center for the teachings of Yogi Bhajan, and offers ongoing classes in Kundalini Yoga and meditation. For more information, see National Listings.

HAWAII

MELE MAUKA CENTER
Box 946
Captain Cook, HI 96704

Daily Ashtanga Yoga sadhana performed in the tradition of K. P. Jols.

EWA SOTOJI
1137 Hulili Street
Ewa, HI 96706

Monthly Sunday morning meditation classes are open to the public.

VIPASSANA HAWAII
882 Nenelea Street
Haliimaile, HI 96796
Tel. (808) 572–0137

Sunday sittings at the center include an instruction period, an hour of silent practice, and a Dhamma talk. Each month there is a full day of mindfulness practice, and throughout the year there are periodic weekend and ten-day retreats. Instruction is in the tradition of Mahasi Sayadaw and U Pandita.

KAGYU THEGCHEN LING
2327 Liloa Rise
Honolulu, HI 96822
Tel. (808) 941–8561

Founded by the Ven. Kalu, Rinpoche, K.T.L. embraces varied meditation practices, selected according to the student's ability, temperament, and background. The center offers chanting and prostration retreats, Vipassana retreats, weekend sittings, and solitary retreats.

NECHUNG DORJE DRAYANG LING
WOOD VALLEY RETREAT CENTER
PO Box 250
Pahala, HI 96777
Tel. (808) 928–8539

Nechung Drayang Ling is a nonsecretarian Buddhist temple and retreat center in Wood Valley on the Island of Hawaii. The temple and retreat were established by the Venerable Nechung Rinpoche in 1973, and frequently hosts visits by high lamas of all lineages of Tibetan

Buddhism. At weekend seminars and month-long intensives, topics range from Buddhist philosophy to esoteric meditation practices. These courses are open to the public, and are announced in the Temple publication, "Drayang." Visitors are welcome to join the daily meditations and special ceremonies held monthly. The main building is a renovated, classic Japanese temple, built at the turn of the century. It is located in a cool, quiet bamboo and eucalyptus forest, at an elevation of 2,000 feet. An excellent library of books on Buddhism, Tibetan culture, and New Age subjects is available to guests. There is also a small book and gift store, with one-of-a-kind items from the East on sale.

IDAHO

THE OPEN PATH
703 N. 18th Street
Boise, ID 83702
Tel. (208) 342–0208

The Open Path offers study groups, workshops, and meditations, and has limited accommodations for those seeking to do private retreats.

KIRPAL ASHRAM
Sagle, ID 83860

For information, contact Sant Bani Ashram, Franklin, NH (see Local Listings).

GOVINDA
801 Church, #3
Sandpoint, ID 83864
Tel. (207) 263–7076

A meditation class and spiritual discussion are offered each Tuesday from 7 to 9 PM.

ILLINOIS

BRAHMA KUMARIS CENTER
7065 Damen Avenue, #2
Chicago, IL 60645
Tel. (312) 262–2828

For further information, see National Listings.

CHICAGO DHARMADHATU
3340 N. Clark Street
Chicago, IL 60657
Tel. (312) 472–7771

Meditation instruction and practice are offered on Thursday evenings from 7:00 to 9:00 PM and on Sunday mornings from 9:00 AM to noon.

HIMALAYAN INSTITUTE
9703 S. Forest
Chicago, IL 60628
Tel. (312) 660–1239

For further information, see the National Listings.

NARAYANANANDA UNIVERSAL YOGA CENTER
2937 N. Southport Avenue
Chicago, IL 60657
Tel. (312) 327–3650

Sri Swami Narayanananda, a sage from India, is the spiritual leader of the Center. Regular hatha yoga classes and group meditation programs are available and open to the public.

THE OASIS CENTER
7463 N. Sheridan Road
Chicago, IL 60626
Tel. (312) 274–6777

The Center was established to provide an environment

.to support the evolution of consciousness—the consciousness of self-awareness and self-responsibility. There are introductory programs, one-day workshops, drop-in events, and one- to two-year training programs.

SHAMBHALA TRAINING
Chicago, IL
Tel. (312) 973–1665

For further information, contact Shambhala Training, Boulder, CO (see Local Listings).

SIVANANDA YOGA VEDANTA CENTER
1246 W. Bryn Mawr
Chicago, IL 60660
Tel. (312) 769–5338

The Center offers classes in yoga, meditation, pranayam, and vegetarian cooking. Daily satsang is open to the public. There is a limited residential program for sincere students.

TEMPLE OF KRIYA YOGA
2414 N. Kedzie Avenue
Chicago, IL 60647
Tel. (312) 342–4600; (800) 248–0024

The Temple provides instruction in beginning, intermediate, and advanced meditation techniques and in hatha yoga. Seminars are offered from time to time by Goswami Kriyananda.

WAT DHAMMARAM
7059 W. 75th Street
Chicago, IL 60638
Tel. (312) 594–8100

Daily morning and evening meditations are open to the public. There is a Buddhist Sunday School program and a course in Vipassana practices which is conducted once every year.

BUDDHADHARMA MEDITATION CENTER
7201 S. Cass Avenue
Darien, IL 60559
Tel. (312) 960–5359

The Center emphasizes the application of the Dharma to everyday life. There are weekend services and meditation sittings, short Vipassana courses, and supervised solitary retreats.

CHICAGO ZEN CENTER
2029 Ridge Avenue
Evanston, IL 60201
Tel. (703) 475–3015

Founded by the Venerable Philip Kapleau, Roshi, and affiliated with the Zen Center, Rochester, NY (see Local Listings).

HIMALAYAN INSTITUTE
1505 Greenwood Road
Glenview, IL 60025
Tel. (312) 724–0300

Swami Rama is the founder and spiritual leader of the Himalayan Institute. See the National Listings for further information about programs.

ZEN BUDDHIST TEMPLE OF CHICAGO
865 Bittersweet Drive
Northbrook, IL 60062
Tel. (312) 272–2070

The Temple provides meditation instruction and practice sessions four days a week. There are monthly weekend-long Soto Zen sesshins.

HIMALAYAN INSTITUTE
109 S. Roselle Road
Schaumburg, IL 60193
Tel. (312) 519–9725

For futher information, see the National Listings.

LIVING TAO FOUNDATION
PO Box 846
Urbana, IL 61801
Tel. (217) 337–6113

Living Tao is a not-for-profit international organization which conducts a full range of cross-cultural events including lecture demonstrations, week- and month-long seminars, concerts, and specialized training courses. The unique core curriculum consists of Tai Ji movement meditation, Qi Gong healing exercises, brush calligraphy, and Taoist and Confucian classics, combined with a parallel diversity of Western disciplines. Under the direction of Tai Ji master artist Chungliang Al Huang, Living Tao provides a common ground for shared learning and personal exchange. The universal concept of Tao is the guiding force for a vision of world peace and harmony; all the programs and activities of Living Tao strive to further the fulfillment of this vision.

THE THEOSOPHICAL SOCIETY IN AMERICA
PO Box 270
Wheaton, IL 60189
Tel. (312) 668–1571

For further information see National Listings.

INDIANA

HIMALAYAN INSTITUTE
2370 E. 52nd Street
Indianapolis, IN 46205
Tel. (317) 253–4700

For further information, see the National Listings.

IOWA

3HO FOUNDATION
GURU RAM DAS ASHRAM
1510 Carrol Street
Boone, IA 50036
Tel. (515) 432–1924

The Ashram is a center for the teachings of Yogi Bhajan, and offers ongoing classes in Kundalini Yoga and meditation. For more information, see National Listings.

VIPASSANA SITTING GROUP
c/o Ray Hock
1920 40th Place
Des Moines, IA 50310

The group meets for weekly sittings on Wednesday evenings at 7:00 PM, at the Thoreau Center in Des Moines.

KANSAS

KANSAS ZEN CENTER
1115 Ohio
Lawrence, KS 66044
Tel. (913) 842–8909

The Center is a residential Zen community, offering daily morning and evening practice and periodic three- to seven-day retreats. There are classes for beginners, and techniques include breath awareness and mantra.

KENTUCKY

LEXINGTON DHARMADHATU
208 Catalpa Road
Lexington, KY 40502
Tel. (606) 266–9714

Meditation practice in the tradition of the Ven. Chogyam Trungpa, Rinpoche.

LEXINGTON ZEN CENTER
345 Jesselin Drive
Lexington, KY 40503
Tel. (606) 277–2438

Daily practice sessions include sitting, bowing, and chanting meditations. Supervised or unsupervised retreats are available monthly.

LOUISIANA

BATON ROUGE DHARMA STUDY GROUP
442 Albert Hart
Baton Rouge, LA 70808
Tel. (504) 766–3126

Meditation practice in the Karma Kagyu lineage of Chogyam Trungpa, Rinpoche.

PERSONAL GROWTH SERVICES
13586 Neil Avenue
Baton Rouge, LA 70810
Tel. (504) 766–7615

Participants in the Personal Growth Services meditation course learn about centering prayer, mantra, the Jesus prayer, Zen, and other approaches. The teachings are presented in the framework of Christian spirituality, but non-Christian participants are free to make their own religious connections. The content of the course includes the study and practice of meditation skills and discussions of the meditative experience. Courses on spirituality and relationship skills are also offered from time to time.

MAINE

KANZEON
33 Ledgelawn Avenue
Bar Harbor, ME 04609
Tel. (207) 288–3569

Genpo Merzel Sensei, Abbot.

DHARMA STUDY GROUP
98 Maine Street
Brunswick, ME 04011
Tel. (207) 729–4204

A Vajradhatu meditation center offering a regular program of group practice and weekly classes.

MORGAN BAY ZENDO
Morgan Bay Road
Surry, ME 04684
Tel. (207) 667–5428

The Zendo offers facilities for solitary retreats. There is a regular schedule of zazen practice and occasional lectures by visiting Buddhist teachers.

MARYLAND

UNITY WOODS YOGA CENTER
4853 Cordell Avenue
Bethesda, MD 20814
Tel. (301) 656–8992

Classes in yoga, meditation, and breathing for students at all levels. The Center also offers weekend intensives and a wide-ranging program of seminars on yoga practice.

AMAR STUDIO
6504 80th Street
Cabin John, MD 20818
Tel. (301) 320–2065

An affiliated center of the Himalayan Institute, Amar Studio offers classes and seminars in meditation, hatha yoga, and yoga philosophy.

WORLD PRAYER CENTER
18400 River Road
Poolesville, MD 20837
Tel. (301) 428–8116

The Center provides bi-weekly classes and monthly retreats, and maintains a constant prayer vigil for the well-being of the earth.

SUNFLOWER YOGA COMPANY
1305 Chalmers Road
Silver Spring, MD 20903
Tel. (301) 445–3882

Yoga and meditation classes and workshops, beach and mountain retreats.

MENGALA RAMA BUDDHIST VIHARA
1708 Powdermill Road
Silver Spring, MD 20903
Tel. (301) 439–4035

A Burmese monastery, offering practices in the tradition of Mahasi Sayadaw. There are weekend and week-long Vipassana retreats, and facilities for solitary retreats.

INTERNATIONAL MEDITATION CENTER/USA
PO Box 314
White Marsh, MD 21162
Tel. (301) 461–8946

The Center offers one weekend retreat each month and four longer meditation courses each year. Practices are taught in the tradition of the Burmese teacher, U Ba Khin.

MASSACHUSETTS

LIVING DHARMA CENTER
Box 304
Amherst, MA 01004
Tel. (413) 259–1611

For information, see Living Dharma Center, Bolton, CT, in the Local Listings.

UNICORN BOOKS
1210 Massachusetts Avenue
Arlington, MA 02174
Tel. (617) 646–3680

As well as being a spiritual book and gift shop, Unicorn serves as a resource center for the local spiritual community, offering classes and workshops on meditation, hatha yoga, and related disciplines. Free introductory programs of meditation and sacred chanting are presented at least four times each year.

THE INSIGHT MEDITATION SOCIETY
Pleasant Street
Barre, MA 01005
Tel. (508) 355–4378

IMS is a meditation center offering scheduled intensive retreats in the Theravadin Buddhist tradition. Weekend, ten-day, and three-month courses are available, as well as work retreats.

MAHA YOGA PUBLICATIONS AND RETREAT
PO Box 9, New Town Branch
Boston, MA 02258

Write for publications and for information regarding

retreats or residence. Maha Yoga offers in-depth experience and study of yogic wisdom, books, meditation, etc.

BRAHMA KUMARIS CENTER
9 Wilson Park, #2
Brighton, MA 02135
Tel. (617) 734–1464

For further information, see National Listings.

SHIM GUM DO ASSOCIATION
203 Chestnut Hill Avenue
Brighton, MA 02135
Tel. (617) 787–1506

Shim Gum Do is a form of active meditation practiced through a combination of martial arts and sitting practice. The Shim Gum Do Association offers instruction and a program of retreats which are open to the public.

NEW AGE TEACHINGS
2-4 Maple Street
PO Box 346
Brookfield, MA 01506
Tel. (508) 867–3754

New Age Teachings offers spiritual guidance channeled through the meditations of Illiana. A monthly bulletin is available upon request.

CAMBRIDGE BUDDHIST ASSOCIATION
75 Sparks Street
Cambridge, MA 02138
Tel. (617) 491–8857

Group sittings and meditation instruction.

CAMBRIDGE INSIGHT MEDITATION CENTER
331 Broadway
Cambridge, MA 02139
Tel. (617) 491–5070

A nonresidential center for the practice of insight meditation, CIMC provides an environment where the contemplative life can be developed and protected amid the
complexities of city living. Larry Rosenberg is the founder
and guiding teacher. The Center offers a regular schedule of classes, retreats, talks, group sittings, and special
programs.

CAMBRIDGE ZEN CENTER
199 Auburn Street
Cambridge, MA 02139
Tel. (617) 576–3329

The Center offers a regular daily schedule of bowing,
sitting, and chanting meditations, monthly retreats, and
bi-weekly interviews with a Dharma teacher. Discourses
every Thursday evening are free and open to the public.

PIONEER VALLEY ZENDO
263 Warnerhill Road
Charlemont, MA 01339
Tel. (413) 339–4000

The Zendo has daily meditation practice, utilizing the
technique of "Shikan-taza," or "just sitting," as taught
by Dogen Zenji. There is a one-day sesshin each Sunday, and a five-day sesshin every month.

VEDANTA CENTRE
ANANDA ASHRAMA
130 Beechwood Street
Cohasset, MA 02025
Tel. (617) 383–0940

For more information see Ananda Ashrama, La Crescenta,
CA, in the Local Listings.

SAMBODHI RAJNEESH NEO-SANNYAS COMMUNE
Conomo Point Road
Essex, MA 01929
Tel. (617) 768–7640

Sambodhi is a commune on the coast of Massachusetts, where disciples of Bhagwan Shree Rajneesh have gathered to meditate, work, and play together. Guests are welcome to visit for a meal or a meditation, a hot tub or a sauna. Wild woods and sea air make it an ideal place for a retreat.

KRIPALU CENTER
PO Box 793, East Road
Lenox, MA 01240
Tel. (413) 637–3280

Founded by the spiritual teacher Yogi Amrit Desai, Kripalu Center is a spiritual community and holistic educational facility located in the beautiful Berkshire Mountains of Western Massachusetts. Offering a wide variety of transformational programs throughout the year in yoga, personal growth, spiritual attunement, and holistic health, Kripalu Center is a nonprofit organization operated by a residential staff of more than 250. Not only do the thousands of guests who visit each year take advantage of retreats, classes, workshops, seminars, and individualized health services, but they also share fully in a unique atmosphere created by those who have dedicated themselves to service and to the maintenance of a balanced yogic lifestyle.

DHARMADHATU
25 Main Street
Northampton, MA 01060
Tel. (413) 584–0974

Chogyam Trungpa Rinpoche, a meditation master of the Kagyu and Nyingma lineages, established the Dharmadhatu Buddhist meditation and study center. Dharmadhatu offers a daily schedule of meditation practice, including occasional all-day meditation sessions. Individual meditation instruction is always available, and there is an ongoing program of open house talks and classes.

YOGA CENTER FOR THE HEALING ARTS, INC.
75 Wendell Avenue
PO Box 1589
Pittsfield, MA 01202
Tel. (413) 442–1823

The Yoga Center offers classes in hatha yoga, meditation, yama and niyama, kriyas and pranayam, as well as workshops in various growth modalities and healing arts.

ANANDA CENTER
c/o Jerry Haslam
PO Box 469
Salem, MA 01970
Tel. (508) 927–5038

For further information see the listing for Ananda World Brotherhood Village, Nevada City, CA in the National Listings.

FULL CIRCLE WORKSHOPS
68 Conway Street
Shelburne Falls, MA 01370
Tel. (413) 625–9587

Full Circle offers a program called Keepers of the Flame, consisting of weekend intensives, bi-weekly meditation/study programs, and community service projects. The spiritual practice of meditation and movement is based on Diane Mariechild's book, *The Inner Dance.* Through meditation and movement, participants develop a strong awareness of body/mind alignment and a link to the dynamic, energizing female principle.

VIPASSANA MEDITATION CENTER
Shelburne-Colrain Road
PO Box 23
Shelburne Falls, MA 01370
Tel. (413) 625–2160

Ten-day Vipassana courses are offered, utilizing the techniques taught by S. N. Goenka. There is no charge for the teachings; donations are accepted only to cover the cost of room and board.

MICHIGAN

ANN ARBOR KARMA THEGSUM CHOLING
734 Fountain
Ann Arbor, MI 48103
Tel. (313) 761–7495

The KTC offers courses in Tibetan meditation techniques and group meditation practice. Lamas from the Karma Kagyu lineage visit regularly.

ZEN BUDDHIST TEMPLE OF ANN ARBOR
1251 Packard Road
Ann Arbor, MI 48104
Tel. (313) 761–6520

Meditation and chanting practice are conducted daily, morning and evening. Scriptural studies are presented in Friday evening sessions and two-month-long summer training sessions. There are one- to three-day sessions five times a year, and a year-round visitor's program.

HEART CENTER KARMA THEGSUM CHOLING
315 Marion Avenue
Big Rapids, MI 49307
Tel. (616) 796–2398

The Center provides instruction and weekly practice sessions in sitting meditation. Facilities are available for private retreats.

SO GETSU-IN
c/o Dan Gerber
Box 39
Fremont, MI 49412

So Getsu-In is a zendo in the Gerbers' home. While they have no formal training program, they do welcome people who would like to come for zazen instruction, for talk about their practice or their interest in practice, or just to sit. So Getsu-In is somewhat remote, and there are no boarding facilities.

MINNESOTA

THE MEDITATION CENTER
631 University Avenue, N.E.
Minneapolis, MN 55413
Tel. (612) 379–2386

The Meditation Center, an affiliated center of the Himalayan Institute, offers classes and seminars in meditation, hatha yoga, and yoga philosophy.

MINNESOTA ZEN MEDITATION CENTER
3343 E. Lake Calhoun Parkway
Minneapolis, MN 55408
Tel. (612) 822–5313

Minnesota Zen Meditation Center is a Soto Zen Practice center under the guidance of Dainin Katagiri Roshi. Regular activities include zazen (two sittings in both morning and evening), chanting services, zazen instruction, one lecture each week, and a family service once a month. Two-day, five-day, and seven-day sesshins are held during the year. Workshops and monastic practice periods are provided at Hokyoji, a monastic and retreat center being developed in southern Minnesota.

TWIN CITIES DHARMA STUDY GROUP
3314 Emerson S.
Minneapolis, MN 55408
Tel. (612) 825–4703

The Group offers Tibetan Vajrayana meditation teachings and Vipassana practice, as well as regularly scheduled courses in Shambhala Training.

YOGA-MEDITATION CENTER
4232 Highview Place
Minnetonka, MN 55345
Tel. (612) 938–1108

Yoga-Meditation Center, an affiliate of Himalayan Institute, offers classes and seminars in meditation, hatha yoga, and yoga philosophy.

ST. PAUL ZENDO
136 Amherst
St. Paul, MN 55705
Tel. (612) 698–8933

The Zendo offers a Sunday evening practice including hatha yoga, discussion, and zazen. The program is open to the public, but participants are expected to commit themselves to regular, weekly attendance.

MISSOURI

KANSAS CITY DHARMA STUDY GROUP
5309 N.W. 59th Terrace
Kansas City, MO 64111
Tel. (816) 487–8260

Meditation sessions on Thursdays at 7:00 PM and Sundays at 9:00 AM. There are monthly introductory programs, to which the public is invited.

ANANDA YOGASHRAMA
PO Box 321
418 Wingate Street
Lee's Summit, MO 64063
Tel. (816) 524–1084

Ananda is a spiritual center offering a course of study in Integral Yoga called "Lessons in Cosmic Union." The lessons were created by Sri Vijnanamaya and Ananda Shanti, and include exercises in Raja Yoga, Kriya Yoga, and Mantra Yoga.

BROTHERHOOD HOUSE
6004 Pershing
St. Louis, MO 63112
Tel. (314) 726–5133

Weekly meditations and cosmic ceremonies.

MISSOURI ZEN CENTER
220 Spring Avenue
St. Louis, MO 63119
Tel. (314) 961–6138

Rosan Yoshida offers zazen practice and bi-monthly Soto Zen sesshins.

MONTANA

3HO FOUNDATION
GURU RAM DAS ASHRAM
421 E. Story Street
Bozeman, MT 59715
Tel. (406) 587–0050

The Ashram is a center for the teachings of Yogi Bhajan, and offers ongiong classes in Kundalini Yoga and meditation. For more information, see National Listings.

OSEL SHEN PHEN LING
PO Box 7604
Missoula, MT 59807
Tel. (406) 542–2110

Meditation practice twice weekly, periodic weekend meditation retreats.

NEBRASKA

KEARNY ZENDO
3715 Avenue F
Kearney, NE 68847
Tel. (308) 236–5650

Kearney Zendo combines the traditional Soto Zen sitting practice with the martial arts disciplines of karate and kobudo. There are daily sittings, and a once-yearly sesshin.

NEBRASKA ZEN CENTER
816 S. 67th Street
Omaha, NE 68106
Tel. (402) 551–4063

Daily sitting and chanting sessions from 5:30 to 6:30 AM.

NEVADA

LIAN HWA TEMPLE
905 N. 21st Street
Las Vegas, NV 89101

A nonsectarian Buddhist group, offering instruction and practice in many forms of meditation.

THE BUILDERS
Box 2121
Oasis, NV 89835
Tel. (702) 478–5112

Norman Paulsen, the founder of The Builders, received a meditation technique from Paramhansa Yogananda that allowed him to experience Christ Consciousness. Individually and as a group, Builders meditate daily using the Sun Meditation Technique. Visitors are welcome to participate in daily meditations and other events.

SILVER MOUNTAIN SANGHA
3060 Sagittarius
Reno, NV 89504
Tel. (702) 786–1484

The Sangha offers group meditations and Zen chanting each Sunday.

NEW HAMPSHIRE

NEW CANAAN ACADEMY
Canaan Street
Canaan, NH 03741
Tel. (603) 523–4385

Classes in T'ai Chi Ch'uan and daily zazen meditation.

SANT BANI ASHRAM
Franklin, NH 03235
Tel. (609) 934–5640

Sant Bani Ashram, founded by and dedicated to Param
Sant Kirpal Singh (who left his earthly body in 1974),
is the international headquarters of the ashrams cur-
rently under the spiritual guidance of Sant Ajaib Singh,
a disciple of Kirpal Singh. Sant Bani offers initiation
into the path of Surat Shabdh Yoga, a path of love and
discipline that embraces the essence of the teachings of
all True Masters. Santi Bani Ashram has six retreat
centers in the United States and Canada. For their locations, see the Local Listings or write to the international
headquarters. Call to arrange for visits.

NEW JERSEY

SIDDHACHALAM
ACHARYA SUSHIL JAIN ASHRAM
RD #4, Box 374
Blairstown, NJ 07824
Tel. (201) 362–9793

Located near the scenic Pocono Mountains, this 108-acre
ashram provides a peaceful environment for the study
and practice of the science of Arhum Yoga, based on
the teachings of the Jain tradition. Siddhachalam offers
retreats, seminars, and summer camps for adults and
children, in such topics as meditation, Kundalini Yoga,
and Jain philosophy.

ZEN TEMPLE OF CRESSKILL
185 6th Street
Cresskill, NJ 07626
Tel. (201) 567–7468

Directed by Dr. Sun-ock Lee, a Korean choreographer,
the Temple offers teachings in the techniques of Zen
dance. Courses emphasize breathing exercises, concentration, mantra, and dance movements.

YOGA MEDITATION SOCIETY OF NEW JERSEY
29 Washington Street
Morristown, NJ 07960
Tel. (201) 540–1677

Classes in meditation, hatha yoga, diet, and nutrition.

SHANTI YOGA INSTITUTE
947 Asbury Avenue
Ocean City, NJ 08226
Tel. (609) 399–1974

Seminars and instruction in all aspects of yoga are
offered by Yogi Shanti Desai in this oceanside retreat.
There is a natural foods store which offers holistic and
·yogic items and the publications of Yogi Shanti Desai.

SRI CENTRE INTERNATIONAL
PO Box 3016
Princeton, NJ 08540
Tel. (201) 359–7383

See Sri Centre, New York, NY, in the Local Listings.

LIFE QUEST
335 Johnson Avenue
River Edge, NJ 07661
Tel. (201) 342–8133

Life Quest, which calls itself "A Center for Positive
Living," provides an extensive program of workshops

and seminars on meditation, kundalini yoga, t'ai chi, and related New Age topics. There is a weekly group meditation, and a children's meditation program, including both instruction and practice, takes place each Saturday. Call or write for a catalog of courses.

TIBETAN BUDDHIST LEARNING CENTER
Rt. 1, Box 306A
Washington, NJ 07882

The TBLC's objective is to convey to its students a basic knowledge of the many facets of Tibetan Buddhism. Write to the Center for details about seminars and about twice-monthly prayer and meditation services and classes.

NEW MEXICO

KARMA THEGSUM CHOLING
139 La Plata N.W.
Albuquerque, NM 87107
Tel. (505) 344-7611

A Tibetan Buddhist meditation center, offering regular evening practices on Tuesdays and Sundays, new and full moon meditations, and special children's classes on Sunday mornings. A three-week meditation course is offered each month.

JEMEZ BODHI MANDALA
PO Box 8
Jemez Springs, NM 87025
Tel. (505) 829-3854

A Rinzai Zen center offering a daily program of zazen, chanting, and work practice. Each spring and fall there are two- to three-month extended training sesshins; shorter retreats are offered throughout the year for students at all levels of practice.

ZEN CENTER OF LAS CRUCES
3810 Paradise Lane
Las Cruces, NM 88005
Tel. (505) 525–2329

Meditation and chanting practice three times a week.

LAMA FOUNDATION
Box 240
San Cristobal, NM 87564
Tel. (505) 586–1269

During the summer, Lama Foundation hosts meditation retreats and other workshops led by teachers from different traditions and disciplines. It is open to visitors on selected days during the year.

KAGYU SHENPEN KUNCHAB
751 Airport Road
Santa Fe, NM 87501
Tel. (505) 471–1152

A residential Dharma center, offering daily meditations in the shrine room of the stupa.

MOUNTAIN CLOUD ZEN CENTER·
Rt. 7, Box 125
Santa Fe, NM 87505
Tel. (505) 988–4396

The Center provides regularly-scheduled meditation and chanting sessions, "Beginner's Nights," and extended sittings. Roshi Philip Kapleau, author of *The Three Pillars of Zen*, is the Resident Director of the Center and gives *teisho* and *dokusan* from time to time.

NEW YORK

SACRED MOUNTAIN HEALING CENTER
106 Philip Street
Albany, NY 12210
Tel. (518) 465–6483

Jack Allison offers a variety of courses, including T'ai Chi Ch'uan, Rebirthing, and A Course in Miracles.

UNIVERSAL LIFE
3101 Grand Boulevard
Baldwin, NY 11510
Tel. (516) 867–6632

Those who are interested in learning from the revelations of the Divine Spirit and from each other are invited to attend Inner Spirit meetings on the second and fourth Friday of each month. Phone for the time and location of the meetings.

UNIVERSAL LIFE
150 W. 225th Street, #7F
Bronx, NY 10463
Tel. (212) 562–6947

At the heart of Universal Life is the Christian Mystery School, called into being by Christ to teach the direct and perfect inner path to God. Students come together on the second and fourth Friday of each month in gatherings called "the Inner Spirit of Christ Church." Phone for the time and location of the meetings.

HIMALAYAN INSTITUTE
841 Delaware Avenue
Buffalo, NY 14209
Tel. (716) 883–2223

For further information, see the National Listings.

ARUNACHALA ASHRAMA
72-63 Yellowstone Boulevard
Forest Hills, Queens, NY 11375
Tel. (718) 575–3215

An ashram based on the teachings of Bhagavan Sri Ramana Maharshi. For additional information see the listing for Arunachala Ashrama, Bridgetown, Nova Scotia, Canada in the Local Listings.

METTA FOUNDATION
Nelson Lane
Garrison, NY 10524
Tel. (914) 424–4071

Group sittings are held each Wednesday at 8:00 PM. Meditation instruction in the Theravadin tradition is available, and one- to seven-day Vipassana retreats are held several times a year. All of the group's activities are open to the public at no charge.

URGYEN CHO DZONG
Box 555
Greenville, NY 12083
Tel. (518) 966–4727

A practice center located in the Catskill Mountains, offering seminars and retreats for beginning and advanced students. The teachings emphasize visualization and breathing practices. Facilities are available for supervised solitary retreats.

NEW YORK BUDDHIST VIHARA
84-32 124th Street
Kew Gardens, NY 11415
Tel. (718) 849–2637

Meditation practice is offered every Saturday afternoon, and there are frequent short Vipassana courses, monthly Dhamma programs, and opportunities for supervised or unsupervised solitary retreats. The Shrine Room at the Vihara is available for devotional and meditational use.

THE ZEN STUDIES SOCIETY
DAI BOSATSU ZENDO KONGOJI
HCR 1, Box 80
Lew Beach, NY 12753
Tel. (914) 439–4566

Dai Bosatsu Zendo is a Rinzai Zen Buddhist monastery dedicated to a strong and compassionate Zen practice by both ordained and lay Dharma students. Located in 1400 acres of maple forest high in the Catskill Mountains, Dai Bosatsu Zendo offers two three-month training periods a year, each including three seven-day sesshins as well as shorter programs. The monastery is open at all times for visits by serious students who wish to come and practice for a weekend, a week, or longer. In addition to a strong, authentic Rinzai Zen practice under the guidance of Eido Shimano, Roshi, there is also a strong program of yoga asana designed to purify the body as the mind is purified through the practice of zazen and the other Paramitas.

VAJIRADHAMMAPADIP TEMPLE
75 California Road
Mount Vernon, NY 10552
Tel. (914) 699–5778

There are group meditations each evening from 7:00 to 9:00 PM, and occasional seven-day Samma Arahang retreats. Both are open to the general public.

MATAGIRI
Mt. Tremper, NY 12457
Tel. (914) 679–8322

Matagiri is a small retreat center in the Catskill Mountains west of Woodstock, NY, which is dedicated to the experiment of living the teachings of Sri Aurobindo.

There is a large library of books and periodicals by and about Sri Aurobindo and The Mother. Visitors are welcome by appointment, and overnight guests can be accommodated for short stays. Contact Matagiri for room and board fees and dates.

> *The sadhana of this Yoga does not proceed through any set mental teaching or prescribed form of meditation, mantras or others, but by aspiration, by a self-concentration inwards or upwards, by self-opening to an Influence, to the Divine Power in the heart, and by rejection of all that is foreign to these things. It is only by faith, aspiration and surrender that this self-opening can come.*
>
> —*Sri Aurobindo*

ZEN MOUNTAIN MONASTERY
PO Box 197
Mt. Tremper, NY 12457
Tel. (914) 688–2228

Zen teacher Sensei Daido Loori leads authentic Zen practice through residential training in this Catskills monastery. Sensei Loori provides direct personal spiritual guidance, which, combined with the monastery's daily schedule of meditation, chanting, work, art, and body practice, makes residency a transformative experience.

CHOGYE INTERNATIONAL ZEN CENTER
OF NEW YORK
400 E. 14th Street #2E
New York, NY 10009
Tel. (212) 353–0461

The Chogye Zen Center offers daily meditation and chanting practice and weekly public talks. There is a monthly day-long or weekend-long retreat.

FIRST ZEN INSTITUTE OF AMERICA
113 E. 30th Street
New York, NY 10016
Tel. (212) 686–2520

The First Zen Institute is a Rinzai Zen center with a regular schedule of zazen and sesshins for members. Meditation instruction is available. Persons who wish information should come on Wednesdays at 7:30 PM. Mail inquiries should include a stamped, self-addressed envelope.

HIMALAYAN INSTITUTE
AT EAST-WEST BOOKS
78 Fifth Avenue
New York, NY 10011
Tel. (212) 243–5994

For further information, see the National Listings.

INDO-AMERICAN YOGA-VEDANTA SOCIETY
330 W. 58th Street
New York, NY 10019
Tel. (212) 265–7719

Classes in yoga asanas, pranayama, chanting, and mantra meditation, and lectures by Swami Bua.

JAIN MEDITATION INTERNATIONAL CENTER
PO Box 270
Radio City Station
New York, NY 10101
Tel. (212) 765–2232

Jain philosophy is based on a deep reverence for all life and belief in the perfectibility of the soul. Programs at the Center are led by Gurudev Chitrabhanu, the first Jain master to teach in the West. Write for a schedule of programs.

KARGYU DSAMLING KUNCHAB
35 W. 19th Street, 5th Floor
New York, NY 10011

Lama Norlha, resident teacher. Meetings Wednesday nights, 7:30 PM. Tibetan language classes. For more information on centers under the guidance of Lama Kalu Rinpoche, write to Kagyu Kunkhyab Chuling, 4941 Sidley St. Burnaby, BC, Canada V5J 1T6.

NEW YORK BUDDHIST CHURCH
332 Riverside Drive
New York, NY 10025
Tel. (212) 678–0305

Chartered in 1938, the New York Buddhist Church represents the Shin (Pure Land) school of Buddhism, and is affiliated with the Buddhist Churches of America in San Francisco. The Church is located on Riverside Drive between 105th and 106th Streets. Services are offered in English every Sunday at 11:30 AM.

NEW YORK OPEN CENTER, INC.
83 Spring Street
New York, NY 10012
Tel. (212) 219–2527

The Open Center offers workshops, classes, and evening events in such areas as health and healing, spiritual traditions, psychology, and the arts. There are ongoing classes and weekend workshops on meditation, and a meditation room which is open to the public on a daily basis. Call or write for information and a free catalog.

SHAMBHALA TRAINING
New York, NY
Tel. (212) 683–6671

For further information, contact Shambhala Training, Boulder, CO (see Local Listings).

SIVANANDA YOGA VEDANTA CENTER
243 W. 24th Street
New York, NY 10011
Tel. (212) 255–4560

The Center offers classes in yoga, meditation, pranayam, and vegetarian cooking. Daily satsang is open to the public. There is a limited residential program for sincere students.

SRI CENTRE INTERNATIONAL
PO Box 2927
Rockefeller Center Station
New York, NY 10185
Tel. (212) 486–1277

Under the guidance of Shyam Bhatnagar, Sri Centre is dedicated to the spiritual, emotional, and physical growth of the individual through individually-designed inner tuning programs. The programs include instruction in meditation, self-massage, and movements for body awareness.

THE ZEN STUDIES SOCIETY
NEW YORK ZENDO SHOBO-JI
223 E. 67th Street
New York, NY 10021
Tel. (212) 861–3333

The Zen Studies Society, which operates under the guidance of Eido Tai Shimano Roshi, maintains two zendos (training centers), an urban temple in Manhattan, and a monastery in the Catskill Mountains. (See separate listing for Dai Bosatsu Zendo Kongoji in Lew Beach, NY.) Founded in 1968, New York Zendo continues to provide a strong tradition of zazen practice in the Rinzai Zen tradition. The yearly schedule includes two five-month training periods, including five weekend sesshins (retreats), two workshops, and an ongoing class in Buddhist Studies. In addition to daily zazen meetings and services, a public meeting is held each Thursday night, at which time newcomers can get basic zazen instruction. All training programs are conducted under the supervision of the Resident Director, a monk trained at our mountain monastery. The emphasis at New York Zendo is on lay practice, with virtually all of its members living and working in New York and the surrounding metropolitan areas. Nevertheless, all serious students are expected to spend some period of time in training at our mountain monastery each year.

THE ZEN CENTER
7 Arnold Park
Rochester, NY 14607
Tel. (716) 473–9180

The Ven. Bodhin Kjolhede, Sensei, successor to the Ven. Philip Kapleau, Roshi, teaches an Integral Zen grounded in the doctrines and disciplines of both the Soto and Rinzai sects, which includes koan practice for experienced students. The Rochester center offers a daily schedule of meditation and chanting with periodic sesshins. Introductory workshops (participation in which is a prerequisite for attending sesshin) are also available. Write for the location of the nearest affiliate center.

INNERLIGHT CENTER
1 Tower Place
PO Box 295
Roslyn, NY 11576
Tel. (516) 484–5384

Calling itself "Long Island's only full-time nondenominational center," Innerlight presents a full range of classes and workshops in meditation, t'ai chi, yoga, and healing arts. There are weekly meditation sessions, and a monthly full moon meditation utilizing Shree Rajneesh's "chaotic meditation" technique.

WON KAK SA BUDDHIST TEMPLE
301-A Clove Road
Salisbury Mills, NY 12577
Tel. (914) 496–4165

Zen meditation and study groups at Won Kak Sa Temple follow the traditions of the Korean Chogye Order, incorporating koan practice, mantra, and breath awareness. The Thursday evening meditation practice and lecture are open to the public.

LONG ISLAND ZEN CENTER
6 Brewster Court
Setauket, NY 11733
Tel. (516) 751–8408

The Zen Center offers twice-weekly sittings and instruction for beginners.

MA YOGASHAKTI MISSION
114-23 Lefferts Boulevard
South Ozone Park, NY 11420
Tel. (718) 322–5856 or (718) 641–0402

Yoga-oriented teaching inspired by Ma Yogashakti Saraswati.

THE BRIDGE, NORTH
10 Locust Avenue
Southampton, NY 11968
Tel. (516) 283–6839

The Bridge offers classes and workshops in methods of utilizing energy to release personal blocks and contact the God-energy within. The techniques taught are a synthesis of many methods, including insight meditation, chanting, and kundalini yoga.

ZEN COMMUNITY OF NEW YORK
114 Woodworth Street
Yonkers, NY 10701
Tel. (914) 375–1510

Tetsugen Glassman Sensei, Abbot.

NORTH CAROLINA

CHAPEL HILL ZEN GROUP
307 Cameron Avenue
Chapel Hill, NC 27516
Tel. (919) 967–9256

Tuesday evening zazen, including sitting and walking meditation.

DURHAM YOGA AND MEDITATION CENTER
1214 Broad Street
Durham, NC 27705
Tel. (919) 286–4754

The "Center" is comprised of a group of meditators who meet each week at the homes of various members for yoga and meditation classes. Weekend, week-long, and ten-day retreats are offered from time to time throughout the year.

SQUIRREL MOUNTAIN ZENDO
Rt. 5, Box 114
Pittsboro, NC 27312
Tel. (919) 542–4379

Sunday zazen, following the forms taught by Joshu Sasaki-Roshi.

PIEDMONT ZEN GROUP
3805 Greenleaf Street
Raleigh, NC 27606
Tel. (919) 833–6200

Zazen practice is offered several times each week; there are occasional half-day or one-day Zen sittings.

THE SHRI SHIVABALAYOGI MAHARAJ CHARITABLE TRUST
816 Vermont Street
Smithfield, NC 27577
Tel. (919) 934–3534

The meditation master Shri Shri Shri Shivabalayogi Maharaj of Bangalore, India, visits the United States annually to initiate interested aspirants into meditation. Initiation is solely for the deepening of meditation; initiates may follow the spiritual paths of their choice. Shivabalayogi's blessing helps to deepen the inner search for God, and can lead to God Realization. There is never a charge for his blessing. For further information, contact Minu Durgesh Kumari.

OHIO

THE LIGHT CENTER
PO Box 29672
Columbus, OH 43229
Tel. (614) 890–3324

Weekly meditation class and practice, utilizing the A. A. Bailey material, and monthly full moon meditations.

OM-ON-O
548 W. Steeles Cross Road
Cuyahoga Falls, OH 44223
Tel. (216) 929–3804

Weekly meditation each Friday at 9:00 PM.

CLEVELAND BUDDHIST TEMPLE
1573 E. 214th Street
Euclid, OH 44117
Tel. (216) 692–1509

The Zen Shin Sangha, sponsored by the Cleveland Buddhist Temple, offers meditation practice every Tuesday evening (for beginning students) and every Wednesday evening (for advanced students). Sitting, walking, and chanting meditation practices are taught. There are monthly one-day sessions and occasional weekend sittings.

OKLAHOMA

UNIVERSAL GREAT BROTHERHOOD
4133 N.W. 23rd Street
Oklahoma City, OK 73107
Tel. (405) 942–0042

Weekly meditations and cosmic ceremonies.

NATIONAL ASSOCIATION OF
METAPHYSICAL EXPLORATION
6320 S. Peoria
Tulsa, OK 74136
Tel. (918) 744–6767

Weekly discussions, lectures, and meditation practice.

OREGON

KEN KEYES COLLEGE
790 Commercial Avenue
Coos Bay, OR 97420
Tel. (503) 267–6412

Ken Keyes College (formerly Cornucopia Institute in St. Mary, KY) was founded by Ken Keyes, Jr., author of *Handbook to Higher Consciousness.* The approach of Living Love and the Science of Happiness is that our separateness and unhappiness are primarily caused by the demands we make on ourselves, other people, and the world in general. Because our expectations are based on our inner models of how things "should" be, we are constantly disappointed by ourselves and others. Ken

Keyes College offers workshops that teach participants how to experience increasingly effective levels of unconditional love and happiness in their daily lives. The teachings are nondenominational, and universal in their practical application.

CENTER FOR SACRED SCIENCES
5405 Donald Street
Eugene, OR 97405
Tel. (503) 687–0148

Meditation and talk every Sundy morning, 11:00 AM.

EUGENE BUDDHIST PRIORY
2255 Hilyard Street
Eugene, OR 97405
Tel. (503) 344–7377

The Eugene Buddhist Priory is a church dedicated to the practice of Serene Reflection Meditation (Chinese: Ts'ao-tung; Japanese: Soto Zen) as taught by the Order of Buddhist Contemplatives at Shasta Abbey in Mt. Shasta, CA (see Local Listings). The Priory's meditation hall is open to the public on Tuesday, Wednesday, and Thursday from 10:00 AM to 5:00 PM and on Saturday from 10:30 AM to 3:30 PM. Anyone is welcome to stop in and meditate during those hours; however, the Priory asks that only those who have received meditation instruction attend scheduled meditation services or one-day retreats. The Priory maintains a Buddhist library and bookshop.

EUGENE VIPASSANA GROUP
2441 Emerald
Eugene, OR 97403
Tel. (503) 683–6280

Weekly walking and sitting meditation practice, and monthly discussion groups.

KAGYU DAKSHANG CHULING
84443 Murdock Road
Eugene, OR 97405
Tel. (503) 485–3961

Tibetan Buddhist practices.

SATHYA SAI BABA GROUP
4466 Fox Hollow Road
Eugene, OR 97405
Tel. (503) 484–9373

Gatherings each Thursday evening at 7:00 PM are open to the public.

SIDDHA MEDITATION CENTER
1628 Lawrence Street
Eugene, OR 97401
Tel. (503) 686–1917

Siddha meditation gatherings are held each Thursday evening at 7:30 PM. They are free and open to the public.

SIKH DHARMA/3HO FOUNDATION
3635 Hilyard
Eugene, OR 97405
Tel. (503) 686–0432

The Sikh Dharma is a center for the teachings of Yogi Bhajan, and offers ongoing classes in yoga and meditation.

TIME TO LIVE
244 S.E. 2nd Avenue
Hillsboro, OR 97123
Tel. (503) 648–1794

Time to Live is a New Age/Metaphysical store offering classes in relaxation, meditation, and related topics.

SHAMBHALA
1644 N.E. Highway 101
Lincoln City, OR 97367
Tel. (503) 994-2488

Shambhala is a nonprofit spiritual center located on
the central Oregon coast. Ishvara, the spiritual leader
of the center, encourages people to discover a deeper
awareness and a greater consciousness of themselves
and those around them. He invites students to view
life as it is: a creative opportunity to become more
unlimited, more unconditional, more One. Meditations and talks with Ishvara are held three times
a week; cassette tapes of these programs are available by mail on request. The center is open daily
from 10:00 AM to 6:00 PM, and all visitors are
welcome.

ANANDA FELLOWSHIP OF
INNER COMMUNION
16200 N.W. Elliot Road
Portland, OR 97231
Tel. (503) 621-3731

Founded by Sri Kriyananda, Ananda Fellowship offers
ongoing classes in Raja Yoga (meditation, yoga, etc.)
based on the teachings of Paramhansa Yogananda.
Other courses are also available, in addition to Sunday
Services and the Festival of Light. For further information see the listing for Ananda World Brotherhood
Village, Nevada City, CA, in the National Listings.

THE CHAPEL OF LIGHT CHURCH
10422 S.E. Division Street
Portland, OR 97266
Tel. (503) 761-3267

The Chapel of Light is a Christian metaphysical church, providing meditation classes, channeled lectures, and discussion groups.

DHARMA STUDY GROUP
2221 N.E. 53rd
Portland, OR 97213
Tel. (503) 281–4993

The Dharma Study Group was founded by the Ven. Chogyam Trungpa Rinpoche, and offers meditation instruction and practice, and classes in Tibetan Buddhism.

HEALING RESOURCES
815 S.W. Second Avenue, #310
Portland, OR 97204
Tel. (503) 228–3081

Weekly group meditation sessions.

INSIGHT SEMINARS
917 S.W. Oak Street, #420
Portland, OR 97205
Tel. (503) 223–9331

Meditation training is available through individual instruction, classes, and retreats.

KAGYU CHANGCHUB CHULING
73 N.E. Monroe
Portland, OR 97212
Tel. (503) 284–6697

Kagyu Changchub Chuling, established in 1974 by the Ven. Kalu Rinpoche, is a center for the study and practice of traditional Tibetan Buddhism. Lama Tinley Drupa, a teacher trained by Kalu Rinpoche, leads regularly-scheduled group meditations and is available for personal consultation.

NEW RENAISSANCE BOOKSHOP
1388 N.W. 23rd Avenue
Portland, OR 97210
Tel. (503) 224–4929

The Ananda Center of Portland, which follows the teachings of Paramhansa Yogananda, offers meditation practice and courses in meditation and yoga at New Renaissance.

OREGON ZEN PRIORY
2539 S.E. Madison
Portland, OR 97214
Tel. (503) 239–4846

The Priory is a Soto Zen Buddhist Church established in 1973 to serve the spiritual needs of lay trainees. Roshi Kyogen Carlson oversees a regular schedule of meditation, classes, retreats, and Buddhist ceremonies. There is a free introductory meditation workshop offered each month.

PORTLAND BUDDHIST PRIORY
1504 S.E. 138th Avenue
Portland, OR 97233
Tel. **(503) 232–0508**

Affiliated with Shasta Abbey in Mt. Shasta, CA (see Local Listings).

THE YOGA STUDIO
1017 S.W. Morrison
Portland, OR 97205
Tel. (503) 227–1726

Classes in meditation, hatha yoga, and kundalini are available for students at all levels.

PENNSYLVANIA

THE CENTER FOR HEALTH ENHANCEMENT
723 S. State Street
Clarks Summit, PA 18411
Tel. (717) 587–4944

The Center for Health Enhancement offers classes and seminars in meditation, hatha yoga, and yoga philosophy.

THE SEARCH AT NORTHEON FOREST
Northeon Forest
RD 4, Box 517
Easton, PA 18042
Tel. (215) 258–9559

The Search attracts those who find that they must look for truth within themselves, without the overt distortion of the normal context of their daily lives. There is a meeting for aspirants every Sunday, 6:00 to 7:00 PM.

B'NAI OR RELIGIOUS FELLOWSHIP
6723 Emlen Street
Philadelphia, PA 19119
Tel. (215) 849–5385

Founded and guided by Rabbi Zalman Schachter-Shalomi, B'nai Or is a nonprofit Jewish fellowship based on the mystical traditions of the Kabbalah and Hasidism. It offers training in meditation, liturgy, chanting, and spiritual leadership on a lay and professional level.

INTERNATIONAL SOCIETY OF DIVINE LOVE
234 W. Upsala Street
Philadelphia, PA 19119
Tel. (215) 842–0300

The International Society of Divine Love, founded by Swami Prakashanand Saraswati, has two main objectives: to spread the knowledge of such traditional scriptures as the Vedas and the Gita, and to teach the process of

Divine upliftment called Divine-Love-Consciousness. Through devotional meditation, the power of the God-head that lies dormant in every human heart is enlivened and its blissfulness dawns in the mind. This is called Divine-Love-Consciousness. Divine names are used for meditation, through internal remembrance or through chanting.

PHILADELPHIA BUDDHIST ASSOCIATION
138 Gorgas Lane
Philadelphia, PA 19119
Tel. (215) 247–3516

The Association offers twice-weekly evening sittings, monthly day-long sittings, introductory workshops, and special celebrations of Buddhist holidays.

ZEN CENTER OF PHILADELPHIA
214 Monroe Street
Philadelphia, PA 19147
Tel. (215) 625–2601

Located near Philadelphia's Center City, the Zen Center is open to the public weekday mornings and evenings. In addition to its daily schedule, the zendo offers a program of workshops and of weekend, week-long, and month-long sesshins. The zendo is under the guidance of the Rev. William B. Lee Milton, a Zen Buddhist monk. Call or write for further information.

HIMALAYAN INSTITUTE
PO Box 6221
Pittsburgh, PA 15212
Tel. (412) 431–6548

For further information, see the National Listings.

HOLY SHANKARACHARYA ORDER
RD 3, PO Box 3430
Stroudsburg, PA 18360
Tel. (717) 629–0481

The Holy Shankaracharya Order was founded in India in the 9th century by the mystic Adi Shankara. The "Ashram Retreat Program" offered by the Order encompasses meditation, Hatha Yoga, spiritual disciplines, and Karma Yoga.

RHODE ISLAND

THE PROVIDENCE ZEN CENTER
528 Pound Road
Cumberland, RI 02864
Tel. (401) 658–1464

Daily practice in meditation and chanting is open to all.

BUDDHIST TEMPLE OF NEW ENGLAND
178 Hanover Street
Providence, RI 02907
Tel. (401) 273–0969

In the Cambodian lineage, the Temple offers morning and noon chanting and Vipassana meditation practice.

THE MEDITATION PLACE
168 Fourth Street
Providence, RI 02906
Tel. (401) 274–4026

The Meditation Place offers instruction and group practice in a relaxed, nondenominational atmopshere. There is a morning meditation every day, several evening sittings each week, and monthly day-long retreats.

TENNESSEE

3HO FOUNDATION
2917 Deanview Drive
Knoxville, TN 37920
Tel. (615) 579–0582

The 3HO Foundation follows the teachings of Yogi Bhajan, and offers ongoing classes in Kundalini Yoga and meditation. For more information, see the National Listings.

BUDDHIST TEMPLE
230 Treutland Street
Nashville, TN 37212

Insight Meditation instructions by the Ven. U Indika and U Vimala.

SADHANA ASHRAM
PO Box 359A
Sevierville, TN 37862
Tel. (615) 428–0426

Daily meditation practice and satsang.

TEXAS

SCHOOL OF AGELESS WISDOM
6005 Royaloak Drive
Arlington, TX 76016
Tel. (817) 654–1018

Monthly full moon meditations.

SHAMBHALA TRAINING
Austin, TX
Tel. (512) 835–6730

For further information, contact Shambhala Training, Boulder, CO (see Local Listings).

THE YOGA CENTER
1710 Houston Street
Austin, TX 78756
Tel. (512) 454-7448

An affiliated center of the Himalayan Institute, the Yoga Center offers classes and seminars in meditation, hatha yoga, and yoga philosophy.

DALLAS-FORT WORTH ZEN CENTER
3602 Cole Avenue
Dallas, TX 75204
Tel. (214) 521-9408

The Center is an affiliate of Rinzai-Ji, and most members of the sangha are students of Joshu Sasaki-Roshi. The Center offers daily meditation, chanting, instruction, and work practice, and weekends of intensive zazen practice.

SHEPHERD'S BUSH CENTRE
c/o Carol Frost
5416 Gaston Avenue
Dallas, TX 75214
Tel. (214) 823-0292

The Centre teaches classes in meditation, self-improvement, prayer work, and healing. It is open to new members. The facilities are urban, with a rural retreat center in New Mexico.

HIMALAYAN INSTITUTE
3833 Diamond Loch W.
Fort Worth, TX 76118
Tel. (817) 589-1484

For further information, see the National Listings.

ESOTERIC PHILOSOPHY CENTER
9441 Roark
Houston, TX 77099
Tel. (713) 271–1863

Seven-week classes taught at the center include meditation, tarot, and astrology. Full moon meditations are conducted each month.

TEXAS BUDDHIST ASSOCIATION
13210 Land Road
Houston, TX 77047
Tel. (713) 434–0211

Meditation practice on Thursdays and Saturdays; monthly weekend sittings.

THE YOGA INSTITUTE
2150 Portsmouth
Houston, TX 77098
Tel. (713) 526-6674

The Yoga Institute offers classes and weekend intensives. Techniques taught include Hatha Yoga, an eclectic variety of meditation methods, relaxation, and breath and body awareness. Books and meditation supplies are available in the Institute's New Age Bookstore.

BRAHMA KUMARIS CENTER
710 Marquis
San Antonio, TX 78216
Tel. (512) 344–8343

For further information, see National Listings.

TRIYANA MEDITATION GROUP
OF SAN ANTONIO
406 Olney Drive
San Antonio, TX 78209
Tel. (512) 826–1971

A heterogeneous Buddhist meditation group, practicing mindfulness meditation and breath awareness.

UTAH

THE BUILDERS
Clearbrook Center
576 E. Vine, #3B
Salt Lake City, UT 84107
Tel. (801) 268–4240

Norman Paulsen, the founder of The Builders, received a meditation technique from Paramhansa Yogananda that allowed him to experience Christ Consciousness. Individually and as a group, Builders meditate daily using the Sun Meditation Technique. Visitors are welcome to participate in daily meditations and other events.

DHARMA STUDY GROUP
1167 E. 200 South
Salt Lake City, UT 84102
Tel. (801) 583–1272

An affiliate of Vajradhatu International, the study group meets weekly for sitting meditation.

FERTILE GROUND CENTER
274 E. 9th South
Salt Lake City, UT 84111
Tel. (801) 521–8124

Weekly classes and monthly workshops are offered in meditation, deep breathing, t'ai chi, and guided visualization. There are also "Earth Meditations," in which participants go into nature, in silence, and allow the earth to lead the meditative practice. Although meetings and classes are open to all, there is special emphasis on working with women and women's spirituality, and some activities (such as the Medicine Woman Retreat, Channeling the Goddess Within, and the Shadow Woman Dance Workshop) are designed particularly for them.

GOLDEN BRAID BOOKS
213 E. 300 South
Salt Lake City, UT 84111
Tel. (801) 322–1162

Since 1983, Golden Braid has functioned as a spiritual resource center, with a focus on self-healing, self-discovery, and self-enlightenment. Seminars, workshops, and meditation practice are offered regularly by teachers from a variety of traditions, and both old and new students are welcome.

GURU RAM DAS ASHRAM
AND 3HO YOGA CENTER
1955 S. 800 East
Salt Lake City, UT 84105
Tel. (801) 466–5001

Healthy, Happy, Holy (3HO) Foundation is a scientific, educational, and spiritual organization founded by Yogi Bhajan. Its philosophy affirms that human beings can use exercise, breath, and meditation to revitalize the physical body and to bring balance and peace to life. The 3HO Yoga Center offers classes and workshops in kundalini yoga and meditation, as well as in male-female relationships, child-rearing, pregnancy and birth preparation, and related topics. Classes are available for both beginners and advanced students, and are open to all. Write or phone the 3HO Yoga Center for a copy of the current class schedule.

NEEM KAROLI BABA SATSANG
611 S. 1300 East
Salt Lake City, UT 84102
Tel. (801) 582–7306

Weekly gatherings focused on the teachings of Ram Dass's guru, Neem Karoli Baba.

PERSON HUMAN
2161 Regent Street, #16
Salt Lake City, UT 84115
Tel. (801) 484–7352

Person Human offers courses and workshops throughout
the year, as well as books, tapes, and private consulta-
tions to aid the individual on the path of spiritual enlightenment. Courses include meditation, hatha yoga,
the chakras, dream analysis, and an in-depth study of
ancient Hindu spiritual texts (such as the Bhagavad Gita
and the Upanishads). Classes are available for the beginner as well as the advanced seeker of truth.

SIDDHA YOGA MEDITATION CENTER
382 L Street
Salt Lake City, UT 84103
Tel. (801) 355–6085

Chanting and meditation are the main practices in Siddha
Yoga. Instruction and practice in both are offered each
Tuesday evening at the Sidddha Yoga Meditation Center. All are warmly welcomed. For more information,
see the National Listings.

WASATCH ZEN CENTER
1118 E. 1700 South
Salt Lake City, UT 84105
Tel. (801) 485–7507

There are regularly-scheduled sessions of zazen, Zen
practice, Dharma talks, and meditation instruction.
Sesshins and Zazenkai (one-day retreats) are scheduled
from time to time. The Wasatch Zendo is open to
members for informal sittings each weeknight.

VERMONT

SUNRAY MEDITATION SOCIETY
PO Box 308
Bristol, VT 05443
Tel. (802) 453–4610

Directed by the Ven. Dhyani Ywahoo, Sunray offers Native American and Buddhist studies in meditation, healing, and earth wisdom.

KIRPAL ASHRAM
Worcester, VT 05682

For information, contact Sant Bani Ashram, Franklin, NH (see Local Listings).

VIRGINIA

SAWAN KIRPAL MEDITATION CENTER
Rt. 1, Box 24
Bowling Green, VA 22427
Tel. (804) 663–9987

Darshan Singh, successor of Kirpal Singh, gives an experience of inner light and sound at the time of initiation, and teaches a method of meditation by which the disciple rises above body consciousness and attains God-realization. There is never any charge for instruction, initiation, or meditation.

BLUE RIDGE ZEN GROUP
214 Rugby Road
Charlottesville, VA 22901
Tel. (804) 973–5435

The group offers instruction for beginners and opportunities for daily practice in the Zendo. There is a rural retreat facility, where periodic weekend sittings are offered.

SAI SHO AN ZEN GROUP
Rt. 1, Box 529
Delaplane, VA 22025
Tel. (703) 592–3701

The group meets on Sunday mornings at 7:30 AM for meditation practice.

SAT GURU DHAM
Lexington, VA 24450

For information, contact Sant Bani Ashram, Franklin, NH (see Local Listings).

KESHAVASHRAM INTERNATIONAL
MEDITATION CENTER
PO Box 260
Warrenton, VA 22186
Tel. (703) 347–9009

Founded on the teachings of Sri Krishna Gopal Vyasji Maharaj, meditation is taught individually, as handed down person-to-person from the ancient rishis and seers. A special one-to-one relationship is established between teacher and student, with spiritual counseling and personal guidance.

WASHINGTON

SAWAN KIRPAL MEDITATION CENTER
5560 Bayvue Road
Birch Bay, WA 98230
Tel. (206) 371–5560

Sant Darshan Singh, spiritual successor of Sant Kirpal Singh, is a modern exponent of the inner science. He teaches, through example, how one may live an active life while achieving the goal of self-knowledge and God-realization through meditation and introspection.

The Center offers meditation programs which are open to the public. No fees are ever charged.

RAJ-YOGA MATH AND RETREAT
PO Box 547
Deming, WA 98244
Tel. (206) 855–1498

This secluded rural retreat, founded in 1974 by Satchakrananda Bodhisattvaguru, is open for short- and long-term stays by mature seekers with a special vocation toward spiritual teaching. Somewhat open-ended and creative in its approach to conscious spiritual growth, it is monastic in nature and very intense in its energy field. It provides excellent experience for the advanced student or for the novice teacher needing an extra push. Personal encounter with, and guidance by, the guru is a necessary part of the growth process. Residents also help in building and maintaining the environment, and in assisting with workshops and retreats.

ST. CLARE'S HERMITAGE
5984 Rutsatz Road
Deming, WA 98244
Tel. (206) 855–1498

Christian-oriented meditative practices are taught within the context of a Carthusian lifesteyle. The Hermitage blends the silent, solitary life with Cistercian-style brotherly love in a beautiful rural setting left rough and natural. All religious approaches and styles are dealt with from the perspective of Christian monastic ideals and practices. Instruction and guidance are offered in Christ-conscious meditation exercises and the contemplation of God.

DHIRAVAMSA FOUNDATION
1660 Wold Road
Friday Harbor, WA 98250
Tel. (206) 378–5787

Dhiravamsa utilizes a blend of Vipassana meditation, dialogue, and body awareness. The Center offers daily group meditations, chanting, and meditative movement. There are weekend and ten-day retreats throughout the summer, and solitary retreat space is available.

NORTH CASCADES BUDDHIST PRIORY
PO Box 152
McKenna, WA 98558
Tel. (206) 458–5075

Members and friends of the Priory meet weekly in Seattle (Wednesday) and Olympia (Tuesday). Day-long retreats are held regularly in Seattle. There is instruction in meditation and private spiritual guidance (sanzen), and memorial and other services are available on request. The practice of the North Cascades Buddhist Priory is Serene Reflection Meditation (Shikantaza). The Priory is affiliated with Shasta Abbey in Mt. Shasta, CA (see Local Listings).

MOUNTAIN OF THE HEART
PO Box 10212
Olympia, WA 98502
Tel. (206) 754–0940

Monthly full moon meditations, solstice and equinox ceremonies.

ANANDA FELLOWSHIP OF
INNER COMMUNION
17544 Midvale Avenue N., #203
Seattle, WA 98133
Tel. (206) 543–8184

Founded by Sri Kriyananda, Ananda Fellowship offers ongoing classes in Raja Yoga (meditation, yoga, etc.) based on the teachings of Paramhansa Yogananda. Other courses are also available, in addition to Sunday Services and the Festival of Light.

BRAHMA KUMARIS CENTER
2571 Westview Drive W.
Seattle, WA 98119
Tel. (206) 282–4028

For further information, see National Listings.

EAST WEST BOOKSHOP OF SEATTLE
6417 Roosevelt Way, N.E.
Seattle, WA 98115
Tel. (206) 523–3726

East West offers meditation instruction and other classes by teachers from many paths.

GOLD SUMMIT MONASTERY
1431 Minor Avenue
Seattle, WA 98101
Tel. (206) 340–0569

An affiliate of the Dharma Realm Buddhist Association, Gold Summit Monastery has an ongoing schedule of lectures and practices throughout the year, including bowing ceremonies, meditation, mantra recitation, and sutra recitation. Weekend sittings, chanting retreats, and bowing retreats are offered periodically. Orthodox Buddhism is taught and practiced, and in meditation instruction the ability to sit in full lotus posture is emphasized.

NORTHWEST VIPASSANA ASSOCIATION
1156 N. 78th
Seattle, WA 98103
Tel. (206) 523–2967

The Association organizes Vipassana courses in the tradition of U Ba Khin, following the techniques taught by S. N. Goenka. Introductory talks are offered each month, and group sittings each Tuesday. Weekend sittings and courses three to thirty days in length are available from time to time throughout the year.

PARAMHANSA YOGANANDA
CHANTING AND MEDITATION GROUP
c/o Alan Pritz
4522 Meridian Avenue N., #302
Seattle, WA 98103
Tel. (206) 547–9718

Basing their practices on the techniques of Paramhansa Yogananda, group members utilize basic concentration/ meditation techniques augmented by a system developed by Yogananda to recharge the body, mind, and spirit with Universal Energy. Each gathering begins with this energizing practice, followed by devotional chanting and a period of silent meditation. Informal sharing about aspects of Yogananda's teachings may follow. The group is dedicated to the spirit and energy of Yogananda as a true guru, and is open to all.

SURAVI RAJNEESH MEDITATION CENTER
615 19th Avenue E.
Seattle, WA 98112
Tel. (206) 322–9288

Daily dynamic meditations at 6:00 AM, and kundalini meditations at 5:30 PM are open to the public. Longer workshops, such as the Mystic Rose Meditation and the No-Mind Meditation, are offered from time to time.

> *Meditation is just being delighted in your own presence. Meditation is a delight in your own being.*
>
> —*Osho Rajneesh*

THREE TREASURES SANGHA
331 17th Avenue E.
Seattle, WA 98112
Tel. (206) 322–2447

A lay Zen meditation group in the tradition of the Sango-Kyodan lineage. There is a daily zazen practice, monthly Zazenkai, and seven-day sesshins twice yearly.

SUFI ISLAMIA RUHANIAT SOCIETY
GARDEN OF NOOR
2117 W. Broadway
Spokane, WA 99201
Tel. (509) 325–5017

The American Sufi leader, Murshid Samuel Lewis, made
the Dances of Universal Peace a central feature of
contemporary Sufism. Murshid Lewis's work with spiritual walk and dance is carried on by the Sufi Islamia
Ruhaniat Society, which sponsors instruction and practice in the dances and in the meditative practice of zikr.

TRANSFORMATION HOUSE
417 W. Cleveland
Spokane, WA 99205
Tel. (206) 327–9791

Guided meditations and a variety of traditional and
nontraditional techniques allow participants to reconnect
with the sources of creativity and power within themselves.

WEST VIRGINIA

BHAVANA SOCIETY
Back Creek Road
Rt. 1, Box 218-3
Highview, WV 26808

Under the guidance of Ven. H. Gunaratana and Bhante
Yogavacara Rahula, the Society offers weekend-long
retreats each month and several longer courses each
year.

ISKCON
322 Beverley Avenue
Morgantown, WV 26505
Tel. (304) 292–6725

A center for the International Society for Krishna Consciousness. Practices include singing, devotional dance, and chanting the names of Krishna. All programs are free and open to the public.

WISCONSIN

MEADOWVALE FARM
Rt. 1, Box 49
Barneveld, WI 53507
Tel. (608) 924–9505

Weekly meditation and yoga instruction in the lineage of Swami Rama.

ANANDA MARGA
1047 Spaight Street
Madison, WI 53703
Tel. (608) 255–4475

Ananda Marga teaches classes in Tantra yoga meditation and postures; individual instruction and group meditation practice are provided, and teachings focus on the integration of spiritual and social philosophy.

T'AI-CHI CENTER
301 S. Bedford
Madison, WI 53703
Tel. (608) 257–4171

In addition to Relaxation/Meditation classes, Taoist Meditation as taught by Master Liu Pei Chung is integrated into T'ai-Chi and Chi Kung courses. The T'ai-Chi Center is also a meeting place for other groups offering meditation classes.

YOGA SOCIETY OF MADISON
AT SHAKTI BOOKS
320 State Street
Madison, WI 53703
Tel. (608) 255–5007

The Yoga Society of Madison (affiliated with the Himalayan Institute) offers classes and seminars in meditation, hatha yoga, and yoga philosophy.

HIMALAYAN INSTITUTE
3581 S. Kinnickinnic Avenue
Milwaukee, WI 53207
Tel. (414) 747–0686

For further information, see the National Listings.

MILWAUKEE ZEN CENTER
2825 N. Stonewall Avenue
Milwaukee, WI 53211
Tel. (414) 963–0526

The Center offers daily morning and evening sitting practice, a weekend study class, and introductory workshops every three or four months.

NARAYANANANDA UNIVERSAL YOGA
ASHRAMA
Rt. 2, Box 24
Winter, WI 54896
Tel. (715) 266–4963

Sri Swami Narayanananda, a sage from India, is the spiritual leader of the Ashram. Ashramites at Narayanananda live a simple and practical spiritual life and take part in a daily program of meditation, work, and other yoga practices. There is a satsang every Saturday. Visitors are welcome, and spiritual retreats are encouraged.

WYOMING

THE YOGA ROOM
Box 639
Wilson, WY 83014
Tel. (307) 733–9260

Day and evening classes and workshops.

Canadian Listings

ALBERTA

AVATAMSAKA MONASTERY
1152 10th Street, S.E.
Calgary, AB T2G 3E4 Canada
Tel. (403) 269–2960

Under the direction of Bhikshu Heng Chang, Avatamsaka Monastery offers a daily program of public lectures and ceremonies from 12:30 to 3:00 PM and from 6:30 to 9:30 PM. Pure Land recitation, Ch'an meditation, bowing repentances, and mantra recitation are conducted daily. Retreats are given monthly, and three- and seven-day recitation sessions are offered several times a year.

FOOTHILLS YOGA SOCIETY
2260 Uxbridge Drive, N.W.
Calgary, AB T2N 3Z4 Canada
Tel. (403) 284–9591

Affiliated with the Himalayan Institute, the Foothills Yoga Society of Calgary offers classes and seminars in meditation, hatha yoga, and yoga philosophy.

BRITISH COLUMBIA

SALT SPRING CENTRE
Box 1133
Ganges, BC V0S 1E0 Canada
Tel. (604) 537–2326

Vipassana retreats include instruction in breathing techniques, meditation, postures, and other practices.

YASODHARA ASHRAM
PO Box 9A
Kootenay Bay, BC V0B 1X0 Canada
Tel. (604) 227–9224

The Ashram was founded in 1956 by Swami Sivananda Radha, a disciple of Swami Sivananda of Rishikesh. It offers a retreat where people of all religions may come to find their center. There are courses in Hatha Yoga, Raja Yoga, and Kundalini Yoga, and workshops which stress the unity of the spiritual life with emotional and physical planes of being.

SRI KIRPAL ASHRAM
Surrey, BC Canada

For information, contact Sant Bani Ashram, Franklin, NH (see Local Listings).

DHARMA REALM BUDDHIST ASSOCIATION (CANADIAN HEADQUARTERS)
301 E. Hastings Street
Vancouver, BC V6A 1P3 Canada
Tel. (604) 684–3754

The monastery's Dharma activities are administered by ordained Bhikshus or Bhikshunis (monks or nuns). Daily practices include chanting of sutras and mantras, trilingual Dharma lectures, daily meditation, and daily recitation of Amitabha Buddha's name. Ch'an meditation, practiced at the monastery, involves investigation of a topic, such as "Who is mindful of the Buddha?," with no attachment to false thoughts that arise. Emphasis is placed on sitting in full lotus posture for sustained periods. Meditation, prostration, and chanting retreats are offered throughout the year.

DHARMADHATU
3275 Heather Street
Vancouver, BC Canada
Tel. (604) 874–8420

Dharmadhatu is a Tibetan Buddhist study and meditation center founded by Vidyadhara the Ven. Chogyam Trungpa, Rinpoche. Meditation periods, open to all, are available several times each week, and a weekly open house offers meditation instruction and a talk on the meditative tradition.

LIONS GATE BUDDHIST PRIORY
1745 W. 16th Avenue
Vancouver, BC V6J 2L9 Canada

Lions Gate Buddhist Priory is a lay meditation and training center directly affiliated with Shasta Abbey, a Buddhist monastery of the Serene Reflection tradition located in Mt. Shasta, CA (see Local Listings). The Priory offers a continuing program of meditation, services, and classes, as well as introductory and advanced retreats and the celebration of Buddhist festivals. In addition, the priest conducts memorials, house-blessings, naming ceremonies for children, and other religious services. Private spiritual counseling is available by appointment. Those who are new to the Priory should receive introductory meditation instruction before attending any other activities; contact the prior to make arrangements.

VIPASSANA FOUNDATION
95 W. 23rd Avenue
Vancouver, BC V5Y 2S8 Canada
Tel. (604) 876–8343

The Foundation offers ten-day meditation courses and introductory talks on Vipassana meditation practices as taught by S. N. Goenka.

ZEN CENTRE OF VANCOUVER
899 E. Pender
Vancouver, BC V6A 1V9 Canada
Tel. (604) 253–2572

Weekly meditation instruction and practice.

VICTORIA ZEN SOCIETY
1149 Leonard Street
Victoria, BC Canada
Tel. (604) 382–9190

Weekly meditation instruction and practice.

VIPASSANA FOUNDATION
79 High Street
Victoria, BC V8Z 5C8 Canada

The Foundation offers instruction in the Vipassana meditation techniques taught by S. N. Goenka.

NOVA SCOTIA

ARUNACHALA ASHRAMA
BHAGAVAN SRI RAMANA MAHARSHI
CENTER, INC.
RR 1
Bridgetown, NS B0S 1CO Canada
Tel. (902) 665–2090

Arunachala Ashrama is a retreat facility for those earnest seekers who wish to deepen their spiritual experiences and stabilize themselves in the practice of Self-awareness and surrender. The retreat is open to those who adhere to any of the various creeds of religious beliefs, and even to those of no belief who earnestly seek peace. The only requirements are a sincere desire for peace and truth and an open heart to receive them. In the quiet, idyllic Nova Scotian countryside, a daily schedule of prayer, recitation, and silence is conducted in the Temple. Time is also set apart for light work, meals, and quiet time alone. A minimum visit of one to two weeks is necessary to absorb the full effect of the Ashrama environment. Facilities are provided to guests without a fixed charge; donations are accepted from those who value the Ashrama's ideals and work.

ONTARIO

ASHTANGA YOGA FELLOWSHIP
RR 1
Ashburn, ON L0B 1A0 Canada
Tel. (416) 649–1136

The Fellowship follows the practices of yoga and meditation taught by Baba Hari Dass.

UNIVERSAL ASHRAM
PO Box 2358
Orillia, ON L3V 6V7 Canada
Tel. (705) 325–8076

Yogi Krishan offers individual training in meditation, monthly workshops, and seasonal retreats.

TORONTO MAHAVIHARA
3595 Kingston Road
Scarborough, ON M1M 1R8 Canada
Tel. (416) 269–5882

Group sittings are held each Saturday morning from 8:00 to 10:00 AM.

BRAHMA KUMARIS CENTER
897 College Street
Toronto, ON M6H 1A1 Canada
Tel. (416) 537–3034

For further information, see National Listings.

ECKANKAR
12 Birch Avenue
Toronto, ON M4V 1C8 Canada
Tel. (416) 926–8946

Eckankar reveals practical, everyday ways to recognize yourself as Soul, moment to moment.

ONTARIO ZEN CENTRE
515 Logan Avenue
Toronto, ON M4K 3B3 Canada
Tel. (416) 482–9168

Practice at the Centre utilizes traditional breath meditation, koan, and mantra practice. Practice sessions, open to the public, are held each Sunday at 7:00 PM.

SAHAJ YOGA CENTRE
745 Markham Street
Toronto, ON M6G 2M4 Canada
Tel. (416) 531–5688

"Sahaj" means natural and flowing, and the power of movement in yoga comes from breath and concentration. The Centre offers yoga exercises, meditation classes and workshops, and a teacher's training program.

SPIRITUAL SCIENCE INSTITUTE
1430 Yonge Street, #223
Toronto, ON M4T 1Y6 Canada
Tel. (416) 964–9628

Each class at the Institute consists of meditation for self-exploration, plus experiential exercises which access the spiritual and psychic abilities within. There are regular weekly meditations each Sunday at 7:00 PM.

THE TORONTO GROUP
359 Sackville Street
Toronto, ON M5A 3G4 Canada
Tel. (416) 960–0783

Affiliated with the Himalayan Institute, the Toronto Group offers classes and seminars in meditation, hatha yoga, and yoga philosophy.

TORONTO KRIPALU YOGA CENTRE
320 Danforth Avenue
Toronto, ON M5A 3G4 Canada
Tel. (416) 960–0783

Yoga, meditation, and movement practices as taught by Yogi Amrit Desai.

UNIVERSAL ASHRAM
453 Keele Street
Toronto, ON M6N 3E1 Canada
Tel. (416) 761–9247

Yogi Krishan offers individual training in meditation, monthly workshops, and seasonal retreats.

ZEN LOTUS SOCIETY
45 Gwynne Avenue
Toronto, ON M6K 2C3 Canada
Tel. (416) 533–6911

Meditation and chanting practice are offered twice daily. Retreats are held five times a year, and a year-round visitor's program accommodates short-term guests.

QUEBEC

ASSOCIATION DOJO ZEN DE MONTREAL
982 Gilford E.
Montreal, QU H2J 1P4 Canada
Tel. (514) 523–1534

Daily zazen meditation practice.

SIVANANDA YOGA VEDANTA CENTER
5178 St. Lawrence Boulevard
Montreal, QU H2T 1R8 Canada
Tel. (514) 279–3545

The Center offers classes in yoga, meditation, pranayam, and vegetarian cooking. Daily satsang is open to the public. There is a limited residential program for sincere students.

ZEN CENTRE OF MONTREAL
10851 Rue Saint Hubert
Montreal, QU Canada
Tel. (514) 388–4518

RAJA YOGA MEDITATION CENTER
1405 St. Cryille
Quebec City, QU G1S 1X1 Canada
Tel. (418) 682–0203

Free meditation instruction.

BRAHMA KUMARIS CENTER
830 des Jesuites, #7
Quebec City, QU G1S 3N1 Canada
Tel. (418) 682–0203

For further information, see National Listings.

SASKATCHEWAN

YOGA MEDITATION CENTER
30 Plainsview Drive
Regina, SK S4S 6K3 Canada
Tel. (306) 586–4133

The Yoga Meditation Center of Regina offers classes and seminars in meditation, hatha yoga, and yoga philosophy.

3

RETREAT
FACILITIES

The following facilities provide individual and/or group retreats (or facilities for them). Individual retreats may range from isolation to directed programs of yoga and meditation—which are also offered by many of the organizations listed in the preceding section. If you cannot tell from the description what a facility that you are interested in offers, write and ask. Some retreats are geared only to people who are part of their own tradition or interested in partaking in it. Many of them have very limited space and are heavily booked. Some are closed in the winter.

Never just arrive at a retreat facility—be sure to write or call first. Try not to require special arrangements at a facility that is not prepared to provide them. If nothing else suits you, a closed door, tent, or cabin is all that is needed.

There is nowhere perfect rest save in a heart detached.

—Eckhart

This list is largely composed of Catholic retreat facilities suitable for an individual retreat or a "day of renewal," as well as (in most cases) for groups. In addition, there are facilities run by other churches, and by synagogues, spiritual groups, and social organizations such as the YMCA.

Retreat Listings

ALABAMA

BENEDICTINE SISTERS' CONFERENCE CENTER
PO Box 488
Cullman, AL 35056
Tel. (205) 734–4622

Sr. Regina Barrett, OSB, Director. Capacity 65.

BLESSED TRINITY SHRINE RETREAT
Holy Trinity, AL 36859
Tel. (205) 855–4474

Sr. Virginia Morris, MSBT, Director. Forty single rooms.

ALASKA

HOLY SPIRIT RETREAT HOUSE
10980 Hillside Drive
Anchorage, AK 99516
Tel. (907) 346–2343

Rev. Vincent Beuzer, SJ, Director. A year-round retreat facility, with 21 single rooms.

ARIZONA

OUR LADY OF SOLITUDE HOUSE OF PRAYER
PO Box 1140
Black Canyon City, AZ 95324
Tel. (602) 374–9204

Sr. Therese Sedlock, OSF, Director. Seven single rooms and four hermitages.

DESERT HOUSE OF PRAYER
PO Box 574
Cortaro, AZ 85652
Tel. (602) 744–3825

Rev. John Kane, Director. Accommodations include 12 single rooms and two hermitages.

PICTURE ROCKS RETREAT
PO Box 569
Cortaro, AZ 85652
Tel. (602) 744–3400

A Redemptorist retreat center. V. Rev. Tony Ross, CSSR, Director. Capacity 75.

FEATHER MOUNTAIN CONFERENCE CENTER
PO Box 670
Paulden, AZ 86334
Tel. (662) 445–0911

Feather Mountain is available to groups for retreats and seminars. Individual retreat space is also available.

FRIENDLY PINES CAMP
7400 Senator Road
Prescott, AZ 86303
Tel. (602) 445–2128

A secluded, rustic camp suitable for groups of 35 to 300 people.

FRANCISCAN RENEWAL CENTER
5802 E. Lincoln Drive
Box 220
Scottsdale, AZ 85252
Tel. (602) 948–7460

Rev. Ray Bucher, OFM, Director.

RIM INSTITUTE
6835 Pepper Tree Lane
Scottsdale, AZ 85253
Tel. (602) 263–0551; (602) 478–4727

Rim Institute has a full schedule of summer classes including Vipassana meditation workshops. Individual retreats are also available.

HEALING CENTER OF ARIZONA
25 Wilson Canyon Road
Sedona, AZ 86336
Tel. (602) 282–7710

The facilities of the Healing Center, located near the Sedona Vortexes, are available for both personal and group retreats. Guided group retreats on such topics as spiritual awakening, relationships, and joyful cleansing can be arranged on request. Meditation classes are available, and the Center has a regularly-scheduled World Peace Meditation each Thursday at 7:00 PM. The meditation room, a spacious geodesic dome with beautiful stained-glass windows, is always open.

HOLY TRINITY MONASTERY
PO Box 298
St. David, AZ 85630
Tel. (602) 586–4642

A retreat center inspired by the Benedictine Abbey in Pecos, NM (see Retreat Listings).

ARKANSAS

ST. SCHOLASTICA CENTER
PO Box 3489
Fort Smith, AR 72913
Tel. (501) 783–1135

Sr. Antonia Lutz, OSB, Director. Capacity 80.

DIMENSIONS OF EVOLVEMENT
Star Rt. 3, Box 47
Melbourne, AR 72556
Tel. (501) 368–4468

Dimensions of Evolvement is a wilderness retreat center in the Ozark Mountains, where one can spend time meditating, learning, or just being. There are ongoing classes and workshops on Kundalini energy development, t'ai chi ch'uan, meditation, and spiritual development.

OZARK THEOSOPHICAL CAMP
RR 1, Box 225
Sulphur Springs, AR 72768
Tel. (501) 298–3594

A summer camp is held each June.

CALIFORNIA

MANRESA JESUIT RETREAT HOUSE
801 E. Foothill Boulevard
PO Box K
Azusa, CA 91702

Rev. Terrance Mahan, SJ, Director. Seventy-five rooms.

ESALEN INSTITUTE
Highway 1
Big Sur, CA 93920
Tel. (408) 667–3000; (408) 667–3005

Esalen is a nonprofit educational center sponsoring workshops and seminars in the area of human potential development; a catalog of seminars is published three times a year. For those who wish to live and work at Esalen for longer periods, an extended student residential program is offered. There is a small meditation center on the property which is available from 6:00 AM to 11:00 PM for quiet sitting. Esalen is nonsectarian, and rather than espousing any particular practice or approach to personal growth, sees itself as a forum for the expression of many approaches.

IMMACULATE HEART HERMITAGE
Big Sur, CA 93920
Tel. (408) 667–2456

A hermitage of the Camaldolese monks. Fr. Aelred Squire, Guestmaster. Ten rooms are available for private, nondirected retreats; both men and women are welcome. A donation is requested.

VAJRAPANI INSTITUTE
PO Box 1
Boulder Creek, CA 95006

A country retreat facility affiliated with the Foundation for the Preservation of the Mahayana Tradition, offering solitary retreat opportunities and weekend courses.

MERCY CENTER
2300 Adeline
Burlingame, CA 94010
Tel. (415) 340–7474

Sr. Mary Waskowiak, SM, Director. Ninety single rooms and nine double rooms.

DOUBLE D RANCH
Star Route, Box 14
Caliente, CA 93518
Tel. (213) 434–3453

The Ranch is a place of sanctuary and a place for spiritual unfoldment. Located on 150 acres, the Ranch offers accommodations in dormitory rooms, double occupancy rooms, or trailers.

RAINBOW RANCH
3975 Mountain Home Ranch Road
Calistoga, CA 94515
Tel. (707) 942–5127

Located in the historic Mayacama Mountains on 80
acres of rolling hills, Rainbow Ranch enjoys an expansive view of vineyards and mountains. The site was
formerly used for Indian ceremonial rites, and is only
five miles from the Calistoga hot mineral springs. Accommodations are in motel-type bedrooms and A-frame
sleeping cabins. Groups have exclusive use of the Ranch
during their stay.

ZEN CENTER
TASSAJARA ZEN MOUNTAIN CENTER
Carmel Valley, CA 93924
Tel. (415) 431–3771 (Students: (415) 863–3136)

Tassajara is a Zen Buddhist monastery where both lay
and ordained students practice a daily schedule of zazen, services, meals, study, and work. Open to newer
students only during the summer months. Also open as
a guest resort during the summer months.

SAN DAMIANO RETREAT HOUSE
Highland Drive, Box 767
Danville, CA 94526
Tel. (415) 837–9141

Rev. Howard Hall, OFM, Director. Programs include
marriage encounters, engaged encounters, and renewal
programs as well as directed and private retreats.

HOLY SPIRIT RETREAT HOUSE
4316 Lanai Road
Encino, CA 91436
Tel. (818) 784–4515

Monthly contemplative sittings. For information, contact Maureen Fox.

VIPASSANA DHURA SOCIETY
PO Box 355
Fawnskin, CA 92333
Tel. (714) 985–0832

A comfortable cabin, located in a pine forest on Big Bear Mountain, is open for retreats in the spring, summer, and fall. The cabin is available for two or three experienced meditators at a time; solo retreats may be arranged by special permission.

ISIS OASIS LODGE
20889 Geyserville Avenue
Geyserville, CA 95441
Tel. (707) 857–3524

Facilities at Isis Oasis include a lodge with dormitory and meeting space, a retreat house, yurts, tipis, and a pyramid with accommodations for 80. There is an Egyptian Temple that may be used for meditation and healing.

SIVANANDA ASHRAM
VRINDAVAN YOGA FARM
14651 Ballantree Lane
Grass Valley, CA 95949
Tel. (916) 272–9322

Founded by Swami Vishnu Devananda, Vrindavan Yoga Farm is nestled in the Sierra foothills of California and offers 60 acres of peace and solitude. Daily programs include two periods of meditation, two asana classes, and two vegetarian meals. There are accommodations for campers, or guests may stay in dormitory rooms in the farmhouse. Work-study and resident programs are available.

> *Health is wealth. Peace of mind is happiness. Yoga shows the way through proper exercises (asana), proper breathing (pranayama), proper diet (vegetarian), proper relaxation (savasan), proper meditation (dhyana).*
> *—Swami Vishnu Devananda*

RIVERRUN RETREAT
c/o Simon Jeremiah
1569 Fitch Mountain
Healdsburg, CA 95448
Tel. (707) 433–6754

Riverrun Retreat is a small community facility on the Russian River, 60 miles north of San Francisco. We encourage visitors to participate in a retreat setting which includes a ceremonial tea hut, a meditation hall, and a library. A small hermitage is available to individuals. River beaches are nearby. Reservations are required.

MEADOWLARK
26126 Fairview Avenue
Hemet, CA 92344
Tel. (714) 927–1343

Located on a 20-acre country estate, Meadowlark provides facilities for both individual retreats and group sessions, including yoga, meditation, and dream analysis.

FAR HORIZONS, INC.
PO Box 857
Kings Canyon National Park, CA 93633
Tel. (209) 565–3692

Far Horizons is a center of spiritual, mental, emotional, and physical refreshment. Programs are designed to meet the needs of a broad range of people, providing both for the interested inquirer, often battered by the rigors of city life, and the serious student, who may have devoted many years to the spiritual path. We offer special attention to the Spanish-speaking community in an attempt to build a bridge of trust and communication based on our common spiritual heritage. The President of Far Horizons is Mr. Beverley Wyatt.

MOUNT MARY IMMACULATE
RETREAT CENTER
3254 Gloria Terrace
Lafayette, CA 94549
Tel. (415) 934–2411

Fr. Leo Dummer, OMI, Director. A year-round facility, offering accommodations in 21 double rooms. Mount Mary hosts a variety of programs during the year.

JESUIT RETREAT HOUSE
662 University Avenue
Box 128
Los Altos, CA 94023
Tel. (415) 948–4491

Rev. Robert St. Clair, SJ, Director. Year-round accommodations.

PRESENTATION CENTER
19480 Bear Creek Road
Los Gatos, CA 95030
Tel. (408) 354–2346

Sr. Doris Cavanaugh, PBVM, Director. Capacity 100.

SKY HI RANCH
Lucerne Valley, CA 92356
Tel. (619) 247–7881

Sky Hi offers a range of workshops, from a two-day introductory weekend to a nine-day intensive. Other programs include individual retreats, structured retreats, and work-study programs. The Ranch is available for rental by other groups for retreats and workshops.

HARBIN SPRINGS
P.O. Box 782
Middletown, CA 95461
Tel. (707) 987–2477

Our 1160 acres of woods, meadows and streams are nestled in the valley of majestic Mt. Harbin and located two hours north of the San Francisco Bay Area. Our community shares this beautiful environment with visitors, both individuals and groups. We operate the facility as a resort, retreat, and teaching center.

DEPAUL CENTER
1105 Bluff Road
Montebello, CA 90640
Tel. (213) 723–7343

The Center offers a variety of retreats throughout the year, including engaged encounters, renewal programs, special retreats, and directed private retreats.

THE EXPANDING LIGHT
ANANDA'S MEDITATION RETREAT
14618 Tyler Foote Road
Nevada City, CA 95959
Tel. (800) 346–5350 (in California, call (916) 292–3494)

The Expanding Light retreat is part of Ananda World Brotherhood Village, a spiritual community located in the foothills of the Sierra Nevada Mountains. Ananda's founder is Sri Kriyananda, a close, direct disciple of Paramhansa Yogananda. The Expanding Light is open to visitors year-round. Guests follow a daily schedule of meditation, hatha yoga, chanting, classes in yoga philosophy and greater awareness, evening inspirational programs, and karma yoga projects with community members. Work-study opportunities are offered, and the facility is available for individual retreats. Accommodations range from comfortable cabins and rooms, to tents, to "bring your own."

PRINCE OF PEACE ABBEY
650 Benet Hill Road
Oceanside, CA 92054
Tel. (619) 430–1306

Ten double rooms.

CENTER FOR SPIRITUAL DEVELOPMENT
434 S. Batavia
Orange, CA 92668
Tel. (714) 771–8275

Sr. Eileen McNerney, SCJ, Director. Capacity 58.

INTEGRATRON
PO Box 1022
Pacific Palisades, CA 90272
Tel. (213) 281–6114

The Integratron, a "modern pyramid," is a powerful center for spiritual awakening and physical healing. It is constructed on a ley line, and features unique characteristics of sound tones. No overnight facilities are available at this time, but the Integratron is ideal for day-long group retreats.

SHENOA RETREAT CENTER
PO Box 43
Philo, CA 95466
Tel. (707) 895–3156

Inspired by the Findhorn Community in northern Scotland, Shenoa was designed to create a similar environment in California. It occupies 160 acres of open meadows and redwood, laurel, fir, and oak forests, and is bordered by the Navarro River. Ancient redwoods in the adjacent Hendy Woods State Park create a natural sanctuary which is both healing and inspirational. Shenoa can accommodate up to 65 people in rooms and cabins, most of which have private baths. Camping is available for an additional 50 people. Shenoa's staff and invited faculty periodically present programs, events, and gatherings, and individuals or groups are invited to make use of the facilities for retreats, seminars, or workshops of their own. (Between November and April, groups must provide their own meal service; special winter group rates apply.)

DOMINGUEZ YOUTH RETREAT CENTER
18127 S. Alameda Street
Rancho Dominguez, CA 90220
Tel. (213) 636–6030

A small, year-round facility. Br. Modesto Leon, Director.

MARY AND JOSEPH RETREAT CENTER
5300 Crest Road
Rancho Palos Verdes, CA 90274
Tel. (213) 377–4867

Sr. Theresa McShane, DMJ, Director, Capacity 64.

MONKS OF MT. TABOR
17001 Tomki Road
Redwood Valley, CA 95470
Tel. (707) 485–8959

Twelve rooms, year-round accommodations.

SPIRITUAL MINISTRY CENTER
4822 Del Mar Avenue
San Diego, CA 92107
Tel. (619) 224–9444

A year-round facility with accommodations for up to
ten people, offering individually-directed retreats.

ST. FRANCIS RETREAT CENTER
PO Box 1070
San Juan Bautista, CA 95045
Tel. (408) 623–4234

Br. Bede McKinnon, OFM, Director. Fifty-seven double rooms plus dormitory accommodations for 25.

MONASTERY OF THE RISEN CHRIST
PO Box 3931
San Luis Obispo, CA 93403
Tel. (805) 546–8103

A retreat center inspired by the Benedictine Abbey in Pecos, NM (see Retreat Listings).

MISSION SAN LUIS REY RETREAT CENTER
PO Box 409
San Luis Rey, CA 92068
Tel. (619) 757–3659

A year-round center with 53 double rooms and one single room.

SANTA SABINA CENTER
1520 Grand Avenue
San Rafael, CA 94901
Tel. (415) 457–7727

A year-round retreat facility, with 14 single rooms and 23 double rooms.

IMMACULATE HEART CENTER
FOR SPIRITUAL RENEWAL
888 San Ysidro Lane
Santa Barbara, CA 93108
Tel. (805) 969–2474

The Center provides a retreat house for those who wish to make private retreats.

LA CASA DE MARIA
800 El Bosque Road
Santa Barbara, CA 93108
Tel. (805) 969–5031

The goal of La Casa is to provide, through its environment and its programs, a place of peace where individuals of all faiths can search for truth, engage in dialogue, realize their own self-worth, experience the sacred, and then, refreshed and renewed, participate more effectively in the creation of a just and peaceful world. The Director is Don George. The facility has 42 retreat rooms and two dormitories; the total capacity is 150.

ST. MARY'S SEMINARY
1964 Las Canoas Road
Santa Barbara, CA 93105
Tel. (805) 966–4829

Rev. James Galvin, Director.

WHITE LOTUS FOUNDATION
2500 San Marcos Pass
Santa Barbara, CA 93105
Tel. (805) 964–1944

A 40-acre mountain center with yurts, indoor accommodations, and creekside campsites. Weekend, seven-day, and 16-day yoga courses are offered, and the facility is available for individual retreats.

VILLA MARIA DEL MAR
1-1918 E. Cliff Drive
Santa Cruz, CA 95062

Sr. Regina Ann, SNJM, Director. Capacity 78.

ANGELA CENTER
535 Angela Drive
Santa Rosa, CA 95401
Tel. (707) 528–8578

Angela Center is an Ecumenical Christian retreat facility sponsored by the Ursuline sisters. Its programs seek to integrate spirituality, psychology, social responsibility, and the arts, believing that religious experience can best be understood through its expression in our daily lives. The facility provides private and semiprivate rooms for 48 people, but larger groups can be accommodated by special arrangement.

MATER DOLOROSA RETREAT CENTER
700 N. Sunnyside Avenue
PO Box 68
Sierra Madre, CA 91024
Tel. (818) 355–7188

ST. ANTHONY RETREAT CENTER
43816 Sierra Drive
Box 249
Three Rivers, CA 93271
Tel. (209) 561–4595

St. Anthony's offers special retreats, renewal programs, and marriage encounter programs, as well as opportunities for directed and private retreats.

ORR HOT SPRINGS
13201 Orr Springs Road
Ukiah, CA 95482
Tel. (707) 462–6277

A hot springs resort/retreat with private cabins, dormitory space, and campsites.

SACRED HEART RENEWAL CENTER
13333 Palmdale Road
Victorville, CA 92392
Tel. (619) 241–2538

Programs at the Center include marriage encounters, engaged encounters, renewal programs, and directed private retreats.

MOUNT MADONNA CENTER
445 Summit Road
Watsonville, CA 95076
Tel. (408) 722–7175

The resident staff at Mount Madonna, students of Baba Hari Dass, offer programs encompassing many forms of personal growth and many varieties of spiritual pathways. The Center also rents workshop space to other compatible groups of 12 to 300 people, and provides facilities for personal or group retreats. Personal retreats are individually designed, and can vary from total seclusion to total immersion in Center activities.

ST. FRANCIS SALESIAN RETREAT
2400 E. Lake Avenue
Watsonville, CA 95076
Tel. (408) 722–0115

Rev. Carmine Vairo, SDB, Director.

LAS BRISAS RETREAT CENTER
PO Box 500
Wildomar, CA 92395
Tel. (714) 229–6161

Las Brisas provides the privacy for quiet study, meditation, relaxation, and reflection. The facility caters to a small number of guests and offers shared or private rooms in an atmosphere of tranquil natural beauty. Las Brisas schedules meditative seminars twice a month, focused on learning to listen to inner guidance. A daily morning meditation is open to guests who wish to participate.

WILBUR HOT SPRINGS
Star Route
Williams, CA 95987
Tel. (916) 473–2306

Wilbur Hot Springs accommodates guests in a unique, turn-of-the-century hotel located at the site of natural hot mineral springs long used as a healing ground by Native Americans. The facility is ideal for private or small group retreats. Reservations are required. Call for a free brochure.

SPIRIT ROCK CENTER
c/o Insight Meditation West
PO Box 909
Woodacre, CA 94973
Tel. (415) 456–8940

Insight Meditation West is establishing Spirit Rock Center on 412 acres of rolling open meadows and hills in rural West Marin County. The core of this Dharma center will be Vipassana meditation from the Theravadin tradition. There is a year-round program of intensive retreats of varying lengths for new and old students; other Dharma-related events, such as classes, lectures, and workshops, are planned. Teachers from a variety of orientations within the Vipassana lineage focus on traditional teachings of liberation through mindfulness practice, on integrating mindfulness and Dharma principles in daily life, and on involvement in the world.

COLORADO

BENET PINES
15780 Highway 83
Colorado Springs, CO 80921
Tel. (719) 495–2574

Year-round accommodations in a four-room cabin and three hermitages.

JULIE PENROSE CENTER
1661 Mesa Avenue
Colorado Springs, CO 80906

Sr. Barbara Hagedorn, SC, Director. Capacity 75.

THE FISHERFOLK
1214 N. Hancock
Colorado Springs, CO 80903
Tel. (719) 687–9237

Mr. James Creasey, Manager. Capacity 30.

SPIRITUAL LIFE INSTITUTE
NADA HERMITAGE
Box 260
Crestone, CO 81131
Tel. (303) 256–4778

SLI is a monastic Carmelite community characterized

by Christian humanism. At Nada Hermitage, guests and
retreatants may participate in the monastic life of the
community, or may make solitary retreats in individual
hermitages. Please write in advance.

TAKOJA RETREATS
4495 Lakeridge
Denver, CO 80219
Tel. (303) 934–3607

Takoja Retreats maintains a spiritual center at Ranchos
Mesclados in the Sangre de Cristo Mountains north of
Taos, NM. The historic 40-acre ranch offers lovely
dome accommodations on the site of a former Indian
campground. A wide spectrum of seminars and workshops on topics ranging from Native American spirituality to Taoism is offered during the summer months, and
the facility is available for rental by groups of 10 to 30
people.

DORJE KHYUNG DZONG
BUDDHIST RETREAT CENTER
PO Box 35
Farisita, CO 81037
Tel. (303) 444–0190

Founded by Chogyam Trungpa Rinpoche for solitary
Buddhist retreat practice, Dorje Khyung Dzong is located on Mt. Greenhorn overlooking the Huerfano Valley in southern Colorado. Open year round, the facility
offers 240 acres of alpine meadows and woods, seven
fully equipped secluded retreat cabins, and two summer
tent sites. For information and reservations contact the
Retreat Coordinator at 1345 Spruce Street, Boulder, CO
80302.

BETHLEHEM CENTER
12550 Zuni
Northglenn, CO 80234
Tel. (303) 451–1371

Mr. Noel Dunne, Administrator.

ROCKY MOUNTAIN DHARMA CENTER
Red Feather Lakes, CO 80545
Tel. (303) 881–2530

The Dharma Center is a year-round contemplative meditation center founded in 1971 by the late Vidhyadhara, the Ven. Chogyam Trungpa Rinpoche. Situated on 350 secluded acres of highland meadows and pine and aspen forests, it provides an ideal setting for programs devoted to the study and practice of Buddhism and to the more secular meditation approach of Shambhala Training. Introductory programs and group retreats are offered frequently for beginning meditators. The Center is part of the Vajradhatu International organization of meditation and study centers.

SACRED HEART RETREAT HOUSE
Box 185
Sedalia, CO 80135

The Rev. Robert F. Houlihan, SJ, Director. Capacity 45.

CONNECTICUT

EPISCOPAL CAMP AND CONFERENCE CENTER
Bushy Hill Road
PO Box 577
Ivoryton, CT 06442
Tel. (203) 767–0848

A year-round facility for large groups.

MONTFORT MISSIONARIES RETREAT HOUSE
PO Box 667
Litchfield, CT 06759

Capacity 34.

WISDOM HOUSE CENTER OF SPIRITUALITY
Clark House Road
RR 3, Box 272
Litchfield, CT 06759
Tel. (203) 557–3163

Ivan Hawk, Administrator. Facilities include a farmhouse and a large main building, so the Center can
accommodate large groups.

MERCY CENTER
167 Neck Road
Box 191
Madison, CT 06443
Tel. (203) 245–0401

Sr. Eugenie Guterch, RSM, Administrator. Twenty single and 42 double rooms.

MY FATHER'S HOUSE
39 N. Moodus Road
Box 22
Moodus, CT 06469
Tel. (203) 873–1581

A year-round facility with a capacity of 150 guests.

EDMUNDITE APOSTOLATE CENTER
Enders Island
Mystic, CT 06355
Tel. (203) 536–0565

Rev. Paul McQuillen, SSE, Director. Thirty-five rooms.

VISITATION CENTER
223 W. Mountain Road
Ridgefield, CT 06877
Tel. (203) 438–9071

Sr. Eileen Kelly, CND, Director.

DELAWARE

ST. FRANCIS RENEWAL CENTER
1901 Prior Road
Wilmington, DE 19809
Tel. (302) 798–1454

A year-round facility with nine double rooms.

DISTRICT OF COLUMBIA

MARIAN HOME OF PRAYER
3700 Oakview Terrace, N.E.
Washington, DC 20017
Tel. (301) 832–2261

Br. Leonard Konopka, MIC, Director.

WASHINGTON RETREAT HOUSE
4000 Harewood Road, N.E.
Washington, DC 20017
Tel. (202) 529–111

Special retreats and private directed retreats. Fifty single and two double rooms.

FLORIDA

CENACLE RETREAT HOUSE
1400 S. Dixie Highway
Lantana, FL 33462

DUNKLIN MEMORIAL CAMP
3342 S.W. Hosannah Lane
Okeechobee, FL 34974

A year-round retreat facility. Mr. Richard Boggs, Director.

HOLY NAME PRIORY
PO Drawer H
St. Leo, FL 33574
Tel. (904) 588–8320

Holy name is open only during the summer, and facilities are for women only. Accommodations include four suites, three single rooms, and 123 double rooms.

ST. JOHN NEUMANN RENEWAL CENTER
685 Miccosukee Road
Tallahassee, FL 32303
Tel. (904) 224–2971

Sr. Christine Kelly, SSJ, Director.

FRANCISCAN CENTER
3010 Perry Avenue
Tampa, FL 33603
Tel. (813) 229–2695

Sr. Catherine Cahill, OSF, Administrator. Capacity 54.

SAN PEDRO SPIRITUAL CENTER
2400 Dike Road
Winter Park, FL 23792
Tel. (305) 671–6322

Forty-eight double rooms plus dormitory space and cabins.

GEORGIA

IGNATIUS HOUSE
6700 Riverside Drive, N.W.
Atlanta, GA 30328
Tel. (404) 255–0503

Rev. George Wiltz, SJ, Director. Capacity 73.

HAWAII

HAWAII INTERNATIONAL CONFERENCE CENTER
PO Box 13
Hawi, HI 96719
Tel. (808) 889–5108

Located at the northern end of the island of Hawaii, the Conference Center has a large meditation room, and offers private or semiprivate accommodations for up to 20 people.

KAGYU THEKCHEN LING
2327 Liloa Rise
Honolulu, HI 96822
Tel. (808) 941–8561

A Tibetan Buddhist center in Honolulu, founded by Ven. Kalu Rinpoche, Kagyu Thekchen Ling has a resident monk and occasionally hosts visiting lamas. The center publishes a newsletter, "The Empty Mirror." Write or call for further information.

SPIRITUAL LIFE CENTER
2717 Pamoa Road
Honolulu, HI 96822
Tel. (808) 988–7800

Sr. Katherine Theiler, MM, Director.

KALANI HONUA
PO Box 4500
Kalapana, HI 96778
Tel. (808) 965–7828

Kalani Honua provides an opportunity for those who are agents of transformation, peacemakers, healers, or teachers, to do their work in an "island paradise" setting. The facility is near the beach, and there is a safe yet active volcano several miles away. Accommodations are in simple, comfortable rooms in four two-story cedar lodges. The calendar of annual events includes yoga, meditation and church retreats, holistic health and Eastern arts workshops, personal growth programs, and individual retreats.

NECHUNG DORJE DRAYANG LING
WOOD VALLEY RETREAT CENTER
PO Box 250
Pahala, HI 96777
Tel. (808) 928–8539

Nechung Drayang Ling is a nonsectarian Buddhist temple and retreat center in Wood Valley on the island of Hawaii. The main temple is a renovated, classic Japanese temple, built at the turn of the century. It is located in a cool, quiet, bamboo and eucalyptus forest, at an elevation of 2,000 feet. The retreat center, with a capacity to accommodate up to 30 people, has a spacious meditation hall, private and dormitory quarters, dining room, and fully equipped kitchen. When not in use for Temple progams and activities, the retreat facilities are available to individuals and groups at reasonable rates.

HALE MAULI OLA HOU
PO Box 1653
Pahoa, HI 96778
Tel. (808) 965–9880

A spiritual healing center located on a beautiful five-acre setting on the ocean. There are accommodations for 20 to 30 people, with such amenities as a hot tub, pool, and hot ponds.

KARMA RIMARY OSAL LING
PO Box 1029
Paia, HI 96779
Tel. (808) 579–8076

Founded by Ven. Kalu Rinpoche, Karma Rimary Osal Ling is a Tibetan Buddhist center located on the island of Maui.

BENEDICTINE MONASTERY OF HAWAII
PO Box 490
Waialua, HI 96791
Tel. (808) 637–7887

A retreat house inspired by the Benedictine Abbey **in** Pecos, NM (see Retreat Listings).

IDAHO

NAZARETH RETREAT CENTER
4450 N. Five Mile Road
Boise, ID 83704
Tel. (208) 375–2932

Contact Laurel M. Rickert for information.

ILLINOIS

KING'S HOUSE CENTER
FOR RETREATS & RENEWAL
North 66th Street
Belleville, IL 62223
Tel. (618) 397–0584

The Center is located on 40 shaded acres, and offers **65** rooms with bath.

CENACLE RETREAT HOUSE
Box 340
Warrenville, IL 60555

Sr. Evelyn Jegen, RC, Director. Capacity 82.

INDIANA

POPE JOHN XXIII CENTER
407 W. McDonald Street
Hartford City, IN 47348

The Rev. Keith Hosey, Director; Maureen Mangen, CPPS, Co-Director. Capacity 45.

FATIMA RETREAT CENTER
Notre Dame, IN 46556

Steve Gibson, CSC, Director. Capacity 80.

MARY'S SOLITUDE
• St. Mary's College
Notre Dame, IN 46556
Tel. (219) 284–5599

Year-round accommodations in 15 private rooms. Sr. Mary Brooks, CSC, Director.

SOLITUDE OF ST. JOSEPH
Brothers of Holy Cross
Notre Dame, IN 46556
Tel. (219) 239–5655

Br. John Kuhn, CSC, Director.

ST. JUDE GUEST HOUSE
St. Meinrad Archabbey
St. Meinrad, IN 47577
Tel. (812) 357–6585

The Rev. Barnabas Gillespie, OSB, Director. Capacity 39.

IOWA

AMERICAN MARTYRS RETREAT HOUSE
PO Box 605
Cedar Falls, IA 50613
Tel. (319) 266–3543

Rev. Frederick Fangmann, Director. The American Martyrs Retreat House hosts a variety of programs year round. Accommodations are in 60 single rooms.

SHALOM RETREAT HOUSE
1001 Davis Avenue
Dubuque, IA 52001
Tel. (319) 583–9786

Sr. Marie Therese Kalb, OSF, Director.

KANSAS

TALL OAKS CONFERENCE CENTER
PO Box 116
Linwood, KS 66052
Tel. (913) 723–3307

A year-round facility suitable for large groups; accommodations for 160 people in single rooms.

ACUTO CENTER
1165 Southwest Boulevard
Wichita, KS 67213
Tel. (316) 945–2542

Sr. Rita Robl, Director. Twenty beds, eight doubles.

KENTUCKY

FLAGET CENTER
1935 Lewiston Place
Louisville, KY 40216
Tel. (502) 448–8581

Steven Wirth, Director. The facility offers accommodations for a hundred guests in single, double, and four-person rooms.

CLEFTROCK RETREAT CENTER
Rt. 1, Box 397
Mt. Vernon, KY 40456
Tel. (606) 256–2336

Matt Beck, Director.

THE RETREAT HOUSE
ABBEY OF GETHSEMANI
Trappist, KY 40051
Tel. (502) 549–3117

The monastic milieu offers a place apart "to entertain silence in the heart and listen for the voice of God—to pray for your own discovery" (Thomas Merton). Communing with the Lord requires a measure of solitude, a stillness and emptiness, a waiting on and attending to the Spirit. Silence fosters and preserves the climate of prayer, and is thus a fundamental part of the Gethsemani experience. There are 25 private guest rooms, each with its own shower, and accommodations for the handicapped are provided. Offerings are on a freewill basis, according to means.

LOUISIANA

MANRESA RETREAT HOUSE
PO Box 89
Convent, LA 70723
Tel. (504) 562–3596; (504) 529–3555

Rev. Thomas Naughton, SJ, Director.

REGINA COELI RETREAT CENTER
Rt. 7, Box 515
Folsom Road
Covington, LA 70433
Tel. (504) 892–4110

For group retreats only. Earl and June Magner, managers.

CARMEL CENTER
PO Box 130
Lacombe, LA 70445
Tel. (504) 882–5613

Sr. Joan Broussard, Director.

HOLY REDEEMER MISSION CENTER
PO Box 218
Lacombe, LA 70445
Tel. (312) 882–5114

Rev. Tomothy Kerner, CSSR, Director.

AVE MARIA RETREAT HOUSE
Rt. 1, Box 0368-AB
Marrero, LA 70072
Tel. (504) 689–3837 (Lafitte, LA)

The Rev. Dan Schuckenbrook, OMI, Director. Fifty private rooms.

THE CENACLE RETREAT HOUSE
5500 St. Mary Street
PO Box 8115
Metairie, LA 70011
Tel. (504) 887–1420

Sr. Agnes Sauer, Director. Forty-nine private rooms.

CENTER OF JESUS THE LORD
1236 N. Rampart Street
New Orleans, LA 70116
Tel. (504) 529–1636

Rev. Emile Lafranz, Director. The Center operates a 24-hour counseling service called "Operation Evangelism"; for counseling call 529–HOPE.

DOMINICAN CONFERENCE CENTER
540 Broadway
New Orleans, LA 70118
Tel. (504) 861–8711

Sr. Mary Ann Culotta, OP, Director.

NAZARETH SPIRITUAL CENTER
4930 Dixon Street
New Orleans, LA 70125
Tel. (504) 486–8258

For information, contact Sr. Loretta McCarthy, SBS.

MAGNIFICAT CENTER OF THE HOLY SPIRIT
Lee's Landing Road
Highway 445
Ponchatoula, LA 70454
Tel. (504) 529–1636

Rev. Emile LaFranz, Director.

ROSARYVILLE SPIRIT LIFE CENTER
Star Route
Ponchatoula, LA 70454
Tel. (504) 294–5039; (504) 466–1476

Sr. Paulette Paille, OP, Director.

ABBEY CHRISTIAN LIFE CENTER
St. Benedict, LA 70457
Tel. (504) 892–3473; (504) 892–1800

Rev. William MacCandless, OSB, Retreat House Manager.

LUMEN CHRISTI RETREAT CENTER
100 Lumen Christi Lane
Schriever, LA 70395
Tel. (504) 868–1523

A year-round retreat center for large groups; facilities accommodate 43 in single rooms and 108 in dormitory space. Rev. Joseph Rayes, OFM, Director.

MAINE

ST. PAUL CENTER
136 State Street
Augusta, ME 04330
Tel. (207) 284–5671

Rev. Robert Levesque, OMI, Director. A year-round facility, with 63 single and 15 double rooms.

MARYLAND

MANRESA-ON-SEVERN
PO Box 9
Annapolis, MD 21404
Tel. (301) 974–0332

Rev. Joseph Currie, SJ, Director. Capacity 60.

MASSACHUSETTS

CENTER OF THE LIGHT
PO Box 540
Great Barrington, MA 01230
Tel. (413) 229–2396

Located on 83 acres in the Berkshire Mountains, Center of the Light is an educational retreat center dedicated to the teaching of healing and spiritual growth. During the summer, the Center presents a full program of experiential workshops; topics include meditation, music, herbal studies, and massage. The Center is also available for individual guests.

CAMP LENOX
Route 8
Lee, MA 01238
Tel. (413) 243–2223

Camp Lenox is a retreat center offering programs on

holistic health, sports, and spirituality. It is situated on 250 acres of land on a hillside overlooking Shaw Lake in the Berkshire Mountains. Accommodations include 22 group cabins, four large community houses, eight two-person cabins, and a tenting area for 150. Camp Lenox is available for group rentals, and is ideal for large retreats of 74 to 375 people.

ROLLING RIDGE CONFERENCE CENTER
666 Great Pond Road
North Andover, MA 01845
Tel. (508) 682–8815

Located on 38 wooded acres along the shores of Lake Cochichewick, Rolling Ridge provides a unique environment for learning and recreation. Semiprivate rooms and dormitories house groups of up to 80 people. Day-use facilities are also available.

ROWE CAMP AND CONFERENCE CENTER
King's Highway Road
Rowe, MA 01367
Tel. (413) 339–4216

The Center provides weekend retreats on psychological, spiritual, and political topics, and longer summer camps for teenagers and families.

CALVARY RETREAT CENTER
59 South Street
Shrewsbury, MA 01545

The Rev. Lucian Clark, CP, Director. Capacity 70.

MICHIGAN

ST. PAUL'S RETREAT CENTER
23333 Schoolcraft
Detroit, MI 48223

The Rev. Pat Brennan, CP, Director. Eighty-eight rooms.

ST. FRANCIS RETREAT CENTER
703 E. Main Street
PO Box 250
DeWitt, MI 48820
Tel. (517) 669–8321

Rev. Lawrence P. Delaney, Director. Capacity 81.

SONG OF THE MORNING RANCH
9607 Sturgeon Valley Road
Vanderbilt, MI 49795
Tel. (517) 983–4107

This beautiful, 800-acre yoga retreat, established to further the teachings of Paramhansa Yogananda, offers ongoing meditations, yoga classes, and workshops.

THE HAVEN
Rt. 1, Box 57
Walkerville, MI 49459
Tel. (616) 898–2360

The Haven seeks to provide a protected space where there is time to reflect and refresh in a setting close to nature. It is located on 295 acres of beautiful woods and fields in the Manistee National Forest, and facilities include dormitories, log cabins, and tents, meditation sites, fire circles, and a Dromenon sweat lodge. The Haven can accommodate groups of up to 250 people, and is also available for individual retreats.

MINNESOTA

CENTER FOR SPIRITUAL DEVELOPMENT
PO Box 538
211 Tenth Street
Bird Island, MN 55310
Tel. (612) 365–3644

Sr. Mary Ann Kuhn, SSND, Director. Nineteen private rooms.

THE CENACLE
1221 Wayzata Boulevard
Wayzata, MN 55391
Tel. (612) 473–7308

Contact Sr. Mary Sharon Riley. Forty-six rooms.

MISSISSIPPI

ST. AUGUSTINE'S RETREAT CENTER
St. Augustine's Divine Word Seminary
Bay St. Louis, MS 39520
Tel. (601) 467–9837; (601) 467–6414

Rev. Thaddeus Boucree, SVD, Director.

THE DWELLING PLACE
Star Route Box 126
Brooksville, MS 39739
Tel. (601) 738–5348

Sr. Clare Van Lent, OSF, Director. A small retreat facility with four single rooms and a hermitage. Open year-round.

ST. MARY OF THE PINES
PO Box 38
Chatawa, MS 39632
Tel. (601) 783–3494

Sr. Jackie Merz, SSND, Director. A year-round retreat facility.

MISSOURI

RETREAT AND CONFERENCE CENTER
CONCEPTION ABBEY
Conception Seminary College
Conception, MO 64433

The Rev. Kenneth Reichert, OSB, Director. Capacity 65.

SHINING WATERS ASHRAM
Rt. 3, Box 560
Fredericktown, MO 63645
Tel. (314) 783–6715

The Ashram, which is affiliated with the Universal Great Brotherhood, has dormitory space for 28 and unlimited camping facilities on 40 acres of land in the Ozark Mountains. It offers weekend workshops and opportunities to join in the daily disciplines of morning exercise, hatha yoga, and meditation.

CHRISTINA HOUSE
PO Box 619
Pevely, MO 63070
Tel. (314) 479–3697

A retreat center inspired by the Benedictine Abbey in Pecos, NM (see Retreat Listings).

OZARK RETREAT CENTER
RR 2, Box 45
Willow Springs, MO 65793
Tel. (417) 469–2439

Beautiful mountain setting with dormitory and cabin facilities.

MONTANA

FEATHERED PIPE RANCH
PO Box 255
Helena, MT 59624
Tel. (406) 442–5138

A rustic, Rocky Mountain retreat center, with a special focus on yoga and holistic health programs.

NEBRASKA

THE MARY J. O'DONNELL CENTER
Creighton University
2500 California
Omaha, NE 68178
Tel. (402) 280–2131

Dr. Robert Gerraughty, Director. Capacity 30.

NEVADA

JOY LAKE MOUNTAIN SEMINAR CENTER
PO Box 1328
Reno, NV 89504
Tel. (702) 323–0378

Joy Lake offers weekend and five-day workshops in personal growth and self-development. Most workshops include a meditation practice, and many different meditation practices are explored during the retreat season. There is a medicine wheel, which seems to be a power site where many people choose to practice meditation. The center is located on 80 acres of land, which includes herbal gardens and a four-acre lake, and is surrounded on three sides by National Forest land.

NEW HAMPSHIRE

DURHAM RETREAT CENTER
33 Demeritt Road
Durham, NH 03824
Tel. (603) 659–6708

This is a Sufi retreat center, offering guided individual and group retreats throughout the year for beginning and advanced students. Retreats are based on the spiritual teachings of Hazrat Inayat Khan and Pir Vilayat

Inayat·Khan, and are called "alchemical retreats." They provide an opportunity to immerse oneself in wazifa, dhikr, meditation, visualization, and light practices. Accommodations are in individual heated retreat rooms and huts in a beautiful country setting.

OBLATE RETREAT HOUSE
200 Lowell Road
Hudson, NH 03051

The Rev. George Capen, OMI, Director. Fifty-eight rooms.

NEW JERSEY

CENACLE RETREAT HOUSE
411 River Road
Highland Park, NJ 08904
Tel. (201) 249–8100

Contact the Retreat Office for information. Capacity 28.

VILLA PAULINE RETREAT HOUSE
Hilltop Road
Mendham, NJ 07945

Sr. Georgeanne, SCC, Director. Capacity 40.

SAN ALFONSO RETREAT HOUSE
755 Ocean Avenue
PO Box 3098
West End, NJ 07740
Tel. (201) 222–2731

San Alfonso is a Redemptorist Spiritual Center situated on eight beautiful acres along the New Jersey coastline. There are rooms for 150 retreatants, a large chapel, spacious meeting rooms, a reading room, and a bookstore. In addition to the various scheduled retreats, San Alfonso offers days and evenings of recollection for adults, for school faculties, and for young people. These can be arranged on mutually agreeable dates, with the program adapted to the needs of the group. Rev. Paul V. Bryan, CSSR, is the Director of Retreats.

NEW MEXICO

ROSE MOUNTAIN RETREAT CENTER
PO Box 355
Las Vegas, NM 87701
Tel. (505) 425–3144

Located at an elevation of 8,000 feet, Rose Mountain is an intertraditional retreat center set in a pristine and ecologically balanced section of the beautiful Sangre de Cristo Mountains. The Center is dedicated to contributing toward the growth of peace and wisdom on the planet. In addition to a schedule of public workshops offered each year, the facilities are available to groups of similar outlook.

OCAMORA FOUNDATION
Box 43
Ocate, NM 87734
Tel. (505) 666–2389

The Foundation offers year-round facilities for personal solitary retreats and for meditative group retreats. The remoteness and beauty of the Ocamora Valley encourage a quiet intimacy with nature. Facilities include private retreat rooms, tipis, and tents; a meditation sanctuary is also available.

BENEDICTINE ABBEY
Pecos, NM 87552
Tel. (505) 757–6415

Located on 1,000 acres in the beautiful Pecos River Valley, the Abbey is best known for being a charismatic monastery. Guests are encouraged to participate in the life of the community, especially through shared prayer and liturgies. Being invited into the family of God has proven to be the most healing experience of all. The Director is Abbot David Geraets, and the Abbey has a capacity of 70.

LAMA FOUNDATION
PO Box 240
San Cristobal, NM 87564
Tel. (505) 586–1269

Lama Foundation offers two hermitages for private retreats. See Local Listings for additional information on Lama's programs.

NEW YORK

PUMPKIN HOLLOW FARM
RR 1, Box 135
Craryville, NY 12521
Tel. (518) 325–3538

Contact: Mrs. Dora Kunz
Hillandale Road
Port Chester, NY 10573

Pumpkin Hollow is a Theosophical Society camp, founded in 1937 to provide a peaceful, harmonious, natural setting in which the essential spirituality of the individual can thrive and be integrated into day-by-day relationships with others. Pumpkin Hollow offers summer workshops in meditation practice, meditation and the development of intuition, the chakras, and related topics. The Farm is also often available for individual retreats.

ST. COLUMBAN CENTER
PO Box 816
Derby, NY 14047
Tel. (716) 947–4708

St. Columban Center is a beautiful retreat house situated on 14 acres of land bordering the shores of Lake Erie. The Director is Rev. Paul J. Priester. The Center offers accommodations for 73 retreatants.

WILBUR HERRLICH CAMP
Holmes, NY 12531
Tel. (212) 431–7470

Contact: Lutheran Community Service, Inc.
33 Worth Street
New York, NY 10013
Attn: Teri Messina

Capacity 35.

YMCA CAMP GREENKILL
Huguenot, NY 12746
Tel. (914) 856–4382

Contact: YMCA of Greater New York
Big Pond Road
Huguenot, NY 12746
Attn: John G. Snowden

Capacity 180.

OPEN SPACE CONFERENCE CENTER
HCR 1, Box 80
Lew Beach, NY 12753
Tel. (914) 439–4566

A program of the Dai Bosatsu Zendo, Open Space offers the facilities of the monastery to groups who wish to pursue their own spiritual paths and have a first taste of Zen practice as well.

ANANDA ASHRAM
RD Box 141
Monroe, NY 10950
Tel. (914) 782–5575

The country retreat center for the Yoga Society of New York.

I.C.S.A.
ANANDA ASHRAM
RD 3, PO Box 141
Monroe, NY 10950
Tel. (914) 782–5575

The aims of I.C.S.A. are to experience one's Self as the center of cosmic self-awareness and to recognize the unity of all beings. Founded by Shri Ramamurti Mishra, I.C.S.A. acknowledges the ultimate reality behind all appearances, and thus does not embrace any single path or creed. Ananda Ashram is the main center for Shri Ramamurti's work and the headquarters of the I.C.S.A. Located on 100 acres in the foothills of the Catskills, Ananda Ashram is an ideal setting for programs related to Yoga, meditation, healing, and expanding awareness. Open to visitors throughout the year, Ananda Ashram offers retreat facilities and special weekend programs.

ZEN MOUNTAIN MONASTERY
Box 197, South Plank Road
Mt. Tremper, NY 12457
Tel. (914) 688–2228

A residential Zen retreat in the Catskill Mountains.

ABODE OF THE MESSAGE
RD 1, Shaker Road, Box 1030
New Lebanon, NY 12125
Tel. (518) 794–8095

A Sufi retreat center, located on 430 secluded acres.

There are summer weekend seminars and longer workshops in a variety of spiritual practices.

HOLIDAY HILLS YMCA CONFERENCE CENTER
2 Lakeside Drive
Pawling, NY 12564
Tel. (914) 855–1550

Facilities for group retreats. Contact Ms. Judy Ferraro.

PHOENICIA PATHWORK CENTER
Box 66
Phoenicia, NY 12464
Tel. (914) 688–2211

This retreat center in the Catskill Mountains has a schedule of workshops as well as opportunities for group retreats.

BETHLEHEM RETREAT HOUSE
Abbey of the Genesee
Piffard, NY 14533
Tel. (716) 243–2220

Bethlehem offers private retreat facilities for both men and women. Great emphasis is placed on personal solitude, silence, spiritual reading, and prayer, and only those prepared to make a serious monastic retreat should consider coming to Bethlehem Retreat House. Bethlehem is supported by donations freely made. There is no fixed fee; offer what you are able to afford and do not be troubled if that is very little or even nothing. For information, contact Fr. Daniel O'Shea, Guestmaster.

OMEGA INSTITUTE
Lake Drive
RD 2, Box 377
Rhinebeck, NY 12572
Tel. (914) 338–6030; (914) 266–4301

Founded in 1977, Omega Institute is an educational/

retreat center offering weekend and week-long workshops and conferences on innovative themes in the fields of health, psychology, spirituality, bodywork, the arts, personal growth, global thinking, and business transformation. Programs are held on an 80-acre lakefront campus, two hours north of New York City. Omega's relaxed community atmosphere includes a lake for swimming and boating, sauna, massage center, flotation tanks, and daily meditation, yoga, and t'ai chi instruction. Accommodations are simple and range from camping spaces to private cabins.

CENACLE RETREAT HOUSE
693 East Avenue
Rochester, NY 14607

Sr. Margie Mayk, RC, Ministry Coordinator. Capacity 40 overnight, 70 day use.

WAINWRIGHT HOUSE
260 Stuyvesant Avenue
Rye, NY 10580
Tel. (914) 967–6080

A stately stone mansion on five acres overlooking Long Island Sound. Courses, workshops, and seminars are offered year-round.

SANANDA
489 Woodlawn Avenue
Saratoga Springs, NY 12866
Tel. (518) 584–1036

Sananda is a spiritual community dedicated to a higher way of learning. Activities include meditation classes, groups for abused persons and for addictive behaviors, and groups for children in need of special attention. There are wilderness retreats to expand the spiritual connection with God/Goddess, seminars led by teachers from the Sananda community, and guest workshops with leaders from all over the country. Study groups focus on the teachings of Sananda, the Great White Brotherhood, the Ascended Masters, and Buddhist traditions.

SILVER BAY ASSOCIATION
YMCA CHRISTIAN CONFERENCE CENTER
Silver Bay, NY 12874
Tel. (518) 543–8833

Dennis M. Blank, Associate Executive Director.

BELLE TERRE CLUBHOUSE CAMP
Attn: Consuelo C. Haus
South Kortright, NY 13842
Tel. (607) 538–9434

Capacity 50 to 100.

CHRIST THE KING RETREAT HOUSE
500 Brookford Road
Syracuse, NY 13224

The Rev. J. Peter Conroy, SJ, Director. Sixty rooms.

ST. ANDREW'S HOUSE
89A St. Andrew's Road
Walden, NY 12586

The Rev. Andrew Ansbro, CP, Director. There are 30 rooms with a capacity of 50 retreatants.

CHALEIGHT
c/o Griffin Gorge Commons
Rt. 30, Box 341
Wells, NY 12190
Tel. (518) 924–2112

This Adirondack Mountain chalet is available for weekly or weekend retreats by couples, families, and small groups. Built using the ancient spatial concepts of Feng

Shui, The Chaleight is located on a secluded pond and offers spring water, swimming, canoeing, and a sweat lodge.

SIVANANDA ASHRAM
YOGA RANCH COLONY
PO Box 195
Woodbourne, NY 12788
Tel. (914) 434–9242

The Ashram provides a daily program including two meditations, two asanna classes, and related activities. Work-study and resident programs are available.

WISE WOMAN CENTER
PO Box 64
Woodstock, NY 12498
Tel. (914) 246–8081

Fifty acres of densely wooded Catskill Mountain beauty, with dormitory and campsite accommodations, a meeting lodge tipi, and a moon lodge tipi. Wise Woman offers accommodations for workshops, intensives, and self-healing retreats.

NORTH CAROLINA

BLUE RIDGE ASSEMBLY, INC.
84 Blue Ridge Circle
Black Mountain, NC 28711
Tel. (704) 669–8422

Rich Gapen, Director of Operations.

NORTH DAKOTA

QUEEN OF PEACE RETREAT CENTER
1310 N. Broadway
Fargo, ND 58102
Tel. (701) 293–9286

Fr. Michael Monshau, OP, Director. Operated by the Catholic Diocese of Fargo and conducted by the Dominican Friars and Sisters. Capacity 56.

OHIO

FRANCISCAN RENEWAL CENTER
320 West Street
Carey, OH 43316
Tel. (419) 396–7635

Rev. Donald R. Halpin, OFM Conv., Director, Capacity 115.

BERGAMO CENTER FOR
LIFELONG LEARNING
4400 Shakertown Road
Dayton, OH 45430
Tel. (513) 426–2363

Bergamo Center offers private retreats, directed retreats, and spiritual direction under the guidance of Sr. Mary-ann Rogers, CSJ, and Fr. Michael Lisbeth, SM. The grounds include an 80-acre nature preserve with developed trails through prairie and forest land.

MARIA STEIN CENTER
2365 St. John's Road
Maria Stein, OH 45860
Tel. (419) 925–4538

Maria Stein is a Catholic retreat/renewal center. There are 60 private rooms. Address inquiries to the Registrar.

OKLAHOMA

OFFICE OF WORSHIP AND SPIRITUAL LIFE
7501 N.W. Expressway
Oklahoma City, OK 73123
Tel. (405) 721–5651

Sr. Mary Kevin Rooney, Co-Director. Capacity 104.

OREGON

OUR LADY OF PEACE RETREAT HOUSE
3600 S.W. 170th Avenue
Beaverton, OR 97006
Tel. (503) 649–7127

Sr. Anne Marie, OSF, Director. Capacity 57.

AESCULAPIA
1480 Dutcher Creek Road
Grants Pass, OR 97527
Tel. (503) 476–0492

Aesculapia offers personal and group retreats for healing, spiritual evolution, and the transformation of consciousness. Facilities include a guest lodge, a wood-heated
sauna, hiking trails through old growth trees, and a
meditation decahedron.

PENNSYLVANIA

DOMINICAN RETREAT HOUSE
750 Ashbourne Road
Elkins Park, PA 19117
Tel. (215) 782–8520; (215) 224–0945

Sr. Rita McManus, OP, Director. Ninety-five rooms.

BLESSED RAPHAELA MARY RETREAT HOUSE
616 Coopertown Road
Haverford, PA 19041

Sr. Dorothy Beck, ACJ, Director. Capacity 47.

ST. VINCENT RETREAT PROGRAM
ST. VINCENT ARCHABBEY
Latrobe, PA 15650

The Rev. William Wurm, OSB, Director. Capacity 50.

WHITE CLOUD
Box 215, RD #1
New Foundland, PA 18445
Tel. (717) 676–3162

A sylvan retreat in the Pocono Mountains.

PRANA YOGA CENTER
SHIVASHRAM RETREAT
2473 Pruss Hill Road
Pottstown, PA 19464
Tel. (215) 326–4143

Swami Vignanananda's retreat center offers classes in asana, meditation, pranayama, and Vedanta in a beautiful, wooded, farmland setting.

RHODE ISLAND

PROVIDENCE ZEN CENTER
528 Pound Road
Cumberland, RI 02864
Tel. (410) 658–1464

The Providence Zen Center, a residential Zen Buddhist meditation community, has facilities available for retreats, conferences and workshops. The Center also offers its own program of monthly retreats and semiannual intensives integrating Zen practice with contemporary issues.

OUR LADY OF PEACE RETREAT HOUSE
Ocean Road
PO Box 507
Narragansett, RI 02882
Tel. (401) 783–2871

Our Lady of Peace offers a broad program of hermitage days, personally directed retreats, and seasonal retreats, as well as seminars and weekend workshops. Sr. Margaret Goldsbury, CND, Director. Fifty-four rooms.

SOUTH CAROLINA

SPRINGBANK DOMINICAN RETREAT CENTER
Rt. 2, Box 180
Kingstree, SC 29556
Tel. (803) 382–3426; (803) 382–9777

Springbank is an Ecumenical Center located in a quiet, rural setting of South Carolina. The Springbank staff feel in harmony with a holistic approach to life, centered in the Word, conscious of the importance of spiritual, mental, and physical health, and of the extraordinary power of creative energy. We hold a deep respect for all of reality, and accept the responsibility to foster freedom and well-being in ourselves as well as in others. Springbank's program includes guided, private, Scripture, directed, and parable retreats. The Center is located on 58 wooded acres with magnificent live oak and magnolia trees. There are overnight accommodations for 25, mostly in private, air-conditioned rooms. Springbank's Director is Ursula Ording, OP.

SOUTH DAKOTA

HARMONY HILL CENTER
RR 3, Box 254
Watertown, SD 57201
(605) 886–6777

A summer retreat facility offering accommodations for up to 50 retreatants in single, double, and triple rooms.

TENNESSEE

CENTER FOR PEACE
Rt. 11, Box 369
Sevierville, TN 37862
Tel. (615) 428–3595

A lodge, campground, and dining cabins in a natural forest and mountain setting.

THE FARM
34, The Farm
Summertown, TN 38483
Tel. (615) 964–3574

A residential community, founded by Stephen Gaskin. Workshops, retreats, and camping facilities can be arranged on request.

TEXAS

CHRIST OF THE HILLS MONASTERY
PO Box 1049
Blanco, TX 78606
Tel. (512) 833–5363

The Monastery is an orthodox Christian community, living by the contemplative observances of the Rule of St. Benedict. Simplicity is the order at the Monastery, with kerosene lamps and woodburning stoves. The monks teach Hesychast spirituality and the Prayer of the Heart, and rise in the middle of the night to keep the night-vigil. There are accommodations for five or six retreatants.

GUADALUPE RIVER RANCH
PO Box 877
Boerne, TX 78006
Tel. (512) 537–4837

The Ranch is located on 360 acres skirting the Guadalupe River, and offers an environment where groups and individuals can design their own programs in a setting of comfort and natural beauty. Accommodations are available for groups of up to 100 people.

OUR LADY OF THE PILLAR
MARIANIST RETREAT CENTER
2507 N.W. 36th Street
San Antonio, TX 78228
Tel. (512) 433–1408

Under the direction of Sr. Marcy Loehrlein, the retreat center has been greatly expanded, enabling it to serve many more religious groups and nonprofit organizations from all over the world. The center continues to offer a variety of retreat programs in both English and Spanish throughout the year. Some programs have a participatory format and others offer time for silent reflection. Each summer the Progoff "Intensive Journal Workshop" is offered for four days; this program encourages introspection and self-discovery through creative writing. The center has a capacity of 82 overnight guests, and fees vary according to the needs of each retreat group.

BENEDICTINE RETREAT ORDER
CORPUS CHRISTI ABBEY
HCR #2, Box 6300
Sandia, TX 78383
Tel. (512) 547–3257, x-23

The Benedictine Retreat Center has been established by a community of Benedictine monks living at Corpus Christi Abbey. One of the apostolates of the community is to provide a quiet place where people can come to be spiritually refreshed through prayer, silence, contemplation, and the enjoyment of natural beauty. Weekend retreats, group retreats, private retreats, and directed retreats are offered at the Center, and all retreatants are invited to pray the Liturgy of the Hours and to celebrate the Eucharist with the monastic community. The facilities of the Center are open to all and can be reserved by individuals or groups of all faiths. Contact Fr. Bartholomew Leon, OSB, or Br. Dominic Mazoch, OSB.

LEBH SHOMEA HOUSE OF PRAYER
La Parra Ranch
Sarita, TX 78385
Tel. (512) 294–5369

Lebh Shomea is a mixed Christian community under the auspices of the Missionary Oblates of the Mary Immaculate. The core community consists of three members, and the lifestyle is contemplative-eremetical. Guests who wish to share the desert silence for indefinite periods are welcome year-round. There is no predetermined schedule, no imposed structure—only the freedom and creativity of solitude. All are invited to share the daily Eucharist, and members of the core community are always available to listen heartfully to anyone seeking to discern God in spiritual direction.

UTAH

LAST RESORT
PO Box 6226
Cedar City, UT 84720
Tel. (801) 682–2289

The Last Resort is a year-round retreat center. The rustic log house, high in the mountains of southern Utah, can accommodate up to 12 people. Workshops in Iyengar yoga and Vipassana meditation are conducted from time to time during the year. When workshops are not in session, the center is available for individual or group retreats.

ABBEY OF OUR LADY OF THE HOLY TRINITY
1250 S. 9500 East
Huntsville, UT 84317
Tel. (801) 745–3784

Private retreats for men. Rev. Emmanuel Spillane, OCSO, Guestmaster. Capacity of 12, mostly in private rooms.

OUR LADY OF THE MOUNTAINS RETREAT HOUSE
1794 Lake Street
Ogden, UT 84401
Tel. (801) 392–9231

Directed retreats are offered for both men and women. Sister Danile Knight, OSB, Director.

VERMONT

MERCY RETREATS
Mt. St. Mary Convent
Burlington, VT 05401
Tel. (802) 863–6835

Sr. Helen Good, Director. Open seasonally.

VIRGINIA

YOGAVILLE
Rt. 1, Box 1720
Buckingham, VA 23921
Tel. (804) 969–3121

Located in the foothills of the Blue Ridge Mountains, Satchidananda's Ashram, Yogaville, is the site of L.O.T.U.S.—The Light of Truth Universal Shrine, an ecumenical temple dedicated to all faiths. All world religions are represented around a common altar of light. Yogaville offers retreats, yoga teacher training courses, meditation and pranayama workshops, individual retreats, and work exchange opportunities.

> *Let us walk together, talk together, think together, live together.*
>
> —*Swami Satchidananda*

SEVENOAKS CENTER
Rt. 1, Box 86
Madison, VA 22727
Tel. (703) 948–6544

A beautiful 130-acre spiritual center, encompassing woodlands, river, pond, and seven ancient oak trees, in the foothills of the Blue Ridge Mountains. Sevenoaks holds retreats and personal growth intensives year-round, and sponsors workshops and conferences with New Age leaders. It is also available for rental by small groups.

THE FRANCISCAN CENTER
PO Box 825
Winchester, VA 22601
Tel. (703) 869–1599

The Center can accommodate 40 overnight guests, each with private room. Facilities include a beautiful chapel, dining room, library, meeting rooms, and a large recreational lounge, situated on 150 acres of land. Br. Paul McMullen, TOR, Director.

WASHINGTON

CLOUD MOUNTAIN
373 Agren Road
Castle Rock, WA 98611
Tel. (206) 274–4859

A nondenominational Buddhist retreat center, Cloud Mountain hosts meditation workshops in the Theravadin, Zen, and Vipassana traditions. It is also available for self-directed individual retreats, and for use by any group that wishes to use the facility for meditative, contemplative practices.

CHINOOK LEARNING CENTER
PO Box 57
Clinton, WA 98236
Tel. (206) 321–1884

Chinook offers seminars, workshops, group meditations, and the opportunity for individual retreats. Located on 64 acres of evergreen forest and meadowland, facilities at Chinook include a restored farmhouse and cedar-log sauna, three small cabins, a retreat house, and camping areas.

RAJ-YOGA RETREAT
PO Box 547
Deming, WA 98244
Tel. (206) 855–1498

Retreats are offered for serious students of yoga and conscious awareness who are not one way/one mind oriented. Seekers experience profound changes and transcendental help in an environment consecrated through many years of intense mantric and meditative work.

The forest and hillside setting has been left mostly in its natural, unsculptured state. Retreat rates are reasonable, and are based on work scholarships.

CAMP INDRALAYA
Rt. 1, Box 86
Eastsound, WA 98245
Tel. (206) 376–4526

A Theosophical Society camp. For information, contact Orcas Island Foundation at above address.

SOLI-TIME RETREATS
3531 108th Street, S.E.
Everett, WA 98208

Soli-Time has hermitages in New Mexico, Washington, and Montana, available for individual, nondirected retreats. Write for a brochure.

SAINT MARTIN'S COLLEGE
Lacey, WA 98503
Tel. (206) 491–4700

Br. Edmund E., OSB, Facilities Coordinator.

BODHI CREEK FARM
7601 Kendall Road
Maple Falls, WA 98295
Tel. (206) 599–2106

Bodhi Creek Farm is a dynamic community and a center for experiential education. Summer programs include workshops in meditation which offer daily practice and guidance in a wide range of cross-cultural meditation techniques to quiet the mind, open the heart, and strengthen the body.

RESORT OF THE MOUNTAINS
1130 Morton Road
Morton, WA 98356
Tel. (206) 496–5885

Overnight accommodations for individuals or groups in beautiful condominiums or a rustic retreat center.

DOE BAY VILLAGE RESORT
Star Route 86
Olga, WA 98279
Tel. (206) 376–2291

Nestled on the edge of Orcas Island, Doe Bay has 60 acres of fir forests, wildflower meadows, and secluded beaches for meditation, quiet walks, and communing with the spirits of the bay. Facilities include cabins, hostels, campsites, and retreat facilities.

ISLAND FARM
Star Route 153
Olga, WA 98279
Tel. (206) 376–2342

A beautiful farm on Orcas Island, with workshop and retreat facilities.

IMMACULATE HEART RETREAT CENTER
S. 6910 Ben Burr Road
Spokane, WA 99223
Tel. (509) 448–1224

Msgr. William Van Ommeren, Director, Sr. Mary Agnes Koenig, OP, Administrator. Capacity 91.

KAIROS HOUSE OF PRAYER
Rt. 5, Box 490
Spokane, WA 99208

Sr. M. Florence Leone, OSF, Coordinator.

HOUSE OF THE LORD RETREAT CENTER
PO Box 34
Tum Tum, WA 99034

Mona Salvatore, Director.

WEST VIRGINIA

JOHN XXIII PASTORAL CENTER
100 Hodges Road
Charleston, WV 25314
Tel. (304) 432–0507

Rev. Edward Sadie, Director. Forty rooms.

NEW VRINDABAN
Route 1, Box 318
Moundsville, WV 26041
Tel. (304) 843–1600

New Vrindaban is an interfaith religious community in the Appalachian foothills. Weekend visitors join with full-time residents of the community in a program of reflection and interfaith fellowship.

LIGHTSTONE
Rt. 2, Box 11
Moyers, WV 26813
Tel. (304) 249–5271

Located on a 560-acre farm in the Appalachian Mountains, Lightstone calls itself "a center for the celebration of life and spirit." There are workshops in alternative farming practices and planetary wholeness, as well as individual and group retreats for spiritual or personal growth. The farmhouse can accommodate up to 20 people; camping is available for larger groups. A new community center is available for group activities, workshops, and food preparation.

PAUL VI PASTORAL CENTER
667 Stone
Wheeling, WV 26003
Tel. (304) 277–3300

Miss Toni Oliver, Director. A year-round retreat facility with 36 double rooms.

WISCONSIN

MONTE ALVERNO RETREAT CENTER
1000 N. Ballard Road
Appleton, WI 54911
Tel. (414) 733–8526

Rev. Kieran Hickey, OFM, Director. A year-round retreat center with 65 single rooms.

MINISTRY AND LIFE CENTER
ST. NORBERT ABBEY
De Pere, WI 54115
Tel. (414) 336–2727

Mrs. Mary Eagan, Director. Capacity 60.

PERPETUAL HELP RETREAT CENTER
1800 N. Timber Trail Lane
Oconomowoc, WI 53066
Tel. (414) 567–6900

Rev. James Springer, Director.

SIENA CENTER
5635 Erie Street
Racine, WI 53402
Tel. (414) 639–4100

The Center, which is ecumenical in scope, offers directed retreats for individuals, days of prayer and reflection, preached group retreats, and special-focus retreats for lawyers, parish secretaries, ecumenical women, couples, and others. There are 55 single rooms. The Director is Mary Michna, OP.

SCHOENSTATT CENTER
W. 284 N. 698 Cherry Lane
Waukesha, WI 53188
Tel. (414) 547–7733

Elizabeth Dingbaum, Director. Year-round center with
28 double and 16 single rooms.

CHRISTINE CENTER FOR MEDITATION
RR 1, Box 245
Willard, WI 54493
Tel. (715) 267–7507

A year-round retreat center with 12 hermitages plus
dormitory facilities. Sister Virginia Barta, OSF, Director.

GEORGE WILLIAMS COLLEGE
LAKE GENEVA CAMPUS
Williams Bay, WI 53191
Tel. (414) 245–5531

Dr. William B. Duncan, Executive Director.

WYOMING

WYOMING CATHOLIC LAYMAN'S RETREAT
743 S. Wolcott
Casper, WY 82601

Year-round retreat facility.

CANADA

BRITISH COLUMBIA

HOLLYHOCK
Box 127
Manson's Landing
Cortes Island, BC V0P 1K0 Canada
Tel. (604) 935–6465

Throughout the summer, Hollyhock conducts a series of workshops, including Vipassana meditation, Tibetan Buddhism, t'ai chi, and shamanism. Hollyhock also offers an unstructured retreat program that allows guests to enjoy the amenities of the facility without enrolling in a program. Retreat guests can decide for themselves how much or how little they wish to participate in daily activities, which include meditation, yoga, and nature walks.

LINNAEA FARM
Manson's Landing
Cortes Island, BC V0P 1K0 Canada
Tel. (604) 935–6976

The Farm encompasses 315 acres of forest, fields, gardens, and lakefront. Hostel-style accommodations are available for group retreats.

KOOTENAY TAI CHI CENTRE
Box 566
Nelson, BC V1L 5R3 Canada
Tel. (604) 352–3714; (604) 352–2468

Located on the shores of Kootenay Lake, the Centre offers t'ai chi classes which include breathing exercises and meditation.

NOVA SCOTIA

SPIRITUAL LIFE INSTITUTE
NOVA NADA
Kemptville, NS B0W 1Y0 Canada

SLI is a monastic Carmelite community characterized by Christian humanism. At Nova Nada, deep in the woods of eastern Canada, guests and retreatants may choose to participate in the monastic life of the community, or may make solitary retreats in individual hermitages. Please write in advance.

ONTARIO

HILL TOP FARM
RR 1
Campbellcroft, ON L0A 1B0 Canada
Tel. (416) 490–1260; (705) 932–5396

Hill Top is a secluded, six-bedroom, century-old farm-house, situated on 100 acres of rolling country land. It is an ideal location for small group workshops or retreats, or for individuals seeking a peaceful setting.

HOLY SPIRIT CENTRE
88 Fennell Avenue West
Hamilton, ON L9C 1E7 Canada
Tel. (416) 385–1222

The Centre offers days of prayer, reflection days, workshop retreats, private retreats, and a Christian meditation group. There are 44 single bedrooms with adjoining bathrooms, two chapels, and ten magnificent acres of natural grounds. Additional accommodations (10 rooms) are available in the attached historic "Auchmar House." The Director is Sister Anastasia Young, SSS.

UNITY RETREAT CENTRE
21 Rosedene Avenue
Hamilton, ON L9A 4W3 Canada
Tel. (416) 389–1364

Located 40 minutes from downtown Toronto, the Centre accommodates up to 50 overnight guests for retreats and workshops.

HOLY FAMILY RETREAT HOUSE
RR 1
Harrow, ON N9Y 2H8 Canada
Tel. (519) 726–6545

Holy Family Retreat House offers directed retreats, preached retreats, workshops, and personal prayer days.

Guests may come whenever they feel the need to be alone, or they may request spiritual direction from the staff. A quiet atmosphere, accommodation in private rooms, and proximity to the chapel enhance prayer and solitude. The Director is The Rev. D. A. Rocheleau.

PHILOXIA
RR 1
Marlbank, ON K0K 2L0 Canada
Tel. (613) 478–6070

Philoxia can facilitate workshops and seminars in a setting that includes nature trails, cross-country ski trails, and a private beach.

MAPLE KI FOREST
Walters Falls, ON N0H 2S0 Canada
Tel. (519) 794–2856

Maple Ki Forest is a macrobiotic guest house, workshop, and retreat center. Accommodations are available for relaxing personal retreats or for small group gatherings. Special workshops are taught once a month, with classes in hatha yoga, meditation, macrobiotic cooking, and the basics of shiatsu and reflexology.

QUEBEC

MAISON JESUS OUVRIER
475 Père Lelievre
Ville Vanier, QU G1M 1M9 Canada

SASKATCHEWAN

QUEEN'S HOUSE RETREAT AND RENEWAL CENTRE
601 Taylor Street West
Saskatoon, SK S7M 0C9 Canada
Tel. (306) 242–1916; (306) 652–9199

Rev. Glenn M. Zimmer, OMI, Director. Sixty rooms.

SUGGESTED READING

Buber, Martin. *Tales of The Hasidim—Early Masters.* New York: Schocken Books, 1947.

Byrom, Thomas, trans. *The Dhammapada.* New York: Alfred A. Knopf, 1976.

Chogyam Trungpa. *Meditation in Action.* Berkeley, CA: Shambhala, 1969.

Chogyam Trungpa. *The Myth of Freedom.* Berkeley, CA: Shambhala, 1976.

French, R.M., trans. *The Way of a Pilgrim.* New York: Seabury Press, 1970.

Goldstein, Joseph. *The Experience of Insight: A Natural Unfolding.* Santa Cruz, CA: Unity Press, 1976.

Goldstein, Joseph, and Jack Kornfield. *Seeking the Heart of Wisdom: The Path of Insight Meditation.* Boston: Shambhala, 1987.

Goleman, Daniel. *The Meditative Mind: Varieties of the Meditative Experience.* Los Angeles: J.P. Tarcher, 1988.

Halevi, Z'ev Ben Shimon. *The Way of Kabbalah.* New York: Samuel Weiser, 1976.

Herrigel, Eugene. *Zen in the Art of Archery.* New York: Random House, 1974.

Kadloubovsky, E., and G.E.H. Palmer. *The Art of Prayer.* London: Faber & Faber, 1966.

Kapleau, Philip. *The Three Pillars of Zen.* Boston: Beacon Press, 1967.

Kempis, Thomas à. *The Imitation of Christ.* Garden City, NY: Doubleday & Co., 1955.

Krishnamurti, J. *Commentaries on Living*. Third series. London: Victor Gollancz, 1962.

Lawrence, Brother. *Practice of the Presence of God*. Mount Vernon, NY: Peter Pauper Press, 1967.

LeShan, Lawrence. *How to Meditate*. Boston: Little, Brown & Co., 1974.

Levine, Stephen. *A Gradual Awakening*. New York: Anchor-Doubleday, 1978.

Lysebeth, Andre von. *Yoga Self Taught*. New York: Harper & Row, 1968.

Mascaro, Juan, trans. *The Bhagavad Gita*. New York: Viking Penguin, Inc., 1962.

Merton, Thomas. *New Seeds of Contemplation*. New York: New Directions Publishing Corp., 1961.

Osborne, Arthur, ed. *The Teachings of Ramana Maharshi*. New York: Samuel Weiser, 1962.

Prabhavananda, Swami, and Christopher Isherwood, trans. *How to Know God: The Yoga Aphorisms of Patanjali*. New York: Signet, 1969.

Ram Dass. *Grist for the Mill*. Berkeley, CA: Celestial Arts, 1987.

Ram Dass and Paul Gorman. *How Can I Help?* New York: Alfred A. Knopf, 1985.

Ram Dass. *Miracle of Love*. New York: E.P. Dutton & Co., 1979.

Reps, Paul. *Zen Flesh, Zen Bones*. Garden City, NY: Doubleday & Co., 1957.

Rodegast, Pat, and Judith Stanton, compilers. *Emmanuel's Book*. New York: Bantam Books, 1987.

Shah, Idries. *The Way of the Sufi*. New York: E. P. Dutton & Co., 1970.

Suzuki, Shunryu. *Zen Mind, Beginner's Mind*. New York: Weatherhill, 1970.

Tarthang Tulku. *Gesture of Balance*. Emeryville, CA: Dharma Pub., 1977.

Vivekananda, Swami. *Karma Yoga and Bhakti Yoga*. New York: Ramakrishna-Vivekananda Center, 1973.

Waley, Arthur, trans. *The Way and Its Power: A*

Study of the Tao Te Ching and Its Place in Chinese Thought. New York: Random House, 1958.

Walker, K. *A Study of Gurdjieff's Teaching.* London: Jonathan Cape, 1969.

Wilbur, K., J. Engler and D. Brown. *Transformations of Consciousness.* Boston: Shambhala, 1986.

Yogananda, Paramhansa. *Autobiography of a Yogi.* Los Angeles: Self-Realization, 1973.

About the Author

RAM DASS is an American psychologist and spiritual teacher who is able to make the spiritual insights· of the East accessible to the Western awareness. He was born in Boston in 1931. He received his Ph.D. in psychology from Stanford University, then taught at Stanford, the University of California at Berkeley, and Harvard University.

Ram Dass's own spiritual journey began during the early 1960s, with his explorations of the effects of psychedelic chemicals on human consciousness. Together with Timothy Leary and other members of the Harvard Social Relations Department, Ram Dass (known then by his Western name, Richard Alpert) began utilizing these substances to explore the dimensions of altered states of awareness. The effects of Alpert's first psilocybin experience in 1961 were profound and transformative, opening him to what he later described as "a place where 'I' existed independent of social and physical identity."

Following that first psychedelic experience, Alpert joined with Timothy Leary and others in a research program at Harvard to further examine the nature of these enhanced states of consciousness. In 1963, he was dismissed from Harvard because of the controversial nature of this work.

Over time, Alpert's interest shifted away from psychedelically-induced consciousness alteration. He began to investigate other methods, and in 1967 continued his spiritual quest by traveling to India—where he understood that there were spiritual traditions which concerned themselves with the exploration of these higher states. After months of traveling about India, Alpert was led to a small temple where he met the man destined to become his guru—Neem Karoli Baba, known to his Western devotees as "Maharaji." Alpert recognized that he had found in Maharaji someone who embodied the wisdom he had been seeking, and so spent many months living at Maharaji's temple in the foothills of the Himalayas, studying techniques of yoga and absorbing the spirit of Maharaji's being. It was during that time that Maharaji gave him the name "Ram Dass," which means "Servant of God."

After some months, Ram Dass returned to the United States, where he began sharing what he had learned—first through classes, and later through books, tapes, and workshops. His spiritual writings include *Be Here Now, Miracle of Love, Grist for the Mill, The Only Dance There Is,* and *How Can I Help?* Since his first visit to India, Ram Dass has returned to the Far East again and again to further nourish his spiritual growth. He has studied meditation with such teachers as Goenka, Munindra, and U Pandita, and has spent months at a time practicing meditation in retreat centers and monasteries in the United States and in the East. In *Journey of Awakening* he shares the insights he has gained through these practices, and offers meditation techniques which can be applied by anyone, regardless of experience or background.

In recent years, Ram Dass has centered his spiritual path on the practice of karma yoga—compassionate action as a technique for spiritual growth. He is a member of the board of directors of the Seva Foundation, an organization dedicated to service as a focus for the spiritual journey. He is also the chairman of the board of the Hanuman Foundation.

"My life is my message."
—*Mahatma Gandhi*